AMERICA GOES TO SCHOOL

AMERICA GOES TO SCHOOL

Law, Reform, and Crisis
in Public Education

ROBERT M. HARDAWAY

PRAEGER

Westport, Connecticut
London

Library of Congress Cataloging-in-Publication Data

Hardaway, Robert M.
      America goes to school : law, reform, and crisis in public
education / Robert M. Hardaway.
            p.   cm.
      Includes bibliographical references and index.
      ISBN 0–275–94951–6 (alk. paper)
      1. Public schools—United States. 2. Educational change—United
States. 3. Education and state—United States. 4. Educational law
and legislation—United States. I. Title.
LA217.H36   1995
371′.01′0973—dc20   94–46171

British Library Cataloguing in Publication Data is available.

Library of Congress Catalog Card Number: 94–46171

ISBN: 0–275–94951–6

First published in 1995

Praeger Publishers, 88 Post Road West, Westport, CT 06881
An imprint of Greenwood Publishing Group, Inc.

Printed in the United States of America

The paper used in this book complies with the
Permanent Paper Standard issued by the National
Information Standards Organization (Z39.48–1984).

10 9 8 7 6 5 4 3 2 1

Copyright Acknowledgment

The author and publisher gratefully acknowledge permission to reprint the
following previously published material: Selected passages by Herbert A.
Walberg, Carol Penclas Whitten, and Brian Weinstein in Gary Imhoff, ed.,
Learning in Two Languages (New Brunswick, NJ: Transaction, 1990).

To

Judy Swearingen

Contents

Preface   ix

Acknowledgments   xiii

One   Introduction: The State of Public Education   1

Two   Public and Private Education   23

Three   The Reform Movements   45

Four   The Origins of Public Education   67

Five   The Legacy of Racial Discrimination   97

Six   Alternative Methods of Segregation: Bilingual and Special Education   131

Seven   School Violence and the Crisis in Due Process   151

Eight   Public School Financing and the Issue of Inequality   159

Nine   Conclusion: Can Our Public Schools Be Saved?   163

Notes   167

Selected Bibliography   197

Index   203

Preface

In discussions of American public education, perhaps no word has become more of a cliche than the word "reform." Second only to the word "crisis," reform has become so overused in this context that it has almost ceased to have meaning. And yet both of these words have become such an integral part of the vocabulary of public education that it has become almost impossible to engage in any serious discourse about the state of American public education without the use of both overworked words—witness the subtitle and chapter titles of this book.

The study of public education has become essentially a study of its reform. For this reason, the thrust of much of this book is histori-cal. Only by understanding the origins of public education can its traditions be fully appreciated. For example, it is not commonly known that much of American education is based on the Prussian model of age segregation and male dominance—what David Tyack has referred to as the "pedagogical harem," consisting of a male principal and a number of female classroom teachers.[1] Indeed, the first principal of the first graded American public school set forth the essential "leadership" elements of the Prussian model: "Let the principal have the general supervision of the whole, and let him have one male assistant or sub-principal, and ten female assistants, one for each room."[2]

The adoption of the Prussian model required the creation of a vast hierarchical bureaucracy of administrators, which in turn led to the abandonment of the one-room schoolhouses, the consolidation of the public schools, and the strict segregation of children according to age. Although laws and public policy with regard to the roles of men and women in public education have changed considerably in recent years, an understanding of the Prussian and sexist origins of public education is essential to a comprehensive evaluation of proposals for educational reform. Without knowing where public education has been, we can not competently propose where it should go.

The Prussian model of administrative leadership and segregation by age has now become so ingrained and accepted in public education that its origins have been forgotten and attempts to challenge its basic premise are fiercely resisted. Only by looking at the past can we understand how the traditional American model of public education was abandoned, and realize that there was once a day in American public education when the classroom teacher had the authority to teach, and to maintain a disciplined and safe learning environment.

A parallel development equally worthy of attention is that of the constitutional law of due process and equal protection. Several chapters in this book will examine how the law has affected the quality of public education. In many cases, the sacrifice of principle to expediency in the application of constitutional principles had led to results totally contrary to those that have been claimed to be intended. The decline in student achievement and performance, racial resegregation, and the vandalism and violence that plague so many of our public schools are but a few examples of these unintended results. It was just such results that led to a Congressional Judicial Committee in 1975 to attribute the violence and vandalism in the schools to a "crisis in due process."

In the context of examining these legal developments, a number of questions will be addressed in this book. For example, why do public schools spend two to three times as much per student as private schools? Why do public schools need ten times as many administrators as private schools? Why do parents who can afford to send their children to private schools do so even though it means far less money is spent on their education? Why do students in such foreign countries as Japan (which spends about a third of what American public schools spend per student, and has classes of over 50 students) rank at the top in international achievement tests, while the U.S. students rank 19th out of 20 (nudging out Jordan)? Why in American public schools are there over 500,000 incidents of physical violence every month compared to 180 in Japanese schools? Why does the achievement of American public schools decline even as more and more money is spent on them? Why do 80% of American parents give the public schools a grade of C, D, or F? And finally, why are studies revealing the lack of correlation between spending and student achievement almost totally ignored by the educational establishment?

Also examined are the various proposals for public school reform, such as privatization, magnets, choice, vouchers, and, of course, the most popular reform of simply spending more money and hiring more administrators. Many of these reform proposals have lofty names (like Goals 2000: Educate America), and set forth even loftier goals (that U.S. students be "first in science and math," and "free of crime and violence"). A virtual torrent of government and private studies reach such startling conclusions as that of the 1990 National Assessment of Educational Progress Report Card, which concluded that American students might perform better if they "read more than five pages for school each day, spent at least some time on daily homework . . . and watched less television." (Indeed, American students were found to be second in the world in the time spent watching television, nudging out Mozambique).

Many of the reform proposals, such as choice and vouchers are revealed to be disguised proposals for public school abandonment. A recent article in *The Atlantic Monthly* warned that "school as we know it is doomed. And every attempt to improve — but fundamentally preserve—the present system will only prolong its death throes and add immeasurably to its costs, both financial and social."[3] It is suggested in the chapters herein, however, that such a view is unduly pessimistic, and that the public schools can be saved. It will require, however, a willingness to learn from our own historical tradition and from the experience of others, to discard methods and policies that have proven again and again to be ineffective, and to recognize the essential elements of quality education elements that most American public school parents already know, but that an entrenched educational and hierarchical establishment persists in denying. It is hoped that this book will cast some light on what course is required to save our public schools.

Acknowledgments

This book would not have been possible without the assistance of my dedicated research assistants at the University of Denver College of Law, Thomas F. Muther, Jr., and Lisa Wentzel.

I would like to give special thanks to Dennis Lynch, Dean of the University of Denver College of Law, for his support of this project. He authorized the generous university stipend which made this book possible.

I thank my secretary Tonia Murphy, who worked long and hard hours preparing the manuscript.

I thank Katie Chase for her excellent editing, and James Dunton and the staff at Praeger Publishers for their help and support.

Finally, I thank Judy Swearingen, to whom this book is dedicated, and without whose selfless dedication and support I could not have undertaken this project. A former teacher, she not only provided the inspiration for this book and gave me the benefits of her valuable insights as a teacher, but tirelessly assisted in the editing of the manuscript.

Chapter One

Introduction: The State of Public Education

> If an unfriendly power had attempted to impose on America the mediocre educational performance that exists today, we might very well have viewed it as an act of war.
>
> *A Nation at Risk*[1]

No other country in the world produces more studies, commissions, reports, plans, assessments, reviews, and statistical abstracts on educational reform, or holds more conferences, symposia, and workshops on the subject.[2] Each report and study in turn spawns dozens, even hundreds, of scholarly and not-so-scholarly responses, articles, and reviews in rapidly proliferating educational journals and publications.[3]

Unfortunately, the sheer number and volume of such studies means that most get lost or forgotten over time, overtaken by the most recently publicized study. Even worse, many of the most comprehensive studies are often deliberately shelved or ignored if they do not comport with preconceived or politically correct assumptions.

For example, in 1966 the U.S. Office of Education produced the most comprehensive government report on public education to date. Later referred to by the name of its chief author, James Coleman, the Coleman Report[4] surveyed and tested over 600,000 students in 3,000 American public schools. This report was commissioned in compliance with the Civil Rights Act of 1964, which required that an investigation be made of the extent of inequality in the nation's public schools. Although the original intent of the study was simply to document the inequalities already known to exist between schools in such areas as financing, teacher-faculty ratios, teacher education and salary, and school facilities, the study went beyond mere documentation and proceeded to make conclusions, based on its own extensive data as well as data accumulated from published studies, about the effects of such inequalities on actual student achievement.

To the consternation of the mortified government bureaucrats who had commissioned the study, the Coleman Report concluded, in the words of a Harvard Study,[5] that "schools are not very important in determining student achievement. Families, and to a lesser extent peers, [are] the primary determinants of variations in performance."[6] For example, the report found no relationship between class size, teacher education, and student achievement.[7] Although a slight correlation was discerned between teacher experience and student performance, even this has since been explained on the basis that experienced teachers with the most seniority are more likely to request teaching assignments in schools with higher achieving students—in other words, causation appears to run from achievement to experience, not the other way around."[8] In short, the Coleman Report revealed that when such inputs as family economic and social background were held constant, the data revealed "no strong or systematic relationship between school expenditures and student performance."[9]

In its own words, the Coleman Report concluded that "schools bring little influence to bear on a child's achievement that is independent of his background and general social context; . . . and this lack of independent effect means that the inequalities imposed on children by their home, neighborhood, and peer environment are carried along to become the inequalities with which they confront student life at the end of school."[10]

The Coleman Report confounded educational and government leaders who were accustomed to relying on perceived school inequalities as the basis for seeking more money and spending as the solution to failures in public education. If there was no correlation between such spending and actual student achievement, their demand for greater spending on education would lose much of its force and credibility.

Not surprisingly, reaction to the Coleman Report was fierce, and critics were unleashed by the educational establishment. The report was simply *not* what they had in mind. It was alleged that the data must somehow be flawed, or the research faulty. Over the course of the decade following publication of the report, the data were subjected to rigorous reassessment and reanalysis by experts in a wide variety of disciplines.[11] After a decade of such interdisciplinary scrutiny, however, even critics who persisted in demanding money as the solution to public education failure were forced to concede that no basic flaw in the data could be found. In 1991, at a Harvard symposium on public school reform, critic Ronald Ferguson conceded that despite much criticism of the Coleman Report, its "general conclusion (has) stood: no one (has been) able to find clear and important effects of school resources on student achievement in the Coleman data."[12]

Follow-up studies soon confirmed that "differences in quality [as measured by students' standardized test scores] do not seem to reflect variations in expenditures, class sizes, or other commonly measured attributes of schools and teachers."[13] Instead of continuing to criticize the Coleman data, many leaders of the educational establishment simply began to ignore the report entirely, or turn their focus to the one area in which the Coleman Report had discerned a slight correlation—that is, between teachers' experience and student performance. Ferguson, for example, published a study confirming that "teachers' experience and test scores are important predictors of test scores for students."[14] As noted, however, even this limited correlation has been explained by the fact that teachers with the greatest seniority tend to exercise their prerogative to choose assignments to schools having the higher levels of student achievement.

PUBLIC EDUCATION POLICY

In any case, it does not appear that policy in public education has been significantly influenced by the findings of the Coleman Report. Indeed, it appears that policy has proceeded as if the Coleman Report had never been published. In 1993 the U.S. Department of Education published a monumental digest of education statistics documenting every conceivable trend in public education during the past 25 years.[15] That digest reveals that since 1970, the expenditure per student in public education (after adjusting for inflation) has almost doubled—from $3,100 in 1970 to $5,700 in 1993.[16] If inflation is not taken into account, spending per student has more than quintupled.

The average pay of public school teachers has also risen dramatically. After adjustment for inflation, public school teachers' salaries rose 18% between 1982 and 1992.[17] Student-faculty ratios improved by one-fourth during the period 1965-1980.[18]

While few would argue that greater expenditure on public school education or higher salaries for teachers is bad social or educational policy in the abstract, the question remains as to the effect this dramatic increase in spending has had on the final product as measured by student achievement. Answers to this question in turn raise questions about how and why this money is being spent.

Although the answer to the first question will be the focus of much of this book, it is interesting to note that the opinions of students, parents, independent studies, and leaders in government do not always coincide with those who have a current vested interest in the status quo of public education.

EFFECTS OF PUBLIC EXPENDITURES

In 1991 U.S. Secretary of Education Lamar Alexander cited polls revealing that 80% of American parents gave the public education a grade A of C or lower.[19]   In 1983 the National Commission on Excellence in Education issued a Report to the Nation and the U.S. Secretary of Education entitled *A Nation at Risk: The Imperative for Educational Reform*. This report declared that the educational foundations of our society are presently being eroded by a rising tide of mediocrity that threatens our very future as a Nation and a people. If a friendly foreign power had attempted to impose on America the mediocre performance that exists today, we might well have viewed it as an act of war.[20]

A Nation at Risk made several startling findings. It found that American students performed poorly on achievement tests when compared to the performance of students in other countries, often finishing dead last.[21] It further found that "average achievement on most standardized tests is now lower than 26 years ago"[22] (i.e., about the time when expenditure on public education began its dramatic rise). The College Board's Scholastic Aptitude Tests (SATs) were found to demonstrate a "virtually unbroken decline from 1963 to 1980. Average verbal scores fell over 50 points and average mathematics scores dropped nearly 40 points."[23] In 1994 the SAT proposed an intriguing solution to the problem of declining test scores: simply "curve" the score norms so that a lower number of correct answers would be needed to achieve a particular score.[24] In such a way declining test scores could be obscured and students would be led to believe they were not scoring lower than their predecessors.

A Nation at Risk concluded that "the average graduate of our schools is not as well educated as the average graduate of 25 or 35 years ago, when a much smaller proportion of our population completed high school and college. The negative impact of this fact (on society) likewise cannot be overstated."[25]

Ten years after the publication of A Nation at Risk, and despite continuing increases in public education expenditures, there appeared to be little improvement in the performance of American students. In March 1991, 9 and 13-year-old students from 20 countries took standardized tests in science and math administered by the Educational Testing Service of Princeton, New Jersey, conducted as part of the second International Assessment of Educational Progress. In February 1992 the results were released. "In almost every category, 13 year olds in the United States ranked among the lowest of all those taking the tests."[26] In math, for example, American 13 year olds finished 19th out of 20, managing only to nudge out Jordan.[27] Finishing far ahead of the United States were such countries as Slovenia and Hungary. Korea finished first, followed closely by Taiwan and Switzerland.[28]

In studying the math results, James Stigler and Harold Stevenson of the University of Michigan concluded that the Asian students' "performance was better than the Americans even in the first grade, and that as the children grew older, the gap widened progressively."[29]

The 1990 Science Report Card, released in 1992, and administered as part of the National Assessment of Educational Progress, tested 20,000 students from across the nation in grades, 4, 8, and 12. The results showed a "fairly decent performance by fourth graders," which "deteriorated over the years, reaching the lowest levels by twelfth grade. Only 45 percent of the high school seniors performed at or above Level 300, and only a pitiful 9 percent could reach 350."[30] The Report Card concluded that "a disproportionately low percentage of these students possess in-depth scientific knowledge or the ability to accomplish even relatively straightforward tasks requiring application of thinking skills."[31]

Education Secretary Alexander acknowledged that the Report Card results were an "alarm bell that should ring throughout the country."[32] Francie Alexander, an assistant secretary of eduction and former associate superintendent of schools in California, remarked that "we have all been led to believe that we are above average. These results should take care of that myth."[33]

REACTION OF THE EDUCATIONAL ESTABLISHMENT

Unfortunately, many leaders of the educational establishment choose to try to explain away the results rather than address the issue raised by them. When it was revealed that students in Montana had among the highest levels of math proficiency, apologists suggested that this must have been because "Montana students spend a lot of time reading because there is nothing else to do."[34] In fact, the study also revealed that Montana had among the lowest percentage of students watching television more than six hours a day.[35]

Other educators complained that the international Princeton testing was unfair to American students, since they represented a cross-section, while those from other countries were from more select schools. In fact, it was reported that "15 of the 20 countries involved tested more or less representative samples of their students."[36] Even if the five countries allegedly testing select students unduly affected the results, this can hardly be adequate consolation for the United States, which came in 19th out of 20. In any case, international testing of select students in the United States reveals no substantial differences in the standings of American students.

In 1986, tests were administered to "top-performing" students in all countries whose students were tested. Although these tests showed "no innate intellectual differences" between first and fifth graders in the United States, Taiwan, and Japan, they did reveal that "in mathematics, only 9 percent of American students performed at the level that requires understanding concepts, while 40 percent of students from Korea, the top-scoring country, were at this level. At the highest level, less than 1 percent of U.S. students could interpret data compared to the 5 percent of Korean students."[37]

In science, top American 9 year olds actually performed fairly well on the international tests. Any optimism that might be generated by these results soon fades, however, when it is realized that the science test was given at an age before most countries offered formal teaching in science. In other words, American students did fine until the damaging effects of American education kicked in and caused their performance rates to fall.[38] Thus, a "study comparing U.S. high school students taking Advanced Placement courses in science with top students in 13 other countries found that American students were 13th out of 13 in biology, 11th of out 13 in chemistry, and 9th out of 13 in physics."[39] These dismal results were achieved by American students representing the top 1% of students in the nation — the best the nation had to offer.

The study concluded that the "indicators cited here compare America's top students with top students overseas, and its youngsters still rank at or near the bottom in all subjects tested."[40]

In 1990, a project mandated by Congress, entitled "America's Challenge: Accelerating Academic Achievement," was released by the National Assessment of Educational Progress. The report revealed that despite dramatic increases in expenditure in education, there had been no progress, and indeed regression in achievement, by students in American public schools. It found that few American students could write or communicate effectively, grasp connections of historical events, or apply basic skills.[41]

Also in 1990, Scholastic Aptitude Tests were released showing that "the average verbal scores of college-bound high school students had dropped to their lowest level in a decade."[42] The director of the Educational Excellence Network responded by noting that "the child entering school today is likely to get a very unsatisfactory education. [E]very indicator of outcomes—employers, SAT scores, international comparisons—show it hasn't changed a thing."[43]

Even more alarming are studies revealing the extent of knowledge of those who are products of the American educational system. A 1992 survey revealed that "only 45% of Americans know that the world goes around the sun once a year. A third believe that boiling radioactive milk makes it safe to drink . . . 54% reject the idea that humans evolved from earlier species."[44]

A northern university survey of 2,000 Americans "representing an educational cross section" revealed that 63% believed that "the earliest human beings lived at the same time as the dinosaurs."[45] Another study revealed that less than 15% knew why it was hotter in summer than winter.[46]

Public schools spend an inordinate amount of time purportedly teaching students "social studies" (sometimes having them dress in multiculturalist garb), but apparently have not gotten around to teaching over half of its students that Canada is north, not south, of the United States. Indeed many public schools do not teach geography at all.

Inadequate secondary education leaves students unprepared for college. A study by the National Assessment of Educational Progress revealed that "only 17% per cent of 17 year olds could solve multi-step mathematics problems such as finding percentages; less than 5% of 17 year olds could interpret historical data at a level expected for college work. . . . Only one in 100 high school seniors could write a coherent response of more than one paragraph to an essay question; and only 7% of high school seniors could read at advanced level."[47]

It should not come as a surprise, therefore, to learn that in 1989, only 45% of mathematics doctorates in the United States were awarded to Americans.[48] Between 1970 and 1989, the number of doctorates earned by Americans dropped to 23,172 from 25,000, while doctorates earned by foreigners at American universities (but educated in the secondary schools of their native countries) more than doubled.[49]

But if students in the public schools are not learning enough math and science to compete with students in such countries as Slovenia and Hungary, what are they learning? In 1994, a report by Elizabeth

Mehren of the *Los Angeles Times* entitled "Reading, Writing, and Therapy" revealed that "touchy-feely programs are popping up in schools all over the country" that focus on "confidence, self-esteem, negotiation enhancement," and even "quick hit sessions on table manners."[50] She perceives in the public school curriculum a "psychologization of education (which) has been slow, subtle, and largely unheralded."[51]

Although many psychologists have questioned the emphasis on such classes on grounds that, while well-intentioned, they have a "low probability of efficacy,"[52] others, such as a psychologist at the University of Washington, defend these programs on grounds that "we think the skills we teach are just like teaching reading."[53]

Unfortunately, experience reveals that the rooting out of "touchy-feely" courses mandated by an entrenched educational bureaucracy may be more easily said than done. When a suburban Denver school district was confronted by parental demands for a "back to basics" curriculum in 1994, school bureaucrats resisted fiercely but finally said they would agree to such a curriculum. Dismayed parents, however, soon discovered that the bureaucrats' idea of a "back to the basics" course in math was one in which children were handed questionnaires asking how they "feel" about math.[54]

Schoolteacher Paquita Hernandez, a critic of this latest educational fad, has observed that such programs are "a way of pacifying our anxiety. We're looking at little ways of entertaining ourselves. You don't give people self-esteem through a work-shop. Self-esteem evolves because you feel competent."[55]

But even if, as tests confirm, such programs have been successful in helping American students whip the foreign competition in the "self-esteem" department, there remains the question of poor performance in academic achievement. Indeed, if the public schools could promote a level of achievement that was competitive with that of other countries, there might be less need to provide our students with courses in "self-esteem."[56]

THE RATIONALIZING OF POOR STUDENT PERFORMANCE

Despite the overwhelming heaps of data, many public education experts and consultants persist in rationalizing the American performance. Typical of such rationalizations is that of a consultant who, in a 1993 article for *Phi Delta Kappan*, takes Albert Shanker, the head of the teacher's union, to task for writing in his weekly *New York Times* column that "the achievement of U.S. students in grades K-12 is very poor" and that "American students are performing at much lower levels than students in other industrialized nations."[57] Shanker's sin? Not "(providing) data" to support his conclusion in his short op-ed piece, despite the fact that the international Princeton tests and Science Report Cards are readily available to all serious researchers. After excoriating *Scientific American* as a "scary example of bias in American media" for reporting findings of educational failure, the article's author goes on to attack "methodical flaws" in the findings, and laments as indicative of media bias the lack of coverage and significance given to the one bright spot in American student performance—that is, that American 9 year olds had done well on international science tests before being given formal science instruction.[58]

Calling *A Nation at Risk* a "xenophobic screen," the previously cited author has joined other members of the educational establishment in hoping that "the days of school bashing are over."[59]

If there are indeed "methodical flaws" in the data, as charged by those who see the mounting tide of data as a form of school bashing, such flaws would appear to be common to all the independently conducted studies, since there is very little in any of the studies to suggest any improvement in the achievement of American public school students. In fact, however, there are relatively few even in the educational establishment who persist in denying the results of the mounting tide of data revealing the failure of American public education. Indeed, many educators have even adopted the findings of educational failure and low student achievement (though ignoring the evidence of a lack of correlation between spending and achievement), and then used the findings of low achievement to support their demands for even greater spending on public schools.

THE EDUCATIONAL ESTABLISHMENT

To a considerable extent, therefore, the educational debate now centers not on the fact of failure, but rather on its causes. Whether this represents a meaningful or even helpful progression in the level of the debate remains open to question, however. Without a consensus on the causes of educational failure, it is apparent that no meaningful reforms can be devised or implemented.

Unfortunately, the determination of causes has been complicated by factors unrelated to the problems of public education itself. It has been suggested that many of the causes of educational failure can be traced directly to the educational establishment, and particularly to its structure, outlook, and relationship to society. Like any of society's major institutions, the educational establishment is made up of members who have substantial vested interests in its policies and structure.

In 1989, state governors and the president of the United States held an historic education summit in Virginia. As a result of recommendations made at this summit, a goals panel consisting of both governors and members of Congress was established to report on the progress of American public education through the year 2000. Although the panel confirmed the findings of other studies to the effect that significant "achievement gaps relative to other nations occur as early as first grade," its chairman also issued a statement recognizing that "a lot of people (in public education) have much to gain from protecting the status quo. . . . The educational system in the United States is huge and diverse and not amenable to change."[60]

The determination of causes has also been complicated by attempts to use the public schools as an instrument of social engineering. In some cases, such action has been entirely justified on grounds of fairness, justice, and constitutional principles of equal protection—as in the cases outlawing racial segregation and invidious discrimination.

In many other cases, however, a social goals agenda unrelated to principles of fairness and justice has been used as a fig leaf and as a means to maintain the status quo and defend the vested interests of an institutional elite. As the chairman of the National Goals Panel observed, the "biggest barrier" to reversing the slide of student achievement in the United States is the people in the educational establishment who claim that "high standards . . . will be used against the poor, (and) the disadvantaged. And in seeking equity, they demand impossible guarantees."[61] The Panel concluded that "inertia and complacency slow systemwide education reform."[62]

In 1991, New York City and State Teacher of the Year John Taylor Gatto finally threw in the towel and quit teaching in the public schools, stating that they have become "a kind of income re-distribution mechanization . . . Only incidentally [do the public schools] exist to educate."[63] Earlier, Gatto had observed that educational reform is "probably impossible. Because the vested interests opposing it go beyond the teachers' and supervisors' unions."[64]

Tragically, as the chapters within will document, it is the poor and disadvantaged who have become the chief victims of a public school educational system mired in the status quo and "eroded by a rising tide of mediocrity." The rich and advantaged have used and will continue to use their own resources to escape the public school system for the privilege of sending their children to private schools, where half as much money is spent per child than in public education.

REACTION AND THE REFORM MOVEMENT

The failure to identify the root causes of deficiencies in student achievement has not inhibited the growth in the number of proposals for reform. In many cases, the cause of failure is simply presumed to be "money" (as if no other explanation is possible), and most proposals for reform are premised on this assumption. Other studies omit any analysis of causes and jump directly to solutions and goals.

For example, the 1989 Virginia summit of the president and state governors appeared to make the leap directly from a recognition of failure to the setting forth of goals, among which were that by the year 2000 public schools would be "free from crime and violence," and that "U.S. students should be first in the world in math and science."[65] (One wonders why, while they were at it, the summiteers did not also set forth a goal of peace and prosperity for all the world.) Admirable goals, to be sure, but hardly realistic given the lack of recognition of the root causes of educational failure and a track record of persistence in pursuing solutions that have time and again proved ineffective. Given the lack of American will to even seriously restrict semiautomatic weapons, let along handguns, such "goals" as reducing the crime in public schools must seem disingenuous if not laughable to foreign observers.

A 1984 government report entitled "Disorder in our Schools" revealed that "282,000 students were physically attacked in U.S. schools each month on school premises. During each month 1,000 teachers were also assaulted seriously enough to require medical attention" or hospitalization, and "125,000 more teachers were threatened with bodily harm."[66] In Japan, by contrast, a country with a population of a little less than half that of the United States, 180 monthly incidents of school violence were reported during the same period.[67] Lest this comparison of 282,000 monthly incidents of violence in U.S. schools to 180 in Japanese schools be attributed to the lack of sufficient expenditures in American schools, it should be noted that the Japanese public schools spend about half the money per student that American public schools spend.[68] By 1988 the number of monthly incidents of violence in U.S. public schools had increased to 500,000.[69]

A study conducted in Boston revealed that 40% of high school students had been victims of crime during a one-year period, and 30% of the students reported carrying guns to school.[70] A study of New York schools revealed that over 1,000 deadly weapons were found on students during a four-month period.[71]

Whatever solutions or reforms have been instituted, or goals announced since the 1984 government report on violence, they do not appear to have had significant effect. In 1993 the National Center for Education Statistics of the Department of Education released statistics revealing that over a nine-month period in 1991, 10% of all African American students and more than 5% of all white students in American public schools had been wounded by deadly weapons at school.[72]

The Virginia summit's goal that U.S. students be "first in math and science" by the year 2000 triggers only slightly less incredulity. Despite a doubling of expenditures on public education, dramatic increases in teachers' salaries, and declines in student faculty ratios, student achievement in American public schools continues its inexorable decline. A more modest goal, such as surpassing Slovenia in math and science achievement tests, while less dramatic, and less likely to grab headlines, would at least have the attribute of realism.

The tradition of substituting goals for making hard decisions about public education has been continued in the 1994 Goals 2000: Educate America Act. This act has been described by an article in *USA Today* as a "rehash of George Bush's education plan. Like Bush's plan, it is pretty much mirrors and smoke screens. Washington offers up some bread and circuses . . ."[73] Like its many predecessors, the act is lavish in goals: by the year 2000, U.S. students will be "No. 1 in the world in math and science," all adults will be "literate and skilled," and "every school will be free of drugs and violence."[74] How to accomplish these lofty goals? The act offers up such solutions as giving more standardized tests, encouraging parents to become more involved in their children's education, teaching more occupation skills, and improving "teacher training."[75] If nothing else, such solutions as more standardized tests will at least provide additional documentation of the low academic achievement of American public school students.[76]

Encouraging parents to become more involved in education is certainly a worthwhile suggestion, but in the meantime, and until it is shown that parents are listening, many school administrators today would be thrilled if parents just disarmed their children of semiautomatic weapons.

Unfortunately, most past recommendations to improve teacher training have been applied as a means of further deprofessionalizing teaching, and entrenching closed-shop unionism by introducing still more certification courses that exclude many of the most qualified professionals from teaching in the public schools. Indeed, one of the reasons private schools today have such an advantage over public schools, despite their lower expenditures on students, is that they can hire the most qualified professionals in a particular field without having to worry about whether they took some certification course.[77] Most private school teachers have heard the story, perhaps apocryphal but illustrative nevertheless, of Robert Oppenheimer, the inventor of the atomic bomb, who after retiring from government work was denied a public high school teaching job in physics because he had not taken a certification course.[78] While most private schools would not hesitate to hire an Oppenheimer to teach physics, public schools are content to select their teachers from a pool of teaching applicants, which one study has determined "rank(s) near the bottom of student groups planning to enter various occupations"—that is, those who choose to pursue a teaching credential.[79]

Thus, in contrast to the act's proposal to "improve teacher training," the Center for Public Policy and Contemporary Issues recently recommended the exact opposite namely, to "eliminate the lengthy certification process for teachers," and, in particular, to allow "retired professionals (and) scientists to teach courses in their areas of expertise."[80]

Although the Goals 2000: Educate America Act does not specifically recommend money as the solution to problems in public education, many of the solutions it advocates would require substantial expenditures. It also authorizes $5 billion in grants.[81] For a country whose students finish 19th out of 20 in 13 year old math and science achievement, but spends more per student than any other country in the world (except Switzerland),[82] the drafters of the act revealed that they have not yet recognized that lack of money is the least of the problems facing American public schools [83] (At least Switzerland achieves some return for its high expenditures, finishing 3rd out of 20 in math and science.)[84] Ironically, some of the fiercest criticism of the act has been directed at its failure to specifically recommend even more money as the remedy for low student achievement. One critic of the act, though claiming to be skeptical that money can solve all public school problems, nevertheless suggests that we "not pretend we have tried that course. [The House has not approved enough] money to fix toilets in New York or buy textbooks in Alabama. Washington offers its Cracker Jack prizes to states that mandate more tests."[85]

For such critics, and there are many of them, it is as if such studies as the Coleman Report and *A Nation at Risk* had never been conducted, and that data (showing that student performance has declined at the same time that expenditures and faculty salaries have risen) simply does not exist. Not surprisingly, once the data and conclusions of these reports are ignored, there is an intuitive tendency to seek solutions that can be solved by the stroke of a pen or the passing of a revenue bill.

THE EDUCATIONAL EXPENDITURE LOBBY

If the educational expenditure lobby were limited to those who had a vested interest in increasing educational expenditures, the task of finding real solutions would not be nearly so difficult. There are, however, many well-meaning and dedicated social scientists who still believe, despite the overwhelming data, that student performance could be significantly increased if only even greater sums of money were spent. Typical of such views is that found in Jonathan Kozol's 1991 book *Savage Inequalities*.

Kozol documents the sad state of public education, describing a high school in Detroit in which only 7,000 of 20,000 entering ninth graders graduate, and the "financial pressures have reached the point of desperation."[86] In Chicago, eighth graders are "taught from 15 year old textbooks in which Richard Nixon is still president. There are no science labs, no art or music teachers. Soap, paper towels and toilet paper are in short supply. There are two working bathrooms for some 700 children."[87] A sad plight indeed, and doubtless typical of many public schools around the country. From such descriptions one can understand the temptation to link such deficiencies as lack of paper towels to low graduation rates and poor student performance. However, the book also reveals that the City of Detroit in which "financial pressures had reached the point of desperation" nevertheless spent $3,600 per student, or a sum almost twice that spent per student in the average American private school[88] and in Japanese and French public schools.[89]

Kozol then goes on to blame the plight of blighted public schools on "savage inequalities" in school financing systems, noting that while Detroit spent $3,600 on each student, the "suburban town of Grosse Pointe spent some $5,700 on each child. Bloomfield Hills spent even more: $6,250 for each pupil. Birmingham, at $6,400 per pupil, spent the most of any district in the area."[90] Not explained, however, is what Birmingham's expenditures have to do with the fact that Detroit, which spends twice as much as private schools spend per student, can not afford to buy toilet paper.

What Kozol and other sincere advocates of reform have done is to confuse two very different issues. The issue of equality in financing public education is a real one. (The reasons for this inequality are largely historical and dealt with in more detail in Chapter Nine). Despite the failure of the U.S. Supreme Court to recognize an equal protection problem in existing school financing systems,[91] some states are addressing the problem by restructuring the traditional property tax system of financing public schools. Clearly, existing school financing systems are inefficient and unfair, and are in need of drastic reform.

But unfair school financing systems can not explain poor student performance and low achievement. Even those American public schools that spend the least on students still spend more than most American private schools and foreign public schools. For example, in 1993 New Jersey spent an average of $10,561 per pupil. Yet even the very poorest New Jersey school district spent "more than the overall average for virtually every state."[92] Placing the blame for poor student performance on financing disparities serves only to detract attention from the real causes of low student achievement. Indeed it appears already to have done so.

THE MONEY MAGNETS

Although there are many examples of how the quest for money as the ultimate solution has resulted in the diversion of attention from the real causes of low achievement, a Kansas City, plan to expend huge sums of money to solve an educational problem is perhaps most illustrative.

In 1985 a federal judge in Kansas City, Missouri frustrated by the failure of court-mandated busing to integrate the public schools, decided to order the creation of "magnet" schools in the city's predominately African American district. The judge's theory was that if substantial sums of money were spent on such magnet schools, student performance would improve and parents in the suburban areas would voluntarily send their children to the schools in the predominately African American district.[93]

Tax increases of up to 50% were imposed on state residents, and more than $1 billion was spent on the magnet schools. Lavish new facilities were built at taxpayer expense, including "a new planetarium, a 25-acre farm, an art gallery, television studios, therapeutic whirlpools and a model United Nations wired for language translation."[94] An Olympic-size swimming pool was built "with an underwater alcove so that coaches [could] film a diver's technique."[95]

As a method of integrating the schools, the billion-dollar experiment was a disaster. After five years, less than 3% of suburban students had transferred to the magnet schools, which remained as segregated as ever with over 75% African American enrollment. It was calculated that the cost of inducing white students to the magnet schools was over $1 million per white student.[96] Moreover, to prevent an even higher African American enrollment, thousands of minority students seeking admission to the magnet schools were cruelly denied admission because of their race. Outraged African American parents, who felt victimized by such a blatant quota system, filed a lawsuit against the school district, demanding that their children be permitted to attend area private schools at state expense[97] —not an unreasonable request in light of the fact that the cost of tuition at the private schools was only $2,000 per student compared to almost $6,000 in the public schools.[98]

When critics dared to object and urged that Kansas City "forget about trying to bribe white students to send their kids to inner-city schools, and to instead focus on creating better neighborhood schools,"[99] their pleas were rejected as politically incorrect. But other outraged critics smelled the stench of racism in the Kansas City quota plan, stating that, despite the claimed good intentions, "its insulting to be told the quality of my child's education depends on the number of white children in the room."[100]

As a result of such plans as that imposed by Kansas City, segregation has intensified in the public schools over the past 25 years. According to a recent Harvard study, the percentage of African Americans attending predominately African American schools in 1972 was 62.9%.[101] After years of court-imposed "desegregation" plans, this percentage rose to 63% in 1986 and to 66% in 1992.[102] Segregation of Hispanics intensified even more severely during this period, rising from 56.6% of Hispanics attending predominately Hispanic schools in 1972, to 68% in 1980, and to 71.5% in 1986.[103]

Political, ideological, and social theory appear to have been of paramount importance to policymakers during this period. The fact that the plans that flowed from those theories did not actually work in achieving their objectives does not appear to have deterred them in the slightest from continuing to implement their plans. As has so often been the case in the past with plans based on ideology rather than experience, the poor and disenfranchised have suffered the most.

In 1991 the Center for Public Policy and Contemporary Issues, headed by former Colorado Governor, Richard Lamm, issued a report entitled "What's Really Wrong with American Education," which was critical of an educational theory and "philosophy that relegates millions of poor and minority students to educational failure."[104] The report called for resistance to "calls for the delineation of a permanent class of 'victims,' presumably the result of endless discrimination, who can never achieve at high levels. (The public schools should) reemphasize the traditional role of schools as the locus of opportunity."[105]

The report recommended that public schools "get rid of the nonsense surrounding the debate over the purpose of the public schools. Schools have never been perfect, nor have they been perfectly sensitive to the relativistic needs of every racial, ethnic, and religious group. We are a county of immigrants —'losers' from every continent—who turned into winners by being assimilated into the complexities of life in a free society by the schools. Schools exist to produce literate and informed citizens, ready to serve the broader national interest."[106]

The example of the Kansas City plan reveals why expenditure of vast sums of money is not the easy solution to such social problems as de facto segregation in the public schools. More important, however, the Kansas City experience shows that money has little or no effect on student performance. Not surprisingly, a later evaluation of the effects of the Kansas City plan revealed that the students in the lavishly equipped magnet schools actually tested lower in achievement than students in other schools that had not enjoyed the largesse lavished on the magnets.[107] Although the explanation for such results is not readily apparent, one might speculate that students in the magnets may have spent too much time in their therapeutic hot tubs, and not enough doing homework.

Had the Kansas City policymakers bothered to read the Coleman Report, they would surely have adopted a more effective plan and made better use of the billion dollars they dissipated in the name of ideology racism and educational theory. The 1993 biennial National Assessment of Educational Progress, sponsored by the U.S. Department of Education, also reveals the lack of correlation between spending and student performance. For example, Iowa, which ranked No. 1 in the nation in SAT scores, ranked 27th in per capita student expenditures. Utah, which ranked dead last among the states in per capita expenditures, finished 4th in SAT scores. In Harrison, Arkansas, the public schools spend only $2,700 per pupil (compared to over $10,000 per pupil in New Jersey), yet rank in the top 5% in student performance.[108]

SOME COMPARISONS WITH COMPETITORS

It has already been noted that the Coleman Report has largely been ignored by the numerous studies and reform proposals that now emanate in a steady stream from the nation's think tanks, government agencies, and institutes. While many of these studies do an excellent job of documenting low student achievement, the solutions proposed almost always involve the expenditure of greater sums of money—that is, like the Goals 2000: Educate America Act they call for increased expenditures on teacher training. Others call for increased salaries, more expenditures on facilities or infrastructure[109] or greater federal aid to education.

The problem, of course, is that the money remedies have already been tried. As noted, real dollar expenditures per student have doubled since 1970, teacher salaries have increased by 18% in real dollars, and teacher-faculty ratios have declined by one-fourth. Between 1965 and 1970, federal aid to education rose 83%, and between 1964 and 1968 "federal aid doubled as a proportion of the nation's total education budget."[110] In 1992 "the Education Department alone spent $27 billion, and that was only 43% of the federal government total expenditures that year."[111]

After such extravagant expenditures, the taxpayer may reasonably ask what the investment return is on per student expenditures that are twice that of such other countries as Japan, and twice that expended on students in American private schools. We have already seen the answer:

declining SAT scores, and international test scores that put American students at the lowest levels of academic achievement.[112]

Were the American public education system a corporation whose existence depended upon its efficiency and productivity, years ago it would have gone into bankruptcy, or at least Chapter 11. Many of today's corporations achieve success by keeping an eye on competitors, and often learning from them. For example, many Japanese corporations learned some of their most effective mass-production techniques from U.S corporations. Unfortunately, we have not taken the trouble to return the favor in areas where we could learn from our competitors. Were we to do so, we would discover some interesting features about the Japanese system of public education that might help in understanding why American educational spending policies have been so unsuccessful.

It has already been noted that Japan spends less than half as much per student in public education as American public schools.[113] Indeed, for some age groups the difference in spending is even more dramatic. In 1988, for example, Japan spent only 24% as much on its 13 year olds as the United States spent.[114] Nevertheless, student achievement in Japan exceeds that of American students.

An international study of mathematics achievement conducted in the 1980s revealed that out of 14 nations, Japanese students placed first with an average of 65.47% correct answers, while the United States finished last with 47.30% correct answers.[115] In a direct comparison between American and Japanese students in science, Japanese students outscored their American counterparts in every age category. Among 6 year olds the disparity was relatively slight (an average 20.1 score to an average 17.1 American score). By age 10, however, the Japanese advantage increased to 21.7 to 12.7, and by age 13 the disparity in scores was 31.2 to 16.2.[116]

Given the overwhelming weight of these and other studies, apologists of the American educational establishment have not seriously challenged these findings. Instead they have resorted to rationalizing the obvious disparities in student achievement—suggesting, for example, that the scores reflect only the scores of the most able Japanese students. A study by H. Stevenson in 1983, however, revealed this to not be true.[117] In a comparison of two random cities (Sendai in Japan, and Minneapolis in the United States), the study found that "the school with the lowest mean in Sendai scored higher than the best school in Minneapolis."[118]   This study has been cited as supplying "further evidence that the academic standards of all children are high in Japan, not merely those of some proportion of more able children who respond well to the competitive and demanding system." Stevenson's conclusions are in accordance with the previously noted 1986 tests of the top performing students.[119]

Other apologists have been reduced to claiming that the test comparisons are unfair because "the Japanese system is too competitive and likely to generate a high level of psychological stress and maladjustment among Japanese school children."[120]   Unfortunately for the apologists, even this scrap of consolation lacks a basis. A 1982 study by H. Eysenck of stress and anxiety of students in Japan and Great Britain found "no differences between children aged ten to fifteen from the two countries."[121]

Other apologists have suggested that Japanese students are not as creative as American students. Again, there can be no consolation. A study by T. Husen has revealed that Japanese children "are at least as strong on the more creative tasks tested in the international achievement investigation."[122]   What, then, is the explanation for superior student achievement in Japan? Whatever the answer, the explanation can not be found in teacher salaries, teacher training, student-teacher ratios, or school facilities.

An international study of teacher training has revealed that "the lengthiest training of teachers occurs in the United States, where the educational standards achieved tend to be low."[123]   It further found that "the correlation between the length of training of primary school teachers and the achievement of 10 year olds in science is zero."[124] Japanese primary school teachers were found to have had only a little more than half the number of years of training of American teachers.[125]

The study found that "Japanese teachers typically teach large classes of 40 or even 50 children."[126]   By comparison, the student-faculty ratio in the United States has been 29 and falling.[127] The study concluded that "in spite of the widespread belief [that smaller classes raises the efficiency of instruction] the results of research on this question have invariably shown no relationship, or at best very little, between the educational attainment of pupils and class size or teacher/pupil ratios."[128]

Teachers' salaries are the single largest item in any educational budget. Benjamin Duke, in his study of the Japanese public schools, observed in 1986 that "a beginning teacher in Tokyo, one of the most expensive cities in the world, starts his career at the equivalent of $10,000 a year, including bonuses. And yet there is great demand by university graduates to enter the teaching profession."[129] The average American public school teacher salary in the same year was over $25,000, and has risen rapidly since that time.[130] Although Japanese teacher salaries have risen modestly in accordance with inflation, they remain far below those of American teachers.

Richard Lynn, in his study of the Japanese school system, reports that "Japanese teachers are paid quite poorly. . . . as compared with those in the United States."[131]   As a result he finds a negative correlation between teacher salary and student performance, reflecting the fact that American teachers are relatively well paid, and "Japanese teachers (are) poorly paid; yet Japanese children performed considerably better than American children."[132]   Nevertheless, Lynn mercifully resists concluding that there is a "direct negative causal relationship in the sense that poorly paid teachers actually produce better academic results than the highly paid. Nevertheless, the evidence presented . . . makes it difficult to avoid the conclusion that the level of teachers' remuneration in different countries has no effect on the educational standards achieved by children."[133]

Finally, the evidence reveals that school facilities and infrastructure in Japan are far less lavish than in the United States. For example, most Japanese schools do not even have central heating, despite the bitter cold and heavy snows common in northern Japan. Duke has described Japanese classrooms as "equipped with simple, rather unsightly, kerosene stoves . . . [T]he students who sat nearest the stove were warm while those farthest from it shivered or kept their heavy sweaters on all day. The hallways, gyms, and toilets are cold and drafty throughout the winter months."[134] A world far removed from the therapeutic hot tubs of the Kansas City magnet schools.

When new Japanese schools were built in the mid-1970s, they were considered luxurious because they were "equipped with individual coal stoves in each room. The children were assigned to carry the coal in buckets to the classroom each day. The teacher made the fire. It often went out. Several years later kerosene stoves replaced the coal stoves but the unsightly chimney pipes remained as the classrooms were modernized at a minimum of expense, and comfort."[135]

Japanese students are issued cheap paperback textbooks costing about a dollar. (In the United States colorful hardback books costing many times as much are typical.) Such school amenities as counselors, cafeterias, or carpets, often considered to be necessities in U.S. schools, are considered to be "nonessential in Japanese schools and are rarely provided for in the school budget. . . . Even the school libraries are poorly stocked. In a large number of schools, the walls need paint. The desks and chairs are often badly worn. In fact, the average Japanese would simply be overwhelmed with the facilities [in U.S. public schools]."[136]

While few American students are required to scrub the floors and hallways of their school before going home, "cleaning the floor on hands and knees at the end of the long day is an old tradition in Japanese schools. It is intended to be an instructive as well as hygienic aspect of the Japanese school. It also reduces janitorial expenses."[137] In American schools such duties are considered to be beneath the dignity of the students, and are relegated to hired help, often at high union wages. Not surprisingly, vandalism is rampant in American schools, while in Japan the students who have maintained the school with their own bare hands are far less likely to destroy their own handiwork by vandalism.

Benjamin Duke's study concludes that " the Japanese school is one of the most frugal institutions among all economically advanced nations. The Japanese experience demonstrates that to be effective schools do not have to be costly . . . [O]perational expenses are kept minimal."[138]

In short, a far different educational philosophy prevails in the Japanese public school, namely, that "education is most effective when it takes place under Spartan conditions. Learning and comfort are not related. Color, brightness, attractive surroundings are irrelevant to the learning process. Simplicity is conducive to learning."[139]

A final feature of the Japanese system is that all elements of society "expect the school to be an effective agent within the infrastructure of the nation. It is taken for granted that the raison d'etre of the school is to produce a literate graduate across the board. . . . Anything less is unacceptable."[140] Japanese industry "expects the new employee coming from any school anywhere in the land to have minimum competencies in the three R's. . . . Anything less is unacceptable."[141]

It has been observed that "the expectations of the school by Japanese society are very high indeed. Those of the United States, in comparison, are far too low."[142] The satisfaction of Japanese employers with the products of their schools may be contrasted with the that of American employers.

A 1992 survey conducted by the National Alliance of Business reported that "fewer than 40 percent of principals surveyed believed that non-college-bound high school graduates are prepared to hold entry-level jobs. Twenty-seven percent of the principals surveyed said that graduates can write adequately; 29 percent believed math skills were up to par."[143]

Many U.S. companies are finding that they must provide the training that American public schools have failed to provide. Motorola is now spending over $2 billion dollars on training, or "$2,500 per employee for the next five years to provide employees with simple training in skills necessary to compete."[144] Collins and Aikman, a textile mill in Georgia, has recently opened its own school and is now spending $1,200 per employee to teach its employees how to "read and write."[145] A recent survey of American business included a "small jewelry manufacturer in Santa Rosa, California (which) has begun offering weekly basic reading and writing skills."[146]

There are other features of the Japanese schools that U.S. schools have declined to emulate. For example, Japanese public school students go to school for 240 days per year, compared to 180 days per year in the United States.[147] Thus, by the time Japanese students are teenagers, they have had the equivalent of several additional years of schooling. American schools insist upon a three-month-long hiatus every year. According to a study by E. W. Turner, students lose much knowledge and continuity is jeopardized during such a long interruption.[148] Although the reasons for such long vacations are historical (farmers needed their children to be free to help harvest the crops), American teachers, parents, and students alike have long grown addicted to long summer vacations during which expensive school resources sit idle.

Nor is the abbreviated academic year made up by longer classroom hours. In the United States, the average public school student attends only 22 hours of class a week—some as few as 17 hours a week.[149] Japanese students attend class almost twice as many hours a week, and also attend classes on Saturday.[150] In China, by way of further comparison, "students go to school from 8:00 A.M. to 5:00 P.M. 6 days a week, 250 days a year."[151]

From the American class hours must be subtracted hours spent on non-academic courses in "self-esteem," "negotiation enhancement," and intermediate "table manners."[152] A typical Japanese class schedule includes mathematics, science, English, Japanese, history, and writing. Although the typical curriculum eschews courses in social studies and self-esteem, it does include two hours a week of "morals."[153]

Although courses in the latter would surely be sneezed at in American schools, a recent National Alliance of Business survey of 100,000 American students revealed that "forty percent would keep extra change given to them by a cashier, thirty three percent would not ask for more work if they finished a task early, twenty five percent would give free merchandise to friends, and thirty percent would cheat on a test."[154]   (Experience reveals that the latter figure, based on admissions by students, may be far too low.)

Even the annual spectacle of 10,000 American teachers who are physically assaulted and the 5% all students   attacked by deadly weapons has not prompted interest in emulating the Japanese by offering a course in morals.[155] Apparently there is no room for such a course in a curriculum already taken up with courses in self-esteem and the like.

Educational establishment apologists for the short year and even shorter week claim that making American students put in such hours would be too "burdensome" and would take away the opportunity to engage in other "youthful and beneficial activities."[156] It is therefore revealing to examine exactly what it is that American students do in the spare time that is so generously accorded them.

Whatever American students do when they are not using drugs, vandalizing their schools, or attacking teachers and fellow students, it does not appear that they are doing much homework.[157] The 1993 Report to the U.S. Department of Education on the Condition of Education compared the number of hours spent by American students on homework with the number of hours spent by students in other countries.[158] It was found that 13 year olds in the United States had a lower percentage of students doing more than two hours of homework than those in 16 of the 19 countries studied.[159] By way of comparison, the report revealed that while 29.4% of American 13 year olds spent more than two hours a day on homework, 63.3% of students in Ireland did so, 55.4% in France, and 79.1% in Italy.[160]

If not doing homework, what do American students do in their spare time? Lest one conclude that American students whip the foreign competition only in the violence and self-esteem departments, it appears that there is one additional category in which they finish first in international competition—namely, watching television.

The 1993 Report on the Condition of Education revealed, in a study of 14 countries, that more American 9 year olds spent more than 5 hours a day watching television than in any other country.[161] Over a quarter of American 9 year olds spent more than 5 hours watching television a day. By way of comparison, 8.5% of 9 year olds in Taiwan spent as much time, and only 9.2% of students in Korea.[162] (Although apologists would surely deny any connection, it may be recalled that in the international math tests of 13 year olds, Korea and Taiwan finished first and second, while the United States finished 19th out of 20).[163]

For 13 year olds, the United States received only a silver medal in television watching. Out of 19 countries studied, one other country had a higher percentage of 13 year olds watching more than 5 hours of television.[164] (Close behind the United States, the bronze medal winner in television watching was Mozambique.)[165]

LESSONS LEARNED

Perhaps even more interesting than international comparisons of public school systems is the lessons that have been learned. For example, what might an observer of Japanese schools conclude about what could be done to improve American public schools? One might expect that the differences in the number of school days in Japanese and American schools might account for some of the differences in student achievement, few of the recent reform proposals have recommended extending the school year, the number of hours of classes, or Saturday classes. The Clinton administration's Goals 2000: Educate America Act made no such proposals.

What about reducing the amount of teacher training to the level of training given Japanese teachers, and use the money saved to provide additional classes? What about hiring teachers based on professional expertise in their subject area rather than on whether they took a designated number of certification courses? Despite the overwhelming data revealing the lack of any correlation between teacher training and student achievement, Goals 2000 recommends that teacher training be extended.[166]

Although Japanese students attain high achievement by using cheap paperback texts, while American students are issued deluxe, colorful, hardback editions costing many times as much, Goals 2000 diagnoses the problem of low student achievement as the result of lack of "instructional materials" and recommends that better instructional materials be provided to American students.

Teaching American students morals or asking them to participate in school maintenance is doubtless so far beyond the pale that its implementation would be inconceivable in American public schools, and would doubtless be considered to be beneath the dignity of American students, particularly the children of wealthier parents.

The problem with implementing any such programs may be that they would not cost much money. Having students keep their schools clean and attend school year-round would actually save money, as would spreading the cost of school overhead over a full year rather than leaving resources idle over the summer. It is also difficult to see how assigning students more homework would cost much additional money. And therein lies the problem. Reforms not involving more money have little attraction for an educational establishment accustomed to expanding its interests and powers with vast infusions of additional tax revenues.

The typical reform proposal inevitably involves a demand for more revenues. It is argued that if public schools such as those in Detroit were just given more money to buy additional toilet paper and paper towels, if facilities could just be improved, instructional materials upgraded, and the training of teachers extended, student performance would rise. And it seems that no amount of data, test results, studies of the lack of correlation between spending and achievement, or experiences such as those in Kansas City appear sufficient to deter the public schools from pursuing their agendas again and again after each failure.

These then are the lessons learned by the educational establishment from the Coleman Report, international student achievement tests, the experience of lavish spending programs such as those implemented in Kansas City, and a comparison with schools in other countries such as in Japan. The educational journals and popular magazines are filled with articles demanding additional spending on education, as if spending alone would manifest a national commitment to education. Often the articles concede, and even document the failure of American public education, but then go on to propose solutions that assume the very correlations that time and time again have been proven not to exist.

For example, one recent article carefully documented that "eighth graders have generally mastered no more than basic arithmetic and are weak in reasoning and problem-solving skills. Less than half of them can figure out the weight of a 30-pound object when it is taken to the moon, after being informed that the moon weight is one-sixth Earth weight."[167]   The author's diagnosis of the problem?: "inadequate government funding . . . over-ambitious text-books; and curricula that try to jam impossible amounts of information into courses."[168]   (To such observations, one is much tempted to respond that, of all the problems facing the public schools, and there are many, over ambition does not appear to be one of them.)

Occasionally there appears a glimmer of inspiration in the studies. For example, in 1990 the National Assessment of Educational Progress Science Report Card, after considerable study, came to the startling conclusion that American students might perform better if they "read more than five pages for school each day, spent at least some time on daily homework . . . and watched less television."[169]

There remains, however, one final point for comparison in determining the causes of public school failure, namely that of the private schools within the United States.

Chapter Two

Public and Private Education

It has already been documented that private schools in the United States spend far less per student than the public schools. For example, it will be recalled that in Kansas City, private schools spent an average of $2,000 per student compared to $5,900 per student in the public schools.[1] Parochial schools spend far less than both public schools and other private schools.[2]

And yet hundreds of thousands of parents in the United States choose to pay for private school tuition out of their own pockets rather than send their children to public schools that spend far more per student educating their children. Why would so many parents spend so much extra money for the privilege of having less spent on their children's education?

When this question is asked of members of the educational establishment, the response is usually defensive and often fierce. Many simply reject the premise of the question and dispute the data on cost comparisons by either calling it "inconclusive,"[3] or claiming that the apparent disparities are due to "massive gaps in accounting in private school data."[4]

In responding to such claims, a 1993 study published by Harvard University Press reexamined the data and did find substantial gaps in the cost accounting—but in the calculation of public school costs, not private school costs. For example, it found that calculations of public school expenditures did not include expenditures on over 20 categories of costs, including pensions, interest, administrative costs, and training programs.[5]

Others members of the educational establishment freely concede the substantial disparities in spending between public and private schools, but nevertheless insist that the question is unfair. "Private schools don't have to educate as many . . . disabled, bilingual, illegal aliens, and disadvantaged students as public schools," they argue, and public schools have more discipline problems. Only rarely are they willing to concede that private schools are more efficient, or provide a better education with far less money and fewer resources. To make any such concession would undermine cherished assumptions about the correlation between spending and achievement, and would undercut their demands for ever greater funding. Each of the claimed grounds of unfairness should therefore be examined before exploring other possible explanations of disparity between public and private school costs.

BILINGUAL EDUCATION

It is true, of course, that bilingual education imposes massive additional costs on the public schools. However, it is also true that these costs have been self-imposed by a government and educational establishment determined to implement bilingual programs even in the teeth of countless studies and cases revealing the ineffectiveness, unfairness, and injustice of bilingual education.

In 1954 the United States Supreme Court for the first time rejected the "separate but equal" doctrine of *Plessy v. Ferguson.*[6] In *Brown v. Board of Education*[7] the Court framed the issue of separation in the schools as follows: "Does segregation of children in public schools . . . even though the physical facilities and other 'tangible' factors may be equal, deprive the children of the minority group of equal educational opportunities? We believe that it does."[8] The Court concluded that "separate educational facilities are inherently unequal."[9]

Despite the principles of fairness, decency, and civility set forth in *Brown*, however, many members of the educational establishment, recognizing language as a primary indicator of race and national origin, have sought to segregate students on grounds of the primary language that they speak. Thus, in many public schools today, Hispanics and other racial groups are put in classes that are segregated from other students in the name of bilingual education. In an attempt to justify such blatant attempts to segregate by national origin, some segregation apologists have claimed that bilingual segregation is necessary to enable students whose primary language is other than English to learn effectively.

The issue of bilingual education is treated more completely in Chapter Six. For our purposes here, it is sufficient to refer to the monumental study of bilingual education published by the Harvard University Press in 1993, which reviewed and assessed the countless studies and reports that have been made on the question of whether there is any merit to such a rationalization based on language and national origin. That study concluded that "on its merits, the case for bilingual education is extremely weak. This is true even for the limited objective of helping children to speak English; one comprehensive review concluded that 71% of the studies of transitional bilingual education showed it to be ineffective or counterproductive as a means of achieving this objective."[10]

Several of these studies are particularly noteworthy. In 1981 DeKanter and Baker made a report to Department of Education's Assistant Secretary of Planning and Budget. In a masterpiece of understatement, the report concluded that there was "insufficient evidence to prove that bilingual education is the most effective approach for language minority children" and called for English immersion as a more effective learning method.[11] In this regard it is interesting to note that when the government itself wants to teach its own employees a foreign language for foreign service, it uses immersion programs. Middlebury College, known for having one of the most successful language programs, employs a program in which "students embark on a systematic program of intensive language learning without depending on their native tongue."[12]

A Study by Diane Ravitch entitled "Politicization and Bilingual Education" notes that "to date (not a single) school district has claimed that the bilingual method succeeded in sharply decreasing the drop-out rate of Hispanic children or markedly raising their achievement scores in English and other subjects." As an example of how bilingual education actually hinders educational opportunity, the study posits that the "child who spends most of his instructional time learning in Croatian or Greek or Spanish is likely to learn Croatian, Greek, or Spanish. Fluency in these languages will be of little help to those who want to apply to American colleges, universities, graduate schools, or employers, unless they are also fluent in English."[13]

In 1990, Rosalie Porter, a researcher in bilingual education for 15 years, published the now acclaimed *Forked Tongue: The Politics of Bilingual Education*, in which she pleaded for programs in which limited-English children are "immersed in the English language, in which they have as much contact as possible with English speakers, in which (all) school subjects, not just social conversations, are the focus of English-language lessons."[14]

When faced with the data revealing the ineffectiveness of bilingual education, apologists have responded by quoting such studies as The Russell Sage Foundation's Report entitled *Laggards in Our Schools*, which claimed that "ignorance of the English language is a handicap that is quickly and easily overcome and has little influence on retardation."[15]

The results of the imposition of such an educational philosophy on the public schools have been tragic indeed. Myron Lieberman recently cited the example of New York City's Con Edison Co., which in 1988 tested 7,000 applicants for entry-level positions. Not a single graduate of the city schools' bilingual programs qualified for a job.[16] Nor is it surprising that "Hispanics are the least educated minority in America, according to a Report by the American Council of Education 50% of all Hispanic youth in American drop out of school."[17]

But if the segregation created by bilingual education can not be justified by more effective learning or enhanced achievement, what justification remains? A 1983 article in the *Columbia Journal of Law and Social Problems* gave a justification similar to that which has been used to justify single-race schools and classes: "bilingual-bicultural education serves to . . . ri(d) the school environment of those features which may damage a language-minority child's self-image . . ."[18] At congressional hearings in 1968, advocates of bilingual education argued that "non-English-speaking children did poorly in school because they had low self-esteem, and that this low self-esteem was caused by the absence of their native language from their classroom."[19]

If the lack of a native language in the classroom were truly the cause of a lack of self-esteem, one would expect government foreign service employees who study in language immersion programs, and those studying a foreign language at Middlebury College's acclaimed immersion courses, to also be suffering from low self-esteem. However, this is clearly not the case. It may be helpful to recall what teacher Paquita Hernandez had to say about self-esteem—namely, that "self-esteem evolves because you feel competent."[20]

The *Columbia Journal* article's reference to "bilingual-bicultural education", however, raises another related issue—that of multicultural-ism. The 1993 Harvard University Press Study of public education had this to say about this justification for bicultural education:

In practice, the advocates of multiculturalism are caught in a dilemma. On the one hand, they decry what they perceive to be the uncritical approval of Western culture and of "traditional" lifestyles. On the other hand, objective treatment of virtually any ethnic or religious group. . . . will include some facts that are not conducive to the self-esteem of its members or adherents. Faced with this dilemma, multiculturalists usually are guilty of the same practice they impute to others; that is, they fail to mention important facts that would presumably weaken the self-esteem of the alleged disadvantaged groups. Multicultural activists are not apt to point out that some African tribes enslaved others for sale. . . . or that some native Americans routinely practiced cannibalism or human sacrifices. I do not cite such omissions to defend conventional curricula, which I would gladly change on other grounds. The point is that intellectual integrity fares no better under multiculturalism than under the curricula that it is supposed to replace.[21]

The predominance of the bicultural rationale for bilingual education became evident when Congress passed the 1974 Amendments to the Bilingual Education Act of 1968, and effectively "encouraged Hispanic children to view themselves as a group apart—permanently culturally distinct."[22] According to this rationale, "even Hispanic children who were fluent in English were entitled to bilingual education."[23]

The theory behind bilingual education appears to bear a striking similarity to the theory behind "special education": identify in advance those students whom administrators suspect have a lower chance of achievement due to some handicap (in this case language), then lower expectations of them, cater to their handicap, and stigmatize them as "special education" or "bilingual" students—but most important, of course, segregate them from other more privileged or advantaged students who suffer no such handicap. When students so stigmatized then perform in accordance with expectations and find it impossible to escape from their predetermined track, the tragic result is then pointed to as confirmation of the original decision to segregate them in the first place.

What then has been the response of the government, the judiciary, and the educational establishment to the data and studies on bilingual education?   Apparently, what is good enough for the government's own employees is not good enough for public school students. In the Bilingual Education Act of 1968, Congress legislated and endorsed massive taxpayer-financed funding of bilingual education.[24] Since then, millions of dollars have been spent on bilingual education, bloating the budgets of many of the nation's pubic schools. By 1974 there were bilingual programs in 23 different languages. Since then, however, more and more groups have demanded programs in their native languages, until by 1990 expenditures had been increased to fund bilingual education in 145 different languages. The list of languages continues to expand.

Ironically, many of those who advocate separate classes for non-English-speaking students are opposed to separate classes for learning disabled students. It is to this subject we now turn.

LEARNING AND PHYSICALLY DISABLED STUDENTS

Unlike the role played by the educational establishment, the federal government and the judiciary in the area of bilingual education, governmental and judicial intervention has had a positive effect in insuring fair educational treatment of physically and learning disabled students. Prior to the Education for All Handicapped Children Act,[25] educational treatment of disabled students by the public schools had often been cruel. Typical of the prevailing attitude was expressed in an opinion by the Supreme Court of Wisconsin,[26] which upheld the expulsion of a child "who had the academic and physical ability to benefit from school, but who drooled . . . had a speech impediment, and exhibited facial contortions."[27]

Congress first addressed the issue of education for the disabled in 1966 when it provided grants for education of handicapped children.[28] There followed the Education of the Handicapped Act of 1970,[29] and the Education for All Handicapped Children Act of 1975, which provided to "all handicapped children the right to a free appropriate public education," and required that "to the maximum extent appropriate, handicapped children . . . are educated with nonhandicapped children."[30]   In 1990, this Act was renamed the Individuals with Disabilities Education Act.[31]

The United States Supreme Court has interpreted this act to require "personalized instruction with sufficient support services to permit handicapped children to benefit educationally from that instruction."[32]   However, the law permits public schools to refer severely disabled students to private facilities at state cost.[33] Thus private schools, as well as public schools, educate disabled students. In fact, in many cases private facilities have the greater burden, since the less severely disabled can be educated in the public schools.

For example, in the case of *Department of Education v. Katherine D.*, a federal court held that a public school could not exclude a child and relegate her to private facilities merely because she required periodic suctioning of mucus from her tracheostomy tube.[34] The Court found that such suctioning could be easily provided by the public school nurse, and that the fact that the child needed such help from time to time was no reason to deprive her of an education in a regular classroom environment.

Such decisions are in accordance with the compassionate spirit and goals of the Individuals with Disabilities Education Act. Clearly, disabled students whose education does not deprive others of their educational rights should have a right to learn in a normal classroom environment. Nor does the education of disabled students necessarily require or justify huge sums of money. In the case of Katherine D., the school nurse was required to devote some additional time to the child; but it is doubtful if such additional time required vast infusions of revenue.

Unfortunately, however, as has so often occurred in other government programs, a fair and well-intentioned policy has been taken to an extreme, which defeats the very purposes of the original policy. In the case of the learning disabled, the definition of "disabled" has been extended to include almost any student who is disruptive, violent, or criminal. As one legal scholar has asked, "Is there any sound educational reason for not treating all disruptive students the way in which handicapped children must be treated?"[35] Terms like "emotionally disabled" and "emotionally conflicted" have been coined to justify the unleashing of such students on other innocent children trying to get an education.

A typical view of how the Individuals with Disabilities Education Act should be extended is that of a professor who recently wrote an article in the Tennessee Law Review. The professor cites the case of "Bruce,"[36] a public school student who "kick(ed) other students . . . (and) attack(ed) other children." There are, suggested the professor, four different ways to "interpret this behavior." One is that the child is in need of discipline; a second is that he is suffering from "psychiatric illness"; the third is that the child does not understand the reason for his behavior and therefore needs to "learn to understand the causes of (his) feelings"; a fourth is that "the institutional structure within which (the child) functions is, to some degree a cause of (his) behavior."

The professor concludes that "both the third and fourth interpretations are in accord with the learning paradigm."[37] In other words, it must be the schools's fault that the child is beating other students over the head.

According to the professor, "when a child misbehaves, educators must get beyond their immediate reaction so that they can analyze the event in the context of the child's history as well as the school's history."[38] The professor goes on to suggest that the behavior of Bruce should be "intimately related to his disability or as raising educational issues," and that in response to Bruce's attacks the school should "re-evaluate the design of his educational program."[39] The professor then laments that "all too often schools treat children whose emotional disabilities lead them to behave inappropriately as bad children who deserve to be punished rather than as children who need to learn to understand . . . their own behavior."[40] (Unfortunately, however, the professor does not address the question of what is to become of the student victims while the attacker is kept in school being psychoanalyzed.)

Other scholars have suggested that behavioral problems, like "cultural traits . . . and beliefs may be interpreted as dysfunctional by educators unfamiliar with the culture," and that therefore students with "high physical and verbal activity" may not be properly "understood or accepted by teachers."[41] Although it is not altogether clear how understanding a student's culture will help to understand why he is physically beating other students, the fact remains that under current law a public school that disciplines or suspends a violent student is likely to face a lawsuit.

A typical example is that of *Chris D. v. Montgomery County Board of Education*.[42] In that case, a public school attempted to protect its students by isolating a disruptive student who had been hitting and causing physical injury to his classmates. The parents promptly sued the school district, challenging the "adequacy of his education program."[43]

Although the school conceded that the child needed extended treatment and counseling, it did not feel it was equipped to do so and argued that such services should be provided by another state agency. The court criticized the school's actions in trying to protect its students, however, stating that simply setting forth rules and imposing penalties on attackers was insufficient. The court insisted that the school's "system of behavioral control . . . has been woefully inadequate. (The School) has sought to keep (the child) quiet and hidden away from other students, rather than attempting to teach him to control his own behavior, an essential approach to educating emotionally conflicted children."[44]

The legal basis[45] for such lawsuits may be traced to the Supreme Court decision of *Honig v. Doe*.[46] In that case, a public school attempted to suspend a student who had, in addition to stealing, extorting money, and intimidating other students, tried to strangle another student. When the suspension was challenged on grounds that it discriminated against a student with an emotional "disability," the school pleaded that the Court recognize at least an exception under the statute for "dangerous students." The Supreme Court callously refused to recognize such an exception, holding that one of the reasons that the Disabilities Education Act had been passed was because "discipline procedures had been used to exclude large numbers of children with disabilities."[47] Thus the Court upheld the right of violent "disabled" students to attend school.

In light of *Honig* and its progeny, it is not surprising that public schools feel greatly inhibited in attempting to impose discipline and protect their students. Were it simply a matter of theory, psychology, and judicial philosophy, the results would not be so tragic. Unfortunately, however, the lives of both students and teachers are involved.

A congressional subcommittee investigating school violence discovered that over a three-year period, homicides increased 18.5%, rapes by 40.1%, robberies by 36.7%, and assaults on teachers by 77.4%.[48] A Report by Education U.S.A. and the National School Public Relations Association revealed that vandalism, thefts, and arson cost schools over half a billion dollars, and that "serious incidents of theft and malicious destruction of educational equipment occurs in 80% of the school districts in the country."[49] It was estimated that "the cost of replacing broken windows in the average big city would build a new school every year."[50]

It must be conceded, therefore, that the costs of such policies on public schools are substantial. A Senate Committee Report on the Education for All Handicapped Children Act reported that "on average, costs for educating a handicapped child are double those of educating a nonhandicapped child."[51] It must also be conceded that public schools have more disabled students than private schools. However, since only a percentage of public school students fall within the definition of "disabled," the fact that teaching disabled students costs twice what is costs to teach nondisabled students can not account for more than a fraction of the disparity in costs between private and public education. And, as has been shown, even these costs have been in large part self-imposed by interpretations of the Disabilities Education Act, which go far beyond what was originally intended.

Although the costs discussed in this section have pertained to costs associated with teaching the disabled, there remains the question of the costs of school discipline unrelated to disabilities.

SCHOOL DISCIPLINE

It is true that the costs of discipline in the public schools are greater than in private schools. Again, however, it is also true that most of these costs are self-imposed. What alternatives are available to a public school administrator seeking to provide protection for students who want to get an education? The Model School Disciplinary Code issued by the Center for Law and Education of Harvard University[52] sets forth standards to be used as a guide to "procedural due process for [elementary and secondary] schools." According to this code, no serious discipline of any kind should be imposed except in accordance with the following procedures:

First, a complaint must be submitted to the head administrative officer of the school alleging "possible student misconduct." Second, the officer shall make a determination of whether the complaint states a "potentially disciplinary" matter. Third, there shall be a "full investigation of the facts" at which the student will be fully advised of his constitutional right to "remain silent if he wishes" (i.e, there must be no requirement that the student in question cooperate in any manner with the investigation). Fourth, if after an investigation the officer determines that there is "evidence that the student has actually committed the conduct charged," and "counselling" does not resolve the complaint, the charge is referred to a "hearing."

The hearing must then be held before an "impartial panel," consisting of representatives from the administration, the teaching staff, and students. "The principal shall be the charging party, and the assistant superintendent shall convene the hearing panel." The student shall then be provided with "written notice of the hearing sufficiently in advance to allow him adequately to prepare his defense" and shall contain, among other facts, a "statement of the specific facts against the student . . . the student's right to be represented by an advocate of his own choice (including legal counsel). . . . (and) the right to present evidence, call witnesses, and cross-examine adverse witnesses."

In addition, the student shall be allowed to "inspect written evidence and is informed of the names of witnesses against him and the substance of their testimony," and shall have the right to submit "rebuttal evidence." The hearing panel is then required to "make a verbatim transcript or tape recording of the hearing, a copy of which shall be made available to the student. The hearing panel shall then issue a written statement" as may be warranted by "clear and convincing evidence."

If the punishment imposed involves a suspension of more than 10 days, the student shall have a "right to a hearing before the school committee, which shall be conducted according to the rules set forth in Section 9 (containing additional procedural rules)." The student must be permitted to remain in school "pending the school committee hearing" unless the panel also decides, on the basis of "clear and substantial evidence," that his behavior presents a "threat to the safety of others" or that his conduct is "extremely disruptive." (Apparently, any evidence less than "clear and substantial" would require the school to retain a student who might be dangerous to other students.)

The hearing panel may only actually expel a violent student if the committee finds "beyond a reasonable doubt" that the student's conduct has been of "an extreme and serious nature." In addition, if the school is seeking to expel the student, the "school committee shall pay for, or retain counsel to represent the student at all stages of the proceedings where the student is unable to pay for counsel." In no case may an expulsion last beyond the school year.

The above is only a brief summary of the procedures required, and many additional details and procedures have been omitted. Since these procedures are to be followed even in elementary schools, apparently even teachers of first graders must be subjected to them. It must also be recalled that if a student's behavior is determined to be the result of "emotional confliction," he is also entitled to all the protections of the Disabilities Education Act.

In light of such procedures, the question must be asked as to whether the public schools are being asked to perform such a variety of social functions that their primary educational mission is jeopardized. No one would deny the need for treatment for emotionally conflicted students. (A psychiatrist in Killeen, Texas, has reported that over a quarter of a million dollars of taxpayer money has been expended in treating a violent student who committed a number of crimes, including burglary and car theft.)[53]

The question, however, is not whether such treatment should be provided, but rather whether such treatment is best provided by the public schools (who must, in the meantime, leave their other students subject to the mercy of the violent ones) or by qualified professionals. In cases of repeated acts of criminal conduct, the question is whether the public schools or the judicial system is better equipped to deal with criminal activity and administer justice in accordance with such procedures set forth in the Model School Disciplinary Code.

Lest the Model School Disciplinary Code issued by the Harvard's Center for Law and Education be considered as manifesting only an extreme viewpoint or an institutional opinion of how discipline is to be conducted in the public schools, it should be noted that the code appears to be in accord with existing law.

In the case of *Goss v. Lopez*,[54] The United States Supreme Court considered the case of students suspended for 10 days for involvement in a violent incident in a school lunchroom. Although acknowledging that the imposition of "elaborate hearing requirements in every suspension case is viewed with great concern, and many school authorities may well prefer . . . to act . . . unhampered by rules about notice and hearing,"[55] the Court went on to hold that "in connection with a suspension of 10 days or less . . . students facing temporary suspension have interests qualifying for protection of the Due Process Clause [of the United States Constitution]."[56] Thus, despite the fact that with regard to the incident arising in the lunchroom "the administrative burden of providing 75 'hearings' of any kind is considerable,"[57] nevertheless, "as a general rule notice and hearing should precede the removal of any student from school."[58]

It should be noted that the "due process clause" of the Constitution cited by the Supreme Court in *Goss* states that no state shall "deprive any person of life, liberty, or property, without due process of law."[59] Since it has been difficult to equate a school suspension with a loss of "liberty," the Court, over the vigorous dissents of Justices Powell, Blackmun, and Rehnquist, was reduced to defining school attendance as a "property interest" in order to apply the clause.

Among the many progeny of *Goss* is *Jordan v. Erie School District*, which held that even the transfer of a violent student to a "center especially designed to meet the needs of behavioral disruptive students"[60] requires the application of a hearing and procedural due process requirements.

Not surprisingly, in light of such procedural and constitutional requirements, many school administrators have felt inhibited in distracting themselves from other duties and expending the time and energy conducting extensive hearings that the protection of innocent students and teachers from violence would entail. The results are often tragic, as in the case of the "shooting death of a teacher in Philadelphia by a junior high student who had continuously caused trouble at the school."[61] A security director for a major school district has written to the Senate Subcommittee on Juvenile Delinquency that "students are robbed, intimidated, raped, bludgeoned and sometimes fatally wounded."[62]

Tragic examples of lax school disciplinary policies are by no means limited to inner-city schools. In 1992, four popular female students at a white middle-class junior high school in Madison, Indiana, apparently became jealous of another 12-year-old female classmate's friends and her jeans.[63] They took her out in a car, locked in the trunk, and for several hours beat her, stabbed her, and sodomized her with a sharp tire iron. When the victim in agony dared to beg for mercy and call out for her mother, her four classmates dragged her out of the trunk, sprayed windex on her wounds, poured gasoline over her and then slowly burned their screaming classmate to death.[64] One of the students later described what she had done by saying "You should have seen it. It was so funny."[65]

In this particular case, the offense was too serious to be handled by the school authorities, so there is no way of knowing whether they would have applied such disciplinary theories as helping the offender to "understand . . . their own behavior" rather than actually punishing them. Several of the students had prior disciplinary problems, but the punishments had apparently been mild.[66] Although all the students eventually pleaded guilty to murder, court transcripts reveal that the lawyer for the chief perpetrator claimed that his client was a "handicapped" student, since her parents had been divorced and she came from a broken home,[67] and that she therefore deserved "probation, living back in the community."[68] The argument that the student was handicapped apparently carried substantial weight. Although the judge did feel compelled to impose a jail term, he went out of his way to tell the chief perpetrator that she could "do something useful with her life after being released from prison."[69]

It is not so much the violent acts themselves that reveal a deficient disciplinary environment. Violent acts occur even in the most disciplined of environments. More revealing is the attitude toward such acts by the perpetrators of violence. In a disciplinary environment in which acts of violence are considered a manifestation of a handicap, it is not surprising that the students in this case felt they were being unjustly punished. One of them smugly commented after her conviction that "I murdered somebody, but I can ask forgiveness and not go to Hell."[70] Another said, "It's so stupid when you think about it. . . . I don't blame me. We just need a little growing up. We were young, and we still are."[71]

Such sentiments seem to express the view of many psychological and educational apologists that it is not a student's fault if she commits an act of violence, but rather someone else's fault or the school's fault. Such sentiments place more emphasis on the perpetrators of violence, and their perceived handicaps, than on the victims of such school violence. In the case of the Indiana torture murders committed by junior high students, the fact that the victim had been privileged to attend a school governed by Supreme Court theories of "due process" were doubtless of little consolation to her grieving parents.

Nor have the courts restrained themselves from intervening in some of the most detailed aspects of public education administration.[72] For example, the courts have reversed a teacher's policy of reducing a student's grade for unexcused absences and ordered the student's grade to be raised,[73] and declared that a school rule against the wearing of dungarees was "unconstitutional" because "liberty" under the due process clause of the Fourteenth Amendment is "large enough to include within its embrace the right to wear clean blue jeans."[74] And, of course, the right of a student to wear his hair anyway he pleases in public school has also been enshrined as a constitutional right that can not be taken away without due process.[75]

THE CRISIS OF DUE PROCESS

The imposition of such judicial and educational philosophy has not come without some resistance, however. In response to legal developments in the area of school discipline, a congressional investigation of school violence reported that "one common thread of particular interest to the Subcommittee running through many of the underlying causes of school violence and vandalism is what may be called the crisis of Due Process"[76] and that "educators and administrators are finding that the extent of student conduct which is sought to be regulated, as well as the methods of regulation, are causing more problems than they are controlling."[77]

Indeed, students themselves have been among the vigorous advocates of school discipline. A Gallup poll has reported that "most adults and high school students surveyed cited the lack of discipline as the chief problem confronting schools today."[78] A National Educational Association study has revealed that, among students around the country, many "spoke of the need for consistent, fair discipline."[79]

Students who are disciplined, however, continue to bring lawsuits against public schools that dare to attempt to impose discipline. Where constitutional principles of student "property" interests or "liberty" interests have not prevailed in curtailing discipline measures, a modern trend is to interject litigation with racial considerations. To end a costly suit, the Cincinnati School System, which had dared to place violent and disruptive students in a separate classroom, agreed to "start tracking the race of the teacher as well as the student in the case."[80] In reporting on the case, a 1994 article in *Time* magazine reported that the racial statistics are to be "factored into the teacher evaluation, though the board insists that it is simply gathering relevant information to understand racial disparities [in imposing discipline] teachers are receiving a far different message. 'We're very worried' says art teacher John Rodak. 'Do we have to start thinking about race every time we discipline a student?'"[81]

The president of the American Federation of Teachers has reacted to the case by predicting that "basically, teachers will throw in the towel and say 'why should I get into any trouble,'" comparing the proposal to "requiring the police to make racially balanced arrests."[82] In other words, such a policy would hardly justify police in refusing to protect African Americans from violence in high crime areas on grounds that the police had not made enough arrests of whites in a low crime area.

Teacher Kathy Neuman predicted that "teachers will simply stop referring students for discipline," while the attorney for the Cincinnati Federation of Teachers observed that school discipline will "be like if this week I've disciplined three black students, then next week I'd better discipline three whites.'"[83]

Tragically, as with so many other government policies that started with good intentions, any such policies inhibiting school discipline will doubtless fall heaviest on minorities, the poor, and the disadvantaged, who now suffer the most from school violence.[84]

In summary, therefore, it must be conceded that the public schools have been burdened with disciplinary costs not imposed on private schools. For example, a 1971 School Public Relations Association study found that a "$60,000 [vandalism] loss, approximately the average loss for a school district, could pay for eight reading specialists or finance a school breakfast program for 133 children for a year."[85] It may also be recalled that "the cost of replacing broken windows in the average big city would build a new school every year."[86] The question that remains, therefore, is whether the costs and restrictions imposed on school discipline are worth the tragic results in terms of the loss of human life, property, and a nurturing learning environment for public school children, particularly minority children.

ILLEGAL ALIENS

Finally, it is argued that cost comparisons are unfair because public schools, unlike private schools, are required to pay the costs and provide free education to foreign nationals and illegal aliens. It is true that the Supreme Court has held that persons who are illegally in the United States nevertheless have a constitutional right under the Fourteenth Amendment to a free education supported by American taxpayers. In *Phyler v. Doe*,[87] a bare majority of the Court struck down an attempt by the Tyler, Texas, school district to charge a fee for illegal aliens to go to the public school.

Four justices, led by Chief Justice Rehnquist and Justice O'Connor, wrote an incredulous dissent, observing that it was totally illogical for the majority to concede that illegal aliens could lawfully be deported, but they could not be denied a free education at taxpayer expense. Were the petitioners fugitives of any law other than the immigration laws, the question would not be if they could obtain free tuition, but rather why they were not being brought to justice. "Would deportation be any less a 'penalty' than denial of privileges provided to legal residents?" the four dissenting justices asked.[88]

The dissent bluntly charged that "if ever a court was guilty of an unabashedly result oriented approach, this case is a prime example. . . . By definition, illegal aliens have no right to be here, and the state may reasonably, and constitutionally, elect not to provide them with government services at the expense of those who are lawfully in the state."[89]

It should be recognized, however, that the situation confronting illegal aliens in the United States is not the fault of the aliens, most of whom are hard-working persons seeking only to better themselves. Once in the United States, however, they find themselves vulnerable to exploitation. Companies that seek high profits by paying low wages take advantage of the immigrants' illegal status, as do the rich, and it could be concluded that immigration "widens the differences in classes in the United States; it keeps down the price of hiring a maid or a gardener for the rich while it makes things worse for the poor."[90]

The Center for Immigration Studies has revealed that racism may play a large role in the present lenient immigration policies of the United States, noting that ever since the Civil War the rich and powerful have encouraged lax immigration policies so that African Americans would not have to be hired to alleviate labor shortages. According to the Center, the economic plight of African Americans has seriously deteriorated since the passage of the 1965 Immigration Act, which "provided an alternative supply of labor so that urban employees have not had to hire black job seekers. . . . Whether intended or not, the present immigration policy is a revived instrument of institutional racism."[91]

As early as 1895, Booker T. Washington made the following plea: "To those who would look to the incoming of those of foreign birth, I say 'cast down your bucket where you are. Cast it among those who have tilled your fields, cleared your forests, builded your railroads and cities.'"[92] But his pleas were ignored by those in power, and lax immigration were policies continued. That such racist policies could be justified under the guise of promoting the dream set forth on the Statue of Liberty only made them all the more attractive to the powerful industrialists.

These policies have continued, and the results have been tragic for the economic aspirations of African Americans. In the 1970s, thousands of African Americans lost their janitorial jobs when wealthy corporations farmed out the work to independent contractors employing waves of new immigrants at slave wages.[93] In 1987, when unemployment of African American teenagers approached 80%, garment makers in Los Angeles petitioned the Immigration and Nationalization Service to permit vast numbers of additional unskilled workers to immigrate on grounds that there was an "unskilled labor shortage."[94] Although apologists claim that the slave wages earned by immigrants reduce the price of goods, the same could be said of goods produced by slave labor in China. Most Americans would pay a little more to achieve social justice.

Meanwhile, California reported that it was spending half a billion dollars just to house over 12,500 illegal immigrants in prisons after they were convicted of crimes, and that in one of its counties (Santa Clara), over 40% of welfare recipients were recent immigrants.[95] At the same time, the *San Diego Union-Tribune* was reporting the case of the daughter of a Mexican millionaire who had received $130,000 in Medi-Cal payments after crossing the border, and the County of Los Angeles was reporting that 23% of its public school budget was being used to educate recent immigrants.[96]

Thus, to the 300 years of oppression imposed on African Americans, lax immigration policies have added an economic burden that has prevented many African Americans from giving their children a level playing field when they begin their education in the public schools.

The case of *Phyler v. Doe*, by inducing even greater illegal immigration with the promise of a free education, may be seen as a perpetuation of those policies that have so harmed the chances for African Americans in the public schools, and represents yet another rejection of the pleas of Booker T. Washington to "cast down your bucket where you are." Although the court would doubtless claim that its ruling was "well-intentioned," this detracts little from its implicit cruelty and reveals yet again the dangers of disregarding legal precedent and taking what the dissent described as "an unabashedly result-oriented approach."

For Hispanics, the ruling has proved to be no less cruel. Attracted by such inducements as a free education, immigrants continue to enter the United States illegally, encouraged by wealthy industrialists and employers fearful of losing an exploitable pool of cheap labor. The result is the passage of immigration laws that represent both greed and hypocrisy. Caught in the middle is the hapless and exploited immigrant whom the American border patrol can not even protect from robbers and muggers along the border.[97]

In conclusion, it must be conceded that public schools are indeed burdened by costs in the area of bilingual education, education of aliens, disabled students, and violent students. It has been seen, however, that many of these costs have been self-imposed by the very government institutions from which the public schools derive their legitimacy. How many of these self-imposed costs are justified is of course a question that must be answered by each tax-paying voter. What seems clear, however, is that many parents who can afford to do so are willing to spend a great deal of money to send their children to schools where less money is spent on them and where their children are spared due process.

Although it has been conceded that private schools enjoy a cost advantage in several of the areas already discussed, it remains to examine some other areas where private schools enjoy an advantage. Such areas include teacher salaries and certification, administrative costs, school facilities, instructional materials, and educational equipment. It should be recognized, however, that these other areas are rarely discussed within the educational establishment, since comparisons between public and private schools in these areas do not conform to cherished assumptions about the correlation between educational expenditures and student achievement.

TEACHER CERTIFICATION

It is no secret that private school teachers earn only a fraction of the salaries of their public school counterparts.[98] Due to an 18% increase in public school teacher salaries between 1982 and 1992 (after adjusting for inflation),[99] American public school teachers earn almost three times as much as a public school teacher in Japan,[100] and more than teachers in many other countries. Since teachers' salaries are the single largest item of any school budget, it follows that differences in salaries between public and private school teachers accounts for a large percentage of the disparity in overall cost between public and private education.

It also comes as no surprise, therefore, to learn that while the cost of educating a public school student (K-12) is now over $6,300,[101] the cost of educating a student in the average sectarian private school (K-12) is $2,711, and $1,200 in a parochial elementary school.[102]

There appear to be several possible explanations for why teacher costs are so much higher in public schools than private ones. The first relates to the manner of teacher certification. For private schools, state certification and regulation of teachers is mercifully minimal.[103] Public school teacher certification is another matter.

A study by C. Emily Feistritzer in 1984[104] concluded that "the certification of classroom teachers in the U.S. is a mess. Each state makes its own rules concerning who can be certified and what they can be certified to teach. The numbers of different types of certificates and what is required to get one within a state, much less nationwide, is staggering. Florida, for example, is set up to certify 410 academic and vocational areas for its school personnel."[105]

Not surprisingly, while the cost of administering such certification programs is also staggering, serious questions have been raised as to the results of such certification requirements. A 1991 study by M. M. Kennedy concluded that "our data suggests that these programs . . . do not necessarily produce better teachers than any other approaches to teacher education."[106]

J. B. Conant's monumental study of teacher certification in the 1960s revealed that "among the 16 most populous states, no two states have adopted the same requirements for entry into the profession on either the elementary or the secondary level."[107] He also used the words "horror" and "shocking" to describe data revealing the percentage of certified teachers teaching subjects in which they had less than nine college hours of credits.[108] He found that "one third of the teachers who taught mathematics and one third of those who taught biology had less than nine college credit hours in those subjects."[109]

Although John Stuart Mill first argued against the notion of teacher certification as early as 1859,[110] more modern exposes of teacher certification include Bestor's 1953 *Educational Wastelands*, and Lynd's *Quackery in the Public Schools*.[111]

The real problem with teacher certification is that basic teaching skills can not ordinarily be taught in a classroom. Nor can methodology courses teaching such topics as the preparation of lesson plans, or what color pen to use in correcting papers, be equated with the substantive knowledge or learning of effective teaching techniques. Institutions of higher learning, such as law schools and medical schools, have known this for years and as a result do not require teaching certificates of their professors.

A typical law school, for example, seeks the most qualified professional in the field in which there exists a teaching need. Careful attention is paid to an applicant's education and professional reputation and experience, particularly with regard to scholarly publications. If the applicant has prior teaching experience, past student and peer teaching evaluations are requested and scrutinized. The applicant is also invited to make a formal presentation to the faculty on a topic of interest. Such a presentation is usually most effective in revealing an applicant's classroom demeanor and presence. Once a teacher is hired, he or she is given time to develop an effective teaching style, and help may be provided by peers upon request. If the teacher fails to develop an effective teaching style, he or she will ordinarily not be given tenure, and will either move on to administration or return to practice in his or her chosen profession.

In short, teaching is properly recognized as an art rather than a science. An applicant might have taken dozens of methodology courses, but still be ineffective in explaining ideas and concepts in a classroom setting. Others have a natural talent and ability to teach effectively. It would probably make as much sense to require that actors and actresses be certified before being able to perform in a play or film. While attending acting school may help a struggling actor as well as provide useful professional contacts, it certainly provides no guarantee of proficiency. The list of great and famous performers who did not go to acting school is no doubt a very long one indeed, as would be the list of outstanding but non certified public schools teachers, were certification requirements to be eliminated.

It is not suggested, however, that public schools should use the same criteria for hiring teachers as institutions of higher learning or professional schools. A professional physician, for example, may be adept at explaining difficult concepts to medical students, but less effective at explaining to a first grader how to add two plus two. In the case of both the physician and the first grade teacher, however, an effective teaching technique is not something that can be learned in a class. In both cases, the first priority should be proficiency and knowledge in the subject area that is taught. Observation, monitoring, and peer development can then cull the effective teachers.

But how did the notion ever evolve that a teacher of advanced physics need not be certified to teach, but that one who teaches basic arithmetic must be taught to teach? The answer may lie less in the development of teaching theory than in the world of politics. Conant's study revealed that, regarding teacher certification, "professional teachers' associations and the states' education departments which they influenced were the most powerful groups in policy decisions. . . . (T)eachers' associations . . . supported certification more than any other group."[112]

The transformation of teaching in the public schools from a professional status to that of a trade union has also played a role. Before 1960 there were few teacher unions in the United States.[113] By 1970 over three-fourths of public school teachers in the United States had joined trade unions.[114] Within a few years, most unions had been given the right to strike. It soon became clear that, unlike teachers in institutions of higher learning, public school teachers had decided that they preferred to be treated as trade unionists rather than professionals. The results have been predictable.

In 1993, Sam Peltzman's study of teacher unionization "looked at what happened to student achievement in those places where the push for teacher unionization was most successful most quickly. In those areas, student achievement tended to deteriorate more than average."[115] According to the study, the reason for such deterioration was that "unions have traditional concerns such as job security, promotions and pay deferential rules that may be in conflict with some educational goals. Union-style job security, for example, is not compatible with flexibility in replacing mediocre or poor teachers."[116]

In many school districts, a siege mentality has evolved between teachers and school boards, with teacher strikes becoming an "annual rite of Fall."[117] In such an environment, certification requirements have been further tightened as a means of maintaining job security and higher pay. Unfortunately, however, these certification requirements have served to deprive the public schools of many of their best applicants for teaching positions.

Feistritzer's study revealed that, unlike in the 1960s, "the best and brightest [women] are now getting degrees in fields other than teaching."[118] Data collected by Lieberman shows that "prospective teachers rank near the bottom of student groups planning to enter various occupations,"[119] and that the SAT of the average preservice elementary teacher was lower than the national average.[120]

In more recent years, however, the tightening of traditional certification programs has had an unintended result. Teacher shortages began appearing in the early 1980s, leading some school districts (such as New Jersey in 1984) to consider alternative[121] means of qualifying teachers. According to the National Center for Education Information, by 1992 the number of states permitting alternative routes to teacher qualification had risen to 40.[122]

Not surprisingly, there has been fierce union resistance to this development. It has been reported that "the Association of Teacher

Educators has all but denounced alternative certification, proposing 22 minimum standards that should be followed by states using alternative routes."[123] As a result of such resistance, the number of public school teachers actually qualified by alternative certification has been minimal. In 1988 there were about 2.5 million teachers in kindergarten, elementary, and secondary education.[124] It has been reported that between 1985 and 1990, "only about 20,000 persons had been certified through a 'true' alternative route."[125]

The ranks of the alternatively certified include those in other professions (such as law, business, engineering), housewives, retired military, and other retired professionals. A 1988 study by J. A. Boser and P. D. Wiley revealed that "talented individuals recruited for an alternative program scored higher on core battery tests than the University-certified teachers."[126]

Not surprisingly, the overwhelming majority of private school teachers agree with the proposition that "recruiting adults who have experience in careers other than teaching would improve America's education system," as do a majority of school board presidents, superintendents, and high school principals.[127] Remarkably, however, 56% of public school teachers have parted company with their union leadership and also agree with that proposition.[128]

Feistritzer reports that "growing numbers of governors, state commissioners of education, deans of education, and other political and educational leaders are stepping forward in favor of some type of alternative certification as a means of improving the quality of the teaching profession, and thereby improving the educational achievement of all of the nation's youth."[129] Needless to say, teachers' unions are not mentioned in this group.

Until public schools make more progress in this area, however, and until teachers decide that they want to be treated more as professionals rather than as trade unionists, the private schools will continue to have a significant cost and performance advantage in teaching. In the meantime, the government's solution to the educational crisis is set forth in the Goals 2000 Act which recommends expanded teacher training.[130] In fact, what is needed is far less "teacher training and more professionalism.

ADMINISTRATION

One unfortunate by-product of the deprofessionalization and unionization of teachers in the public schools has been the expansion and aggrandizement of administration. With teachers reduced to the role of executors of administrative policy, it becomes necessary to hire more and more administrators to formulate those policies, and tell the teachers how and what to teach. The bureaucracies in large school districts have become particularly top heavy.

For example, the New York City Board of Education supports and feeds an army of over 3,500 highly paid administrators. The New York City parochial schools, on the other hand (whose students number 40% of students in the public school systems), can not afford such an administrative burden since they do not have vast infusions of tax money to support it. Instead, they spend their limited funds on actual teaching,[131] and get by with fewer than 50 administrators for the entire City of New York.[132]

It is not surprising, therefore, that in 1989 only 32% of the New York City school operating budget went for teaching purposes.[133] The Texas Auditor's Office recently cited a "Texas County, that had 12 school systems—with 12 school boards, 12 superintendents and so forth—that together enrolled only 5,000 students."[134]

Taking on an entrenched educational bureaucracy determined to preserve its own powers, privileges, and prerogatives has proved to be no easy task. Once a school district concedes that it could function without an army of administrators, it can no longer justify its ravenous demands for ever-increasing tax revenues. Nevertheless, on occasion the attempt has been made.

In 1992 *Fortune* magazine reported that during the previous five years, the mayor of Baltimore had taken drastic action to reduce the administrative overhead of the city's public school system. Over fierce resistance from an entrenched bureaucracy, and warnings of dire disaster, the mayor eliminated over 200 administrative positions.[135] The result was not only an improved educational system, but substantial savings to the taxpayers.[136] A study of the effects of the mayor's action revealed that the elimination of the administrative positions had "transform[ed] the city from the second-highest cost jurisdiction in Maryland to the third lowest."[137] In 1992 the Cincinnati school system "slashed its administration by 51%." Sixty five positions from assistant superintendents to supervisors were abolished, saving the city "16 million dollars"[138]   A later study of the action concluded that "public schooling's vast infra-structure from those who change the light-bulbs to those who push the paper has grown so widely . . . that it is more often a hindrance than a support to education."[139]

Comparisons with public schools in other countries also provide some insight. A study of the Koln-Holweide school district in Germany revealed a program that would doubtless send chills down the spines of school administrators if implemented in American public schools. It was found that "teachers, rather than administrators, make all instructional decisions at this school."[140]   Freed from their administrative albatross, the teachers made some important changes, among which was the extension of the school day from 8:15 to 4:15, and the devotion of one or two periods a day to study halls in which students, regardless of their home situation or socioeconomic background, could do their homework without interruption. As a result, the drop out rate was reduced to "a rate of 1%, as compared with a West German average of 14%, and an astonishing 60% rate of admission to four-year colleges, compared with a national average of 27%, and this despite the fact that Koln-Holweide's student body is far from an elite one. Best of all, the kids seem to enjoy their education. Parents report that they can't wait until the holidays end, so that they can get back to school."[141]

Were public school teachers returned to the professional status now enjoyed by professors in institutions of higher learning, they would be trusted to teach as they see fit. Law school administrators hire the best and most qualified teachers they can find, and then let them do what they are paid to do: devise a syllabus, choose a textbook, and develop an effective teaching technique. Rarely are such professors second-guessed by administrators. In any case, if administrators knew how to teach better than the teachers, they would doubtless be better employed in the classroom than in shuffling papers. It makes no pedagogic sense, let alone economic sense, to create a superfluous additional layer of authority between the student and a school's educational mission.

Every school, whether public or private, requires a headmaster or principal. An assistant, a registrar to keep records, and a nurse may also be required. From age 9 to 12, I attended a British grammar school that taught children aged 5-14. The school had three administrators: a headmaster, an assistant headmaster, and a registrar. All other educational responsibilities were given to the teachers, who were hired because they knew how to teach Latin, Greek, mathematics, science, history, and English. For an administrator to have told them how to teach would not only have been impractical; it would also have been greatly resented, and would have been considered an intolerable intrusion of the teachers' professional prerogatives.

Despite such examples as the New York parochial schools and Koln-Howeide, it is doubtful that American public schools will follow their lead. The care and upkeep of administrators involves the distribution of literally billions of dollars that might otherwise have to go for teaching. In today's public school classrooms, "teachers constitute fewer than 40% of all educational employees." [142] If for no other reason, administrators and other members of the educational establishment are needed to compile data and statistics showing why more money is needed to maintain the administrative establishment. Thus, for the foreseeable future, private schools will continue to enjoy a substantial cost advantage in the area of administration.

SCHOOL FACILITIES AND EDUCATIONAL MATERIALS

In 1987 James Coleman and Thomas Hoffer wrote a sequel to the 1966 Coleman Report to the U.S. Office of Education. Entitled *Public and Private High Schools*,[143] the book carefully documented the differences both in cost per student and student performance in the nation's public and private high schools. Among its other findings, it revealed that private parochial schools have, in effect, enjoyed a great advantage—namely, a lack of funding. As one student of Coleman's second study has observed, "with less money, parochial schools are less flexible and retain traditional curriculum and academic structures that have fallen victim to pop trends and political pressure in pubic schools since the 1960s,"[144] and that parochial schools "elicit greater achievement, even from students with comparable family and socioeconomic backgrounds."[145]

It will be recalled that the first Coleman Report revealed that resources that depend primarily on money, such as teacher salaries, teacher training, and student-faculty ratios, have little if any correlation with student achievement.[146] The experience in the Kansas City magnet schools showed how expenditures on lavish physical facilities make no difference in student achievement, and in fact may adversely affect it;[147] and a comparison with Japanese schools revealed that high student performance can be achieved without either lavish school facilities or fancy textbooks. The second Coleman study, however, revealed that schools nevertheless can make a difference in student achievement. The task, therefore, is to identify those features of a school that contribute to student achievement.

THE TREND TOWARD PUBLIC SCHOOL ABANDONMENT

Perhaps the most unfortunate result of public school failure in America has been the movement toward abandonment of the public schools. Parents who can afford it are sending their children to private schools, while the middle class has fled to the suburbs and abandoned the city schools to an inner-city underclass. In short, millions of Americans have simply thrown up their hands and given up on the public schools.

In many respects this trend is understandable. Parents fear for the safety of their children in a public school system where application of due process principles have made discipline impracticable and often virtually impossible, where over 5% of students are harmed with weapons every year, and vandalism destroys the very infrastructure of the schools.[148] Misguided judicial interference has resulted in the exact opposite of what the courts claimed they hoped to achieve, often accelerating the trend toward public school abandonment. After years of court-imposed plans, schools are more segregated today than in 1972.[149] In desperation, parents and educators have also turned to solutions that promise to further hasten implementation of a strategy of abandonment.

Chapter Three

The Reform Movements

SCHOOL CHOICE

Most of the educational-type reform proposals, such as school choice, magnets, and vouchers, are all variations of a strategy of abandonment—that is, they are premised on the underlying assumption that most public schools are beyond redemption. Schemes are then conceived in which children of parents who are best able to take advantage of the scheme can get their children into the best available schools. The concept of choice then serves as a fig leaf for what would otherwise be considered unfair, and educationally or constitutionally unsound. Unfortunately, however, such schemes usually turn out to be zero-sum games in the sense that ultimately only a few can go to the "best" schools.

Take, for example, the concept of choice as proposed by John Chubb and Terry Moe in their widely quoted book *Politics, Markets, and America's Schools.*[1] This book built on an earlier model of economic efficiency developed by renowned economist Milton Friedman—namely, that "if parents could choose any school, with state support through vouchers, this would break the monopoly of the public schools and increase educational competition."[2] Friedman's ideas were based on the sound economic principles of competition. If consumers had a choice, they would take their business to the producers who provided the best service at the lowest cost. Successful enterprises would then thrive, while the unsuccessful ones would fail or wither on the vine. In a strictly economic sense, the choice schemes that have been tentatively implemented by some legislatures have confirmed the soundness of theory—that is, parents (the consumers) have flocked to the best schools to try to get their children admitted.

For example, when a magnet/choice plan was implemented in San Francisco, parents with high socioeconomic status quickly discerned which schools were the best and attempted to get their children admitted. Since the student demand exceeded the number of seats available in such schools, however, the best schools had the luxury of choosing from among many applicants. Not surprisingly, the magnet schools ended up accepting students from the "highest socio-economic level."[3]   In a corporate world of economic competition, the most desirable schools would be able to raise their tuition to the point where supply equaled demand. In the world of free public education, however, the imposition of high tuition would be inconsistent with the goal of a free public education for all children.

Another typical choice program was implemented by Wisconsin pursuant to the 1990 Milwaukee Parental Choice Program.[4] That plan enabled "one percent of a school district's low income students to attend private, nonsectarian schools while the state pays participating schools approximately $2,500 for each student enrolled in the program."[5]   Like the San Francisco plan, the scheme worked well for the 1% or so of gifted students it served.

Among the conclusions of reports that have studied school choice plans are that "school officials have used choice to select and admit the most academically gifted of the students";[6] that choice has become "a gatekeeper for school administrators, not parents";[7] that "there is little proof that private and suburban schools readily accept minority children from the city even when choice is an option";[8] and that "urban choice appears to exacerbate social divisions because middle class students have disproportionate access to the best public schools."[9]

In evaluating school choice systems, I am reminded of my experience as a teenager riding the Paris subway system. The subway cars were divided into two classes First and Second. Ordinarily, the price of a First Class ticket was about three times that of a Second Class ticket. However, I never discerned any appreciable difference in the physical facilities offered in the First and Second Class cars. The only difference was that First Class was less crowded and more quiet, and appeared to serve a more respectable class of clientele—well dressed citizens and businessmen in suits. Every Tuesday afternoon between 2 and 5, however, as a gesture to egalitarianism, passengers with a Second Class ticket were permitted the "choice" of traveling in First Class for no additional charge. All of a sudden it was the First Class compartment that became crowded and noisy, and the Second Class cars became quiet and uncrowded.

In a similar way, the public schools that become most desirable to parents are not necessarily those that have the best teachers or most lavish facilities. (It may be recalled that when Kansas City spent a billion dollars lavishly equipping its magnet schools, it attracted only 3% of the suburban students who studied in schools with inferior facilities.)[10]

In the early 1980s the British government implemented a school choice plan in Scotland that permitted parents to choose any school in Scotland for their children, regardless of where they lived. To the consternation of school officials, well-off parents from all around Scotland began choosing to send their children to a run-down, old Victorian, red brick school named Paisley Grammar School, which had been slated to be closed down.[11] Although Paisley had nothing special to offer in terms of teachers, programs, or facilities, wealthy children traveled miles and miles from home just to attend. Children from less wealthy families also sought admission, although the long distance to the school made this more difficult for them as a practical matter.

What did the parents who sent their children to Paisley like so much about the decrepit old school? According to a study, "they like(d) the royal blue blazers that students were required to wear, in an era when more and more schools were dropping their uniforms. They like(d) the standards of behavior that students were held to. They like(d) the teachers' way of dressing, in business clothes rather than jeans."[12]   In short, Paisley had the attributes of many of Scotland's most exclusive and traditional private schools.

Unmentioned, but a very likely factor in choosing Paisley, was the opportunity to be with other children who wanted the opportunity to be educated in a learning environment. A later poll of parents revealed that a significant number of parents admitted that they sent their children to Paisley in order to "avoid the local school"; while 36% mentioned "reputation" as a reason, only 4% mentioned the quality of teaching.[13] Although administrators pleaded with parents to stop applying to Paisley, suggesting that they had not properly evaluated or compared the qualities of neighboring schools, parents persisted in having their children apply to Paisley.

It will be recalled that the choice theories espoused by such critics as Chubb and Moe predict that efficient schools with good educational programs will siphon students from inferior schools, with the consequence that the less popular schools will either emulate the high standards of the popular schools and improve the schools, or else "go out of business." It is difficult to imagine what the Scottish schools who lost their students to Paisley could have done to stop the flow. They already had greater funding, better school facilities, better teachers, and a more diverse curriculum. (In Scotland, unlike the United States, schools serving poor neighborhoods receive more funds than those in richer neighborhoods.) Perhaps they could have tightened their rules or required uniforms. But Paisley's most attractive feature would have been hard to duplicate. What made Paisley most attractive was that the best students were already going there.

In any case, the predictions of choice theory did not occur in Scotland. A study conducted by Glasgow University of Scotland's school choice system noted that while "proponents (of school choice) argued that choice would encourage schools to . . . improve . . . that has not happened."[14]

Nor did less popular schools end up going out of business. While schools competing with Paisley did in fact wither, a study revealed that despite falling enrollments, "it's difficult to find any school that has closed since 1981 simply because it was abandoned by its students. Closures here are as wrenching as they are anywhere in the world, and just about as popular politically." [15] The net result was simply that students from "families where there was no great interest in education (were) left in the unpopular schools."[16]

VOUCHERS

Voucher systems are basically choice systems that include private schools. Under a voucher system every parent in the state is provided by the legislature with a voucher that may be applied toward an education at either a public or a private school within the state. The theory is the same as the theory of choice within the public school system—that is, parents will vote with their vouchers, give their business to the best schools, and the bad schools will "wither on the vine" if they do not react competitively and improve their educational service.

In practice, the voucher system suffers from the same problems as the choice and magnet systems—namely, that it favors parents in high socioeconomic groups who are more adept at exploiting the system in favor of their own children. Children from low socioeconomic families are either not in a position to take advantage of the system due to such practical factors as distance from the better schools, or their parents do not have the diligence or inclination to jump through the proper hoops necessary to accomplish a school transfer. As in Scotland, "families where there is no great interest in education are left in unpopular schools."[17]

A study of a voucher system enacted in Alum Rock, Arkansas, between 1972 and 1977 found that "information regarding the voucher programs were much higher among white parents with high incomes, and the parents' educational backgrounds proved to be an especially important factor."[18] It was further found that wealthy "parents were much more likely to use the vouchers and to choose schools that offered the best possible education."[19]

Not surprisingly, choice systems, whether or not taking the form of a voucher system, rarely result in any significant improvements or redistribution of students or educational resources. In the case of *Green v. County School Board*, decided by the Supreme Court in 1968, it was found that a freedom-of-choice plan resulted in virtually no transfers between schools, which remained as segregated as before the plan was implemented. Indeed it found that "not a single white child chose to go to the black school where 85% of the black children continued to attend."[20]

Such experiences reveal that, for many parents, a school is not just an educational institution, but an inherent part of a neighborhood and the culture of that neighborhood. The only real choice made by most parents is the one they make when they choose a particular neighborhood to live in. Such a choice is, in turn, almost always significantly influenced by the economic status of the parents.

However, the most serious problem with voucher systems is that, when they are enacted, they almost never provide a voucher sufficient to pay completely for an education at any private school within the state. Vouchers that only partially pay for a private school education are in fact only disguised subsidies to parents who can otherwise afford or almost afford to send their children to private schools.

Some states have attempted to create voucher systems by creating vouchers in the form of tax credits that can be used to offset the cost of private school tuition. In *Committee v. Nyquist* the Supreme Court struck down such a New York scheme on grounds that such credits "actually amount(ed) to tuition grants to the parents of children attending private schools."[21] Since most of the private schools in New York were sectarian, the decision was based on the establishment clause of the Constitution (forbidding the government to establish religion.)[22]

In *Mueller v. Allen*, however, the Supreme Court upheld a Minnesota scheme that provided a $500 tax credit to be used for expenses at either a public or a private school.[23] Since expenses at the public schools were negligible, the scheme appeared to be a thinly disguised attempt to avoid the religious establishment problem of *Nyquist* by appearing to give "neutral" tax credits to parents to be used at either public or private religious institutions. If so, it was an adequate disguise, as the Court viewed the subsidy as neutral and upheld the scheme.

Regardless of their constitutionality, however, such schemes are of doubtful educational value, particularly if they provide only partial assistance for private school tuition. Even voucher systems that provide total reimbursement for private school education foster a general and overall strategy of public school abandonment and do little to solve what should be the ultimate objective of improving public education.

A decision to abandon the public schools may ultimately be found to be necessary in light of continued failure of the public school mission. Many critics now believe the present system is beyond redemption. A recent article in *The Atlantic Monthly* proclaimed that "school as we know it is doomed. And every attempt to improve—but fundamentally preserve—the present system will only prolong its death throes and add immeasurably to its costs, both financial and social."[24]

In 1993 the president of the University of Southern California and a member of the Van de Kamp Education Commission warned that "our public education is the worst of any industrialized nation. Indeed, students in Third World nations receive a better education than many American youngsters . . . our inner-city schools are in a state of virtual anarchy. . . . The United States is on its way to becoming a Third World economy due to the lack of skills among the majority of our high school graduates. And, indeed, average personal income (after inflation) in this country has already dropped 20 per cent in the past two decades."[25]

Should the public schools ultimately be abandoned, such abandonment should be done directly and forthrightly, and not undermined gradually by the implementation of choice or voucher systems. But if the public schools are to redeem themselves with reforms that give all American children an opportunity to learn in a suitable educational environment, they must do so before control is lost to those in the forefront of a growing movement toward privatization.

THE PRIVATIZATION MOVEMENT

Some of those most exasperated with public school failure have suggested that the public schools might be made more responsive to educational needs if they were simply required by law to be so. An associate general counsel for the Department of Health, Education and Welfare recently proposed in a monumental law review article that the law impose a "new legal duty . . . on urban public schools to educate [in basic skills] the vast majority of its students, regardless of race or income."[26] Such proposals, however, might be more persuasive if the law and the courts had a better track record in exerting a positive influence on public education. Many others believe sincerely that there is no hope for public education, and that only privatization can restore its legitimacy.

In 1993 it was reported that "the Edison Project, entrepreneur Chris Whittle's ambitious attempt to create a private school system educating 2 million students on 1,000 campuses, [would] announce its prototype . . . to open its first schools in 1996." In addition, 11 private foundations introduced "visions of redesigned schools they had drafted under the auspices of the New York American Schools Development Corporation."[27]

A Minneapolis company called Education Alternatives recently signed a contract with the City of Baltimore to run nine of its public schools for the same amount of money the city spends per student, and predicted that it would make a 25% profit even while it reduced the student-faculty ratio to 1:15.[28] It would do so, the company maintained, by strictly controlling costs, particularly land and construction costs. Although resisted by the teacher's union, which blocked the company's attempt to replace paraprofessionals at reduced salaries, the company's prototype school at South Pointe in Florida was described by the local press as bursting with "happy kids, newly energized teachers, enthusiastic parents . . . all in a school where 80% of the kids are poor enough to qualify for a free lunch."[29] Although skeptics of the venture in Baltimore abound, Education Alternatives is now on the forefront of a privatization movement.

There is clearly much to be said for the privatization of the public schools, just as there is much to be said for privatization of just about any human activity that does not require the imprimatur or legitimacy of government.

But the vision of free and public education for all citizens is ultimately a vision of all of society's self-interest. Educated citizens are more productive and more law-abiding. Citizens who gain knowledge of where they came from, how the world works, and who understand ideas and concepts based on reason are more likely to employ reason in their relations with each other. That instruments of government in the United States have thus far failed to accomplish their educational goals in public education is not in and of itself a reason to abandon the original vision. Nor should the search for an alternative system provide an excuse for failing to improve the present one.

Before the public schools are abandoned, a final effort should be made to diagnose their problems and find fresh solutions. Any such quest, however, must proceed unencumbered by ideology, preconceptions, and any emotional attachment to past remedies that have so often proved futile. It also requires a willingness to learn from the experience of others.

THE QUEST FOR AN EQUAL PLAYING FIELD

One reason for the failure of public education is that it has not adapted to changing social conditions. For example, in 1960 the number of American children under 18 experiencing the divorce of their parents was less than 1%.[30] By 1990 that number had increased to 50%.[31] During that same period, the percentage of mothers returning to work within one year of a child's birth increased from 17% to 53%, and the percentage of married women in the labor force with children under six years old increased from 18% to 60%.[32]

Although it is beyond the scope of this book to review all the social changes during the past 30 years, it is clear from these figures that young children today receive far less attention from a parent in the home than they did 30 years ago. School children in the 1960s were much more likely to return home to a parent, usually a mother, who would be there to monitor the television and provide a quiet time to do homework. Preschool children were much more likely to receive stimulation in the form of parentally supervised play or reading.

A responsible educational response to such changes would have been to increase the length of the school day, and provide monitored study halls to accommodate students and "latch-key" children who would otherwise return home to an unsupervised environment. Another appropriate response would have been to increase the length of the academic year to accommodate the increasing number of children with two working parents whose vacations rarely exceed three weeks in the summer. The most important response, however, would have been to initiate free, if not mandatory, public education for children aged two or three.

A 1994 report by the Carnegie Institute revealed that there is now growing scientific evidence that the learning environment provided to children prior to age three "determine(s) their brain structure and ability to learn."[33] In addition, "advances in molecular biology and neurology have shown that children's experiences in these early years can influence how many brain cells, or neurons, they develop, and how many connections, or synapses, are formed between them" and that "underused synapses are naturally pruned from the infant brain."[34]

The U.S. educational establishment, however, has decided that the most critical years of a child's learning development are the very years the public schools should completely ignore. State laws often mandate education until age 16 or 18, often hiring an army of truant officers to enforce such laws and round up truants. By then, of course, it is too late. The most likely truant is one who entered school at age six already so irremediably behind in learning development that he can never catch up even if properly motivated. The synapses in his brain, permanently pruned through under use at age two, can not provide the intellectual horsepower needed to learn at even an average rate.

The child may then be singled out as "learning disabled" and put in a special education track in which it may cost the state two to three times as much to keep him in school, and even then sometimes only by physical force.

If ever there were an issue in education that cried out for application of constitutional principles of equal protection and due process it would be on the question of preschool education. Only by providing all children with a stimulating learning environment prior to age three can all children be provided with an equal opportunity to an education. It would be far better to reduce the mandatory age for education from 18 to 14 if that meant that children could be put in a learning environment prior to age three, than to deprive children of a learning environment in their early years while physically forcing them to stay in school later.

Instead, however, the educational and judicial system's idea of equal protection and due process is to make it impossible to protect children from violent students who have already been victimized by an educational establishment that deprived them of the opportunity to learn during the most critical stage of their development. In such a context, the whole philosophy of the educational and judicial establishment is revealed not just as misguided, put perverse.

Educators occasionally concede the desirability of public preschool education but dismiss the idea as too costly. It is ironic that concerns about cost do not arise when plans are made to install therapeutic hot tubs in schools such as those in Kansas City, but become insurmountable obstacles to providing education in the most critical years of a child's development.

There are many ways, however, in which free preschool education could be provided without increasing costs. First of all, preschool teachers require less training and command lower salaries than, say, a teacher in high school with an advanced degree in mathematics or physics. What is most important in a preschool learning environment is stimulation, which can take the form of creative play, building blocks, playing games, and the like. Building blocks and games cost much less than advanced computers, televisions, and lab equipment. Nor do school facilities have to be elaborate, with alcove swimming pools, hot tubs, or carpets. As in Japan, young students can be taught responsibilities of chores and cleanup.

It may be recalled that in public schools, only 40% of the personnel consist of teachers. This could easily be raised to 80% or higher by getting rid of administrators and bureaucrats. It is disconcerting to think that young children are now being permanently deprived of their capability of learning in order to finance, feed, and care for highly paid administrators who shuffle paper and tell teachers how to teach.

Until this tragedy in our public schools is remedied, however, there remains the question of how to provide the best learning environment for students now in the public schools.

INGREDIENTS OF EFFECTIVE EDUCATION

What do parents look for in a school for their children? It has already been seen that lavish facilities, hot tubs, swimming pools, armies of counselors, television studios, art galleries, and colorful glossy textbooks are not among the most important features of a successful school. Even student-faculty ratios and the training and experience of the teachers are not considered most important.

Rather, what most parents seek for their children is a learning environment that is safe, disciplined, and orderly, and that will provide learning incentives and have high expectations of student performance. That is why parents in Scotland chose Paisley over other schools with better facilities and more experienced teachers. It is why suburban parents declined to send their children to the more lavishly equipped and maintained inner-city schools in Kansas City. It is why parents and employers in Japan express satisfaction with the learning experience provided in their spartan and frugally equipped public schools. Indeed, so important to parents and children are these features, that parents, disdaining the public schools, will spend money out of their own pockets to obtain them for their children. They have been voting with their feet by abandoning the public schools.

Despite this evidence of what parents seek, studies and reports continue to set goals that are oblivious to this preference. The 1994 Goals 2000 Act authorizes $5 billion in grants over the next five years,[35] and sets forth "teaching development and standards [as the] top priority."[36] The courts continue to insist upon enforcing due process on the backs of innocent victims of school violence.[37]

The question has therefore become how schools can provide a suitable learning environment for children who want to learn, while still accommodating due process for the others. Schools have experimented with a variety of methods of accomplishing this, ranging from segregation (via special or bilingual education), magnet schools, voucher systems, and ultimately private alternative education.

While all of these solutions do help provide in some measure a more suitable learning environment for more advantaged students, all these solutions, though often disguised, are ultimately based on separation. Such solutions are short-sighted, even in providing a learning environment for the more able, because they all serve to hasten the abandonment of the public schools, and deny access to those students whose ability has not been permitted to develop.

An alternative solution that would guarantee a learning environment for all students who want to learn is the creation of magnet classrooms—based not on institutional preconceptions about a child's ability, but rather on a mutual commitment to the preservation of a learning environment.

THE MAGNET CLASSROOM

I first discussed the concept of the magnet classroom in an article in the *Atlanta Constitution* in 1991.[38] A magnet classroom is one within a neighborhood public school, admission to which is open to all students who are willing to make a formal commitment to learning. It differs from the idea of magnet schools and tracking in several significant respects.

First, unlike magnet schools, which physically separate by long distances those who qualify for admission to the magnet school from those who do not, a magnet classroom exists within an integrated neighborhood school.

Second, the concept of the magnet classroom differs from tracking, in that it would not depend upon an institutional preconception or predetermination of a student's ability. The sole requirement for admission to the magnet classroom would be that a student and his or her parents jointly sign a written commitment to participate in the creation of a disciplined classroom environment. This commitment would include an agreement to abide by rules of discipline as set forth by the classroom teacher, and a waiver of all disciplinary due process rights to which the student would otherwise be entitled by law.

The classroom disciplinary rules would be determined by the classroom teacher, who would be free to adopt a model disciplinary code recommended by the school district. The essential ingredient of such a code would be that if a student becomes disruptive, or at the sole discretion of the teacher is determined to have violated the agreement signed by student and parents, the student is deemed, by breaking the agreement, to have requested a transfer to a regular (i.e., nonmagnet) classroom. The teacher is given the means to insure a safe and orderly classroom environment, thereby releasing energies that would otherwise be expended on discipline to be focused on teaching.

Three possible initial objections to the magnet classroom should be discussed. First, it may be objected that the concept gives too much power to a teacher, and provides no review of a teacher's power to punish students by expelling them from the class. In response to this objection, it should be noted that no "punishment" of any kind is involved. Student and parents sign an agreement to abide by certain rules as the price of admission to the magnet classroom. Students at all times retain the right to withdraw from the agreement. This can be done by simply informing the teacher of the decision to withdraw, or by manifesting withdrawal by violating the agreement and being disruptive. Thus there is no expulsion from the classroom—only a voluntary decision by a student to withdraw from the agreement. The consequences of voluntary withdrawal would not carry any stigma or indicia of punishment. No black marks would be indicated on a student's transcript, and no other discipline of any kind imposed on the student. The student's manifestation of withdrawal would no more be a punishment than if a tenant of an apartment building were to indicate to a landlord that he has decided not to pay any additional rent. It would go without saying that a decision to stop paying rent is tantamount to a decision to vacate the premises. In neither case would the voluntary decision to terminate the agreement be considered a punishment of any kind.

To claim that transfer to a regular classroom was punishment would be to also claim that attending a regular classroom in our public schools today is punishment. While some critics of our public schools might indeed make that claim, the courts have decided that students have a right to attend regular classrooms where all the rights of due process are accorded. No parent would ever be required to have his or her child attend the magnet classroom. Withdrawal from a magnet classroom would mean only that a student had decided to attend a regular classroom where he or she would be entitled to all the benefits of due process that the law provides. Indeed, it would be every student's right to make that decision, either through formal request or by breaking the code of conduct for the magnet classroom.

Nor would there be any denial of due process in the magnet classroom. It is an essential tenant of constitutional law that even fundamental constitutional rights may be waived if there is informed consent.[39] For example, every citizen has a right under the Fourth Amendment to the Constitution to be secure against "unreasonable searches and seizures."[40] However, the law is clear that Fourth Amendment rights may be waived by the giving of an informed consent.[41]

All students applying for admission to a magnet classroom would be fully informed of the standards of behavior expected in the magnet classroom, and would also be informed that the teacher would have sole discretion in determining compliance with the agreement signed by the student and parent. In other words, there would be no second-guessing, appealing of such a determination by the teacher, or resort to due process protection, since such protection would be specifically waived by each student and parent after being fully informed of the consequences of that waiver.

The law does provide that there are limits to the conditions that can be imposed in return for a waiver of constitutional rights. For example, courts initially held that it was not constitutionally permissible to condition interstate travel on a scheduled airline on the waiver of rights against search and seizure of baggage without probable cause.[42] The argument was that is was unfair for the government to require a citizen to give up a fundamental right as a condition of enjoying another basic right. Although the right to travel was considered a basic right, the courts soon reversed themselves and decided that it was not unfair to condition that right upon the agreement by passengers to waive their constitutional rights to be free from a search of their baggage without probable cause.[43]

In the case of the magnet classroom, there would not even be a question of giving up a basic right in return for the waiver. The only consequence of declining to sign a waiver would be that the student would be assigned to a regular classroom. A regular classroom would simply be the kind of classroom that exists in public schools to-day—that is, a classroom in which students are free to be disruptive and are given all the rights of due process. It is difficult to imagine that a court could ever hold that it is unfair to assign students to a class where they enjoy full due process if they decline to sign a waiver which would make them eligible to attend a class that has no due process. For a court to do so would be to arrive at the tautologically illogical conclusion that it is a basic constitutional right to be denied due process.

Although the legal basis for the magnet classroom is clearly sound, there remains the question of whether it is good educational policy to vest teachers with so much authority to control their classrooms. For example, an argument might be made that it would be better to allow administrators to second-guess a teacher's decision, and to not permit a teacher to determine that a student has terminated the agreement, until after extensive consultations with an "administrator". The whole idea of a magnet classroom, however, is that it would enable teachers to devote their entire energies to teaching rather than to discipline. Teachers selected to teach in magnet classrooms should be selected for their abilities to perform well in such a teaching environment. To make the teacher's action subject to approval by the administrator is to assume that the administrator, who is far removed from the classroom, is in a better position to judge the propriety of the decision than the teacher. If the administrator is in fact very good at making such decisions, he or she might be a prime candidate to be a teacher in a magnet classroom.

Teachers who abused their classroom authority in the magnet classroom would of course themselves be subject to review and evaluation by the school principal, but their individual decisions would not be second-guessed. Rather they would be evaluated by their overall and long-term success in the classroom.

An analogy might be made to the judge in a courtroom. The analogy is not a perfect one since the courtroom is subject to a number of considerations of due process that would be waived in a magnet classroom. However, even judges are given wide discretionary contempt powers to control their courtrooms. A judge may, for example, unilaterally order the removal of disruptive persons from the courtroom without having to check with higher authority before making the decision. Of course, like the teacher, the judge is still subject to overall evaluation and review for abuse of that discretion, just as the teacher would be subject to overall review and evaluation by the principal. But the judge is nevertheless given broad discretion and authority to control what goes on in that courtroom because it is recognized that justice can not proceed without order and discipline in the courtroom.

A student who, either by formal request or misbehavior, is deemed by the teacher to have requested transfer to a regular classroom, should have the opportunity after an appropriate period of perhaps several weeks, to request re-admission to the magnet classroom.

Both student and parents would be required to reconfirm their commitment to abide by the rules of the magnet classroom.

INTERNAL TRACKING

The issue of tracking students according to ability and achievement has always been a controversial one. Under a typical tracking system, students are given tests to determine their ability and achievement level, and then assigned to a class with students of similar ability and achievement. While tracking does enable more currently proficient students to benefit from learning with students of comparable ability, it denies many others the opportunity to progress.

Students assigned to lower tracks often find that the expectations of their performance is low, and that they are not challenged to develop their full potential. It has been found, for example, that tracking makes it "increasingly difficult for students (assigned to lower tracks) ever to climb up the academic hierarchy. In this way, low expectations and mindless bureaucrats crush the potential of thousands of students assigned to lower tracks."[44] It has also been found that tracking systems consistently "underestimat(e) rather than overestimate(e) students' ability to handle difficult course material."[45]

At least 90% of students assigned to lower academic tracks (as well as to separate bilingual tracks), never rise to a higher track level.[46] Aptitude tests are often administered to students at very early ages. Inevitably students who have had developmental training in preschool or who have had the benefit of a stimulating learning environment at home perform better on these tests and are tracked accordingly. The remainder are assigned to lower tracks from which they rarely rise to a higher ones. Some schools have even been known to deliberately assign students to lower tracks in order to qualify for extra federal subsidies for teaching "special education" students.[47]

In the case of *Hobson v. Hansen*, a federal court permanently enjoined the superintendent of the public school system in the District of Columbia from operating its track system in the public schools, finding that "track assignments are made (on the basis of) standardized tests, which although given on a state-wide basis, are completely inappropriate for use with a large segment of the student body,"[48] and holding that the resultant tracking assignments resulted in unconstitutional discrimination on the basis of race and economic background.[49]

Although social scientists disagree on the extent to which aptitude is due to environmental factors as opposed to genetic factors, virtually all agree that a student's aptitude is strongly affected by the environment provided in his or her earliest years.[50] It will be recalled that a 1994 Carnegie Institute report revealed that the learning environment provided to children prior to age three "determines their brain structure and ability to learn."[51] The question, therefore, is whether it is appropriate to deprive ten-year-old students of a stimulating learning environment based on the fact that they were denied such an environment during the first three years of their lives.

The only long-term solution to the tracking dilemma is to provide free public preschools to all American children. In the meantime, however, a system must be adopted that fairly balances the right of high academic achievers to realize their maximum potential with the right of students deprived of early developmental training to realize their maximum potential as well. A system of internal tracking within the magnet classroom concept achieves this delicate balance.

THE BROCKHURST MODEL

One model of an age-desegregated school is that of the Brockhurst School in Berkshire, England, a private school for children aged 5-15.[52] The experience has been described by a former student. This school did not assign students to "grades," but rather to "forms." Form Seven was the lowest and Form One was the highest. Form assignments were based not on age, but rather on a student's particular level of academic achievement in each separate subject. Indeed, age was considered quite irrelevant. As students mastered one level of achievement, they were permitted to rise to the next highest form at their own pace.

For example, when a 10-year-old student arrived at the school from America, it was found that he had a very low achievement level in Latin. This was not surprising to the school headmaster, since in public school in America the student had never taken a class in Latin. After a short interview with the headmaster, it was determined that he would attend the Form Seven Latin class.

The American student was the oldest student in the class. At first it was disconcerting for the 10 year old to be in a class with 6-9 year olds. Many of the younger children looked at him with the same awe with which they would look upon an assistant teacher, and he became a mentor to several of them. However, it was soon realized that he had an advantage in English language skills and experience that enabled him to more quickly master that level of Latin, and within four months his teacher recommended that he move up to the Form Six Latin class. Within two years he was in the Form Four Latin class, which had a majority of 10-12 year olds.

During the same 15-minute interview in which the headmaster determined that the student should be assigned to the Form Seven Latin class, it was also determined that he had a proficiency in reading skills that would place him in Form Three, where he was two years younger than the average student in the class. Indeed, there were several 14 year olds in the class. Despite average math aptitude test scores from his last school, however, he was placed in a Form Five math class because he had not yet taken geometry, and also because he had told the headmaster that he felt he needed to learn math at a slower pace. As a consequence he took over two years to advance to the next higher form in math, but he felt much more comfortable learning at the slower pace in the lower form.

Had this been an American school, he would have been subjected to a battery of multichoice tests, after which his grade assignment would have depended upon whether the school was controlled by the trackers or antitrackers. The antitrackers would doubtless have insisted that he be placed in a Latin class with students of his own age who had already reached a high level of achievement in Latin. The fact that he would have been hopelessly frustrated in a higher Latin class, and that he would surely have frustrated his classmates and teacher, would have made no difference to the trackers, who would have insisted that if he were not placed in the higher form, he would feel stigmatized and be the victim of discrimination.

The trackers, on the other hand, might have looked at his American test scores and determined that he should be in a higher math form despite the fact that he learned at a slower pace in math and did not want to feel pressured to keep up with the math wizards who pressed forward with maniacal speed in the higher form math classes. At all levels, however, he was encouraged to progress at a rate commensurate with his abilities.

This system of forms organized by student achievement levels also had advantages for students who would be classified as remedial under American standards. One 12-year-old student at Brockhurst, who would surely have been labeled as "learning disabled" in an American public school (and who would thereby justify educational expenditures two or three times that of nonlearning disabled student), was assigned to Form Seven in all his subjects. Far from feeling stigmatized and discriminated against, he was, as was the American student in the Form Seven Latin class, looked upon as a mentor by his much younger classmates, who often sought his assistance during free learning periods.

In an American public school, this learning disabled student would probably have suffered one of two sad fates. Either he would have been assigned to a special education or remedial class out of which he would most likely never have escaped; or he would have been mainstreamed into a class where he had little hope of keeping pace, could never achieve the satisfaction of excelling, would have been the source of continual frustration to his teacher, and might have been ostracized by his classmates. (In either case, his disabled status would likely have entitled his school to substantial additional federal subsidies.) Instead, at Brockhurst he was permitted to progress without stigmatization at a level and at a pace that was suitable to his abilities. While he took longer to achieve threshold proficiencies, he ultimately did so with dignity and pride.

In some subjects, such as history, there was little difference in the age of students in each form. A history teacher is not faced with the same kind of problems as a Latin teacher in teaching to students of different ability levels. In other words, a history teacher need not make substantial pedagogical adjustments in teaching the date of the Battle of Hastings to gifted students.

In addition, in many areas of school, such as sports and extracurricular activities, students had ample opportunity to socialize with students in their own age group regardless of the fact that they attended different classes in such subjects as Greek, Latin, or advanced mathematics.

Two other aspects of education at Brockhurst hold possible lessons for American schools. A daily mandatory team sports program served not only the beneficial purpose of keeping all students physically fit; it also served to physically exhaust the more hyperactive students. In American public schools, students described by apologists as having "high verbal and physical activity" are handled with generous expenditures of money and due process. At Brockhurst, their energies were expended in sports, or in working off demerits given for disciplinary infractions. Demerits could be worked off at the rate of one demerit per hour by raking leaves, scrubbing floors, and cleaning windows. Needless to say, there was virtually no vandalism.

Perhaps the most important feature of education at Brockhurst was the incorporation of study hall classes in the daily schedule. There were at least two one-hour study halls assigned to each student every day. A student prefect monitored each study hall, and was given the authority to give demerits for such infractions as whispering or rustling papers. More serious offenses, such as talking or giggling, required calling the teacher on duty. During breaks, students were permitted to ask the teacher on duty for help on homework assignments.

Study halls guaranteed to each student two hours each day for doing homework. Most important, however, study halls served to level the playing field for all students. In American public schools, some students go home to an environment in which parents control the watching of television and provide a learning environment for study or for help on homework. These students thus gain an enormous advantage over students who come from families who are disadvantaged or who provide little educational stimulus or discipline to their children.

There have been a considerable number of changes in the British school system since the cited student went to Brockhurst. The point to be made from the previous discussion, however, is that tracking can take many forms and can be employed in ways that serve the interests of both gifted and disabled students.

A responsible tracking program would track only in those subjects in which teaching must be adapted to the students' ability level, such as advanced mathematics, physics, or languages. The *Hobson* notion that slow math learners must be put in a classroom with students learning advanced calculus is as curious as it is incomprehensible.

Indeed, if an educator set out with the specific purpose of lowering the self-esteem of a slow math student, forcing that student into a class with students learning advanced integral calculus would seem to be a perfect way to accomplish that objective. Such a policy would unnecessarily retard the learning pace of the advanced students, while providing little if any benefit to the slower student, who could not even hope to absorb such advanced material. Classes in history and geography would not ordinarily require tracking; nor would a homeroom class that met for an hour a week to discuss current events.

If classes were organized on the basis of achievement levels rather than age, there would be less need for tracking of any kind. In American public schools, however, a fetish has been made of age segregation. As a result, students who learn faster than others are not permitted to advance as their ability permits, and those who learn more slowly are forced to advance to the next grade whether they are ready or not. As a result, the rare child who is determined to have failed a grade and held back is stigmatized.

Educators express alarm whenever a parent asks that a child be held back or advanced by even one grade, citing vague psychological or social reasons for age segregation. In fact, the Prussian system of segregating students by age makes no more sense than segregating students by race, religion, or socioeconomic status. Children of different ages have as much to offer each other as children of different cultures and races. Apparently educators see no psychological problems in dumping slow learners into special education classes from that they have little chance of escaping, or creating programs that serve to segregate students according to their socioeconomic status. But permitting students of different ages but similar achievement levels to learn together must be avoided at all costs, even if it occurs for only a small percentage of the total school day.

It may be that the fetish of age segregation (based on the Prussian model of education) has become so ingrained in the American educational establishment that it can not be reformed. If so, limited tracking may still be necessary to meet the needs of both fast and slow learners.

In any case the magnet classroom provides all students, regardless of their socioeconomic status, with the right to learn in a safe and disciplined environment. Wealthy parents pay thousands of dollars to send their children to private schools in order to provide them with such an environment. The rationale for magnet classrooms is that all students should be given that opportunity, and not just children from families of high socioeconomic status. Any student who signed the pledge to abide by the code of behavior, and waive legal right to due process would be admitted to the magnet classroom within which a teacher could devote all his energies to teaching.

Once a magnet classroom program was implemented, there would be opportunity to incorporate many of the other features of private schools, such as study halls, more homework, a longer school day, and uniforms.

UNIFORMS

Many American private schools, as well as foreign public schools, provide uniforms for their students. Studies reveal that wearing a uniform instills in students a sense of identity and pride in their school.

More important, however, uniforms foster a sense of equality and democracy.

As early as 1915, the great educational reformer John Dewey observed in his book *Democracy and Education* that "a truly democratic society must overcome class barriers," and that "schools must provide an environment in which differences in economic class carry no weight, neither privilege nor stigma."[53]

Ironically, however, many educators who cite democratic principles in support of bilingual education and against tracking, do not favor uniforms in the public schools. A recent study published in *The Education Digest*[54] revealed that students "delay or do not purchase books and supplies, instead using their money for clothing."[55] Others "skip school or work long hours after school — or worse become involved in illegal activities—to finance fashionable wardrobes. . . . (S)chool (has become) a major arena in which to display the latest fashions."[56]

When a Maryland high school recently implemented a uniform policy, the school's principal noticed an "increase in honor-roll students."[57] A number of reports indicate "positive changes in student behavior when dress codes and uniforms are used."[58]

In schools without a uniform policy, children from wealthier families often flaunt their more expensive and stylish clothes to other students from poor or disadvantaged families. A caste system is often created based upon who wears the most expensive and stylish clothes. Resentment, envy, and sometimes violence erupt. Parents often spend considerable time, money, and energy each fall buying their children a fashionable wardrobe for school.

Ample opportunities exist outside of school for children to express their individuality by wearing extreme modes of dress. School, however, should be one arena where class distinctions should give way to the creation of a learning environment. It is for this reason that private schools, as well as public schools in many foreign countries, provide their students with uniforms. It will be recalled that the parents in Scotland who sent their children to Paisley cited uniforms as one important reason they chose that school.

However, groups like the American Civil Liberties Union have demanded the right of students to dress any way they please. For this reason, it is not realistic to suppose that uniforms will ever be provided to students attending regular classrooms in the public schools.

Uniforms could be provided to students attending magnet classrooms, however, since students may waive their liberty and due process rights in the magnet classrooms. In these classrooms, at least, schools could provide an "environment in which differences in economic class carry no weight, neither privilege nor stigma."[59]

CONCLUSIONS

What most parents and students seek in a school is not lavish facilities, certified teachers, or armies of counsellors and administrators.

Rather they seek a safe and orderly environment in which children who want to learn will be permitted a safe and orderly environment in which they can do so. Once teachers are freed from the intolerable burden of enforcing discipline, they can devote their full time and energies to teaching. They will also be able to give more time to disadvantaged students who have the desire to learn.

Teachers should be hired based on their understanding and knowledge of the field in which they are to teach. Once the best teachers are hired, they should be given authority to control their own classrooms.

There is at present no practical way under existing law to provide a safe learning environment in the regular classrooms of the public schools. Students who want to learn have a right to be provided such an environment. The creation of magnet classrooms would provide such an environment to all students who are willing to make a commitment to abide by the rules of behavior. Those children who wish to retain all their rights of due process are free to remain in the regular classrooms and receive the kind of education they are now receiving in the public schools. Reformers can continue to try to reform the regular classrooms by spending more money on lavish facilities, expanding certification programs, reducing student-faculty ratios, dumping students in dead-end programs, and financing ever-expanding armies of administrators.

Parents, teachers, and students in the magnet classrooms would ask very little in terms of money or resources. They would ask only for the right of teachers to control their classroom, establish study halls, provide uniforms, and track only those courses necessary to enable the gifted to advance as fast as they are able, and the disabled to progress at their own pace without stigmatization. The magnet classroom would be available in every neighborhood school and open to every student willing to waive due process and to make a written commitment to abide by a code of behavior necessary to the creation of a safe and orderly learning environment.

The school year should be extended to 240 days a year, and the school day should be lengthened to eight hours from 8:30 to 4:30, including at least two monitored study halls so that all students are given an equal opportunity to study.

Segregation, either by race, religion, sex, or age, should not be permitted; nor should such programs as bilingual education be permitted to camouflage a policy of segregation according to national origin or primary language. Rather, students whose primary language is other than English should be provided the opportunity to learn English by the means the government provides to its own employees studying for the foreign service—namely, by the method of immersion.

Disabled students should be provided with a safe and orderly environment for learning, and should be eligible for admission to the magnet classrooms on the same basis as non-learning disabled children. A distinction should be acknowledged between students who are truly physically or learning disabled, and disruptive students who by committing violent acts deprive other students of their right to an education.

Procedures should be adopted whereby disruptive students can be transferred to special facilities where they can receive proper treatment and their special needs accommodated. In some cases, such facilities might be provided within a school, such as private booths where disruptive students could be periodically monitored and supervised and where they would be permitted to study without contact or interference from other disruptive students. A policy of simply dumping such students on to the streets where they can commit additional crimes on an unsuspecting public should be discouraged. When students commit acts that violate criminal laws, however, they should be referred to the criminal justice system.

Finally, the importance of intellectual development in the preschool years *must* be recognized. Free public preschool education should be provided to all American children so that they are provided with an equal playing field and with equal opportunities in elementary school.

One possible problem with implementation of these proposals is that as a package they do not involve additional money and thus can not be made the basis for increased spending demands. In fact, it might be more practical to implement these proposals if public school budgets are reduced to the level of that of private schools. Once funding levels are reduced, public schools will have no choice but to follow the example of schools such as the parochial system in New York, which hired only 50 administrators for their schools in the entire New York City area (as compared to 3,500 public school administrators).

The cost of hiring public school teachers could be reduced to the level of the costs of hiring private school teachers if, like the private schools, public schools hired teachers most qualified in their subject areas rather than on the basis of whether they took certification courses.

The cost of facilities could also be greatly reduced once it is realized that fancy carpets, hot tubs and television studios are not necessary to the creation of a disciplined learning environment.

The creation of magnet classrooms would by itself involve neither an increase nor decrease in spending. A student uniform policy, however, would save both parents and students a great deal of money.

Lengthening the school year would make more efficient use of existing resources, rather than letting resources sit idle for almost half a year. It is true that extending the school year and day, and providing free preschool education would involve more spending, but these costs would be more than covered by the savings in administrative and teaching costs.

In order to compare these proposed programs with the existing educational system, it is necessary to have a more complete understanding of how the present system came into being. For example, the reason that most public schools have a such a long summer vacation is mostly historical (farmers needed their children to help harvest the crops).

The next chapter reviews the history of American public education with a view toward understanding today's educational public school system.

Chapter Four

The Origins of Public Education

An understanding of public education today requires knowledge of its heritage. Without this knowledge, it is not possible to assess current policies or promote workable reforms that take into proper account the culture and society within that public education has developed.

American public education can trace its earliest roots to education in Renaissance and post-Renaissance Western Europe. Prior to the Protestant Reformation, education consisted primarily of the learning of Latin and Greek and was taught at the institutions of higher learning that, after the eleventh century, had spread northward from Italy into the heartland of Europe.[1]

After Martin Luther translated the Bible into German in 1523, the leaders of the Protestant Reformation recognized that the success and acceptance of their religion depended not upon the classical education of the nobility, but upon the vernacular education of all children. The invention of the printing press made such education possible. Luther was on the forefront of this movement, declaring that "in my judgment there is no other outward offense that in the sight of God so heavily burdens the world, and deserves such heavy chastise-ment, as the need to educate children." The example of sectarian vernacular schools in Lutheran Germany was soon adopted in the neighboring countries of Europe, including England.

Prior to the mid 1700s, over 90% of the immigrants to colonial America came from England, where rates of literacy and education soon surpassed those of other European countries.[2] In 156,[3] Parliament passed the Statute of Artificers, and later the Poor Laws, which provided for the apprenticeship and education of poor children.[4] The notion that it was in the interest of society to provide for the education of all its members was a revolutionary one. By 1640 literacy in London exceeded 50%, a remarkable rate for those times. The printing presses of Elizabethan England poured out literary works penned by Johnson, Bacon, and Marlowe, and even those on the very lowest rungs of the social scale flocked to watch the plays of Shakespeare.[5]

To what may such remarkable achievements in literacy be attributed? In addition to schools established to train the poor to be scholars for the church, by 1510 Latin grammar schools had been established. By 1600 most of the larger towns had such schools. Educational historian Sheldon Cohen has described these grammar schools as "conducted in an austere, formal, and stringent manner. The schoolhouse was usually a small, ascetic structure, holding an average of 50 boys. It was open on a year-round basis with sessions held from early in the morning until later afternoon. Discipline was usually strict, although sympathetic school masters were not unknown, and many teachers were university graduates."[6]

Professor Carl Bridenbaugh has estimated that during this period "there was one public secondary school for every 5,687 persons in the (British) realm"[7] and that the percentage of population enrolled in institutions of higher learning was greater than at any time up until the early nineteenth century.[8]

But there is another explanation for the educational achievements of this period. When the Coleman Report concluded in 1966 that "families, and to a lesser extent peers, (are) the primary determinants of variations in performance,"[9] it had discovered a feature of education that was not unique to modern-day America. Cohen has observed that in the 16th century, "the belief that social . . . and parental desires were the chief determinants of educational attainment were common both on the continent and within England."[10]

Such was the educational heritage of the motherland from which the American colonists came. There were many factors that influenced the subsequent development of education in the colonies, not the least of which was the desire to establish religious independence from the Church of England. Although there exists considerable debate about the extent to which colonial America transplanted educational traditions from its mother country,[11] it is clear that religious considerations played a major role in early colonial educational development.

The Puritans, for example, though apprehensive about the effect on the family structure if the task of education was delegated to the state, nevertheless recognized their limitations in being able to provide an education to their children in a hostile physical environment. They also believed that "the absence of adequate education would mean the collapse of their attempt to implant pure religious societies in the New World."[12]

The response of the colonial government was measured, though perhaps understandable given the more pressing demands of survival in an undeveloped land. The Educational Law of 1642 passed by the Massachusetts General Court did little beyond exhorting parents to educate their children and "condemning the great neglect of many parents and masters in training up their children in learning, and labor and other employments that may be profitable to the common wealth."[13] It did, however, purport to hold parents, and the small communities within which they lived, responsible for teaching their children an "orthodox catechism."

An important educational landmark was achieved in 1647 when Massachusetts passed the "Old Deluder Laws," which purported to require towns of over 50 families to provide education in reading and writing to its children, and required towns of over 100 families to establish a Latin grammar school. The preamble of these laws clearly stated the purpose of requiring an education—namely to foil "that old deluder, Satan (who kept) men from the knowledge of the scriptures, as in former times by keeping them in an unknown tongue. . . . that learning may not be buried in the grave of our fathers in the church."[14]   Many communities were simply financially unable to comply with the law and became legally liable for fines for noncompliance. However, enforcement was sporadic, and there is little documentation of legal proceedings to enforce such laws. Nevertheless, the example had been set for a tradition of compulsory public education.

Those communities that did manage to provide a schoolhouse often did so with the barest of resources. A typical colonial schoolhouse was described in 1681 as a small spartan structure of about 20 by 25 feet in which "the glass broke, the floor was very much broken and torn up to kindle fires, the hearth spoiled, the seats some burned and others out of kilter, that had well nigh as good keep school in a hog site as in it."[15]

THE REVOLUTION IN EDUCATIONAL PHILOSOPHY

The American Revolution significantly altered the popular view about the purposes of public education. Before the Revolution, education was seen primarily as a means of preparing each individual to lead a devout life in accordance with principles upon which the foundations of both church and state rested.[16] The Revolution, however, shattered many beliefs about the sanctity of authority, both religious and political. It was seen that no absolute authority rested either in princes of the church or the state. Torn from the relative security of a well-ordered monarchy, the colonists, who at first reveled in their newfound independence as would seamen who had just thrown their captain overboard, soon faced the threat not of tyranny but of anarchy among themselves.

Scarcely had independence been won when internal rebellions broke out, such as the one instigated by Daniel Shays in Massachusetts. Great Britain, still smarting from its humiliation and loss of colonies, began a policy in which "America was to be treated as a 'lien country,' totally shut off from that commerce which has been the cause of all its prosperity and on which its very existence (depended)".[17] This slow policy of economic strangulation prompted a royal advisor to inform King George in 1784 that if the policy of economic strangulation were continued, the colonists would "in less than twelve months, openly concert measures for entering into something like their former connections with Great Britain."[18]

The first attempts by the colonists to form a united government were dismal failures. The Articles of Confederation gave the colonial

Congress no power to regulate commerce, raise money, or even enforce its own laws. When Congress attempted to "assess" the states for funds, many refused to pay, and some even declined to send delegates to the Congress. When the Congress sent John Adams to the Court of St. James to negotiate an end to the Crown's policy of economic strangulation, he was literally laughed out of London with the parting shot: "What did Adams represent? One, or thirteen nations? What was the use of making an agreement with Congress, when each state could repudiate it? Congress had the power to contract loans, but no power to pay for them."[19]

While concerted action by the colonies might have brought about concessions in the British policy of strangulation, each colony instead adopted its own policy, preferring to follow its own economic interests by erecting trade barriers against its sister states rather than Great Britain.

While the economies of the colonies were gradually degenerating into chaos, disorders spread and several states began pursuing their own confederations and amalgamations. George Washington watched the descent into anarchy and wrote despairingly: "What a triumph for our enemies to verify their predictions. What a triumph for the advocates of despotism to find that we are incapable of governing ourselves, and that systems founded on the basis of equal liberty are merely ideal and fallacious. . . . Thirteen colonies pulling against each other."[20]

It was at this point that Americans first began to realize that they were truly on their own. They had to create the institutions that would allow them to preserve and enjoy the freedom they had won. The Constitution of the United States was the product of what would prove to be one of the greatest strengths of the American people—the art of compromise. It was this spirit of compromise, tempered by a sense of reality borne of war, which led to the creation of a delicate system of checks and balances. The Republican form of government within which this system functioned freed Americans from dependence on authority from which there was no responsibility, and provided the foundation for long-term political stability.

Amid such political upheaval, there took place an equally historic revolution in attitude toward the role of education. After the Revolution, it was no longer enough for education to enable citizens to read the scriptures in order to "live a godly life and to confer status."[21] Rather, education was seen as an important foundation stone of a system of self-government that was as yet insecure and had yet to prove itself to a skeptical world. Indeed, self-government had not been successful in the history of mankind since the days of the Athenians and certainly not on so broad a scale as that envisioned by the founding fathers. As educational historian Joel Spring has observed, the attitude toward education after the American Revolution was that education was necessary to "build nationalism, to shape the good citizen, and to reform society."[22]   This new educational philosophy contained both a principle and a corollary.

It is from this transformation in educational philosophy that the roots of all that is both right and wrong about American education can be traced. The guiding principle of that transformation—that a system of self-government can not long survive without the education of the citizenry that is to do the self-governing—became self-evident in the aftermath of breaking the bonds of dependence on external political authority. But the corollary of that principle—that education is to be society's vanguard and repository for social reform and political change—has done much to undermine, and indeed swallow, the original principle.

THE POLITICIZATION OF THE PUBLIC SCHOOLS

The politicization of the American public schools has had severe consequences that have served to undermine their primary mission of educating the citizens upon whom the system of self-government depends.

Politicization has meant that the public schools have been used to carry out a social or political agenda that other institutions of American society have, for one reason or another, failed to carry out. That public schools might be used as a place to further a social or political agenda is why politicians and power interests alike have long sought to control the public schools. As a result, the public schools have not only been saddled with tasks for which they are ill-equipped, but more seriously have been diverted from their basic task of education. In the process, priorities have been distorted, and the very process of enacting social change has been set back and compromised.

For example, one of the first and most serious consequences of politicization of the public schools was observed shortly after the Civil War. In California the political agenda of those in power was to use Chinese immigrants to build railroads and work in factories. However, those in power also perceived Chinese Americans to be "yellow barbarians and potential economic rivals,"[23] and pursued a social agenda of excluding Chinese Americans from other occupations and to deport them. When other American institutions failed to carry out this social agenda, the politicians turned to the public schools, which they controlled, to carry out their social reform of protecting jobs from "yellow barbarians."

In 1884 the power brokers who politically controlled the public schools in San Francisco issued the following policy statement: "Guard the doors of the public schools that they (the Chinese) do not enter. . . . (This is) the inculcation of the doctrine of true humanity by which . . . we justify and practically defend ourselves from this invasion of Mongolian barbarism."[24]

That the San Francisco politicians of 1884 justified the saddling of the public schools with their social agenda by resort to principles of "true humanity" carried a touch of irony in the early 1990s when several prestigious California universities were caught employing quotas as a means of excluding qualified Asian Americans under the guise of

a benign program of racial discrimination. It will be also be recalled
that in 1985 the power brokers in Kansas City adopted a policy of
excluding, on grounds of race, African Americans who desperately
sought admission to the best magnet schools in Kansas City[25] (see
Chapter One).

There were of course differences in the policies adopted by the
politicians in the above cases. In the case of the San Francisco program
of racial discrimination, the policy was to protect the jobs of a favored
racial group; in the two latter cases the policy was to insure a certain
number of school admissions for other racial groups. But the common
denominator in all these policies was that an institution of learning was
chosen as the place to pursue a social agenda justified on whatever
theory of "true humanity" the power brokers happened to adhere to at
any given time.

The point to be considered is not whether one particular social
policy is good or bad. Views of what is good and bad social policy
change over time. The question is what institutions in American society
are best suited to pursuing a social agenda. The backs of little children
trying to learn may not be the most appropriate place for pursuing
such political and social agendas.

Segregated schools were established around the country after the
Civil War. African Americans were confined to segregated schools not
only in the South but in most Northern states as well. The "separate
but equal" doctrine was enshrined in 1896 by the United States
Supreme Court in *Plessy v. Ferguson*.[26] In that case the Court upheld
the segregated schools established by politicians as a means of pursuing
a social agenda "for the promotion of the public good."[27]

Politicization of the public schools is often justified, however, on
the grounds that since other American institutions have failed to
accomplish the politicians' agenda, there is no other place to pursue
that agenda except in the schools. Politicization is further justified on
grounds that a particular social agenda is a benign one. The San
Francisco school board was convinced it was serving "true humanity."
The Kansas City policymakers were sure they were pursuing a benign
policy in denying African Americans admission to the best magnet
schools on grounds of their race. Unfortunately, however, politicization
has not only undermined the educational mission of the public schools;
it has also failed utterly to achieve the purported social objectives.

It will be recalled that racial segregation has intensified since the
implementation of such desegregation plans as those implemented in
Kansas City, and that the percentage of African Americans attending
predominately African American schools in 1992 was greater than the
percentage in 1972.[28] But most tragic of all, the achievement of
students in public schools has deteriorated dramatically (see Chapter
One).

Politicization has also resulted in bilingual and special education
programs that stigmatize and segregate students according to their
cultural heritage, their primary language, or according to intelligence
tests administered long after there is any hope for children to make up

for deficiencies in their preschool education. Students who are able to advance more rapidly in such subjects as math and science are denied the opportunity to advance at their own pace, and all students are subjected to an environment of fear in schools which are inhibited from providing discipline by a multitude of political obstacles and psychological theories.

Courses in multiculturalism and self-esteem have become political footballs thrown by special interests against each other. Those who have saddled public schools with such courses have chosen to ignore the pleas of teachers like Paquita Hernandez who have observed that "you don't give people self-esteem through a workshop. Self-esteem evolves because you feel competent."[29] And it is precisely in the competence department that American public schools have fallen so tragically short.

Politicization has also resulted in a bloated, top-heavy, and extravagant administrative empire, which has not only consumed and dissipated vast sums of tax dollars that might otherwise have been spent on preschools, study halls, or lengthened school days, but has emasculated teachers and sapped them of their energy and enthusiasm for teaching. The classroom authority of teachers has been so diminished that teachers have fought back in the only way they know how—by forming unions that have served only to accelerate the process of politicization.

When New York City and State Teacher of the Year John Taylor Gatto finally quit teaching in 1991 on grounds that schools had become a political "re-distribution system. . . . Only incidentally [do the public schools] exist to educate,"[30] he spoke for hundreds of thousands of alienated teachers in public schools around the country. One often hears the plaintive cry that we must "get politics out of the schools." But until priorities are reordered to make education the primary mission of our public schools, politics will continue to plague the public schools and ultimately drive all but the very poorest children to private education.

The notion recently expressed by an educational historian that "control of knowledge can be used as an instrument of power"[31] must give way to a recognition that knowledge and competence are themselves empowering for those who achieve it, and that the use of the educational system to achieve power or promote a political or social agenda is contrary to the primary goal of imparting school consolidation and the quest for efficiency.

By the middle of the nineteenth century, most American communities in the North were making some attempts to provide education for their children. In the South, where a class system was more firmly entrenched, children of the rich tended to be educated by tutors or in small private schools, and other children had only a very limited access to education.[32] Because America was still predominately rural, most schools were the small one-room schools that have since faded into the romantic folklore of American heritage.

Historian Andrew Gulliford has observed that "for almost 250 years the country school was the backbone of American education. As late as 1913, one-half of the school children in the United States were enrolled in the country's 212,000 one-room schools. . . . [T]he country school continues to be a powerful cultural symbol to many Americans."[33] By 1931 the number of one-room schoolhouses had been reduced to 143,391;[34] by 1958 there but 25,341, and by the mid-1960s they were virtually all gone.[35]

The period of school consolidation began at the turn of the century as educational experts and administrators began to enter education armed with theories about efficiency and age segregation. The new administrators considered the one-room schoolhouse to be inefficient, since it did not permit the creation of a class of teaching specialists. Consolidation, it was thought, would permit the merger of resources at a central location. Perhaps most important, however, consolidation would create a need for an army of administrators to coordinate the activities of a large school system.

It was not until the roads of America began to be paved in the 1930s, however, that consolidation became feasible on a wide scale. Children could be bused long distances to a central location in any weather. Great emphasis was placed on the modernization of facilities. Consolidation permitted the building of newer facilities, modern toilets, and centrally heated buildings.

In this process of consolidation, little consideration was given to preserving the educational values of the one-room schoolhouse. Consideration of the fruits of experience in educational community and discipline took second place to considerations of bricks and mortar. Only recently have educational historians begun to look back at what was lost in the process of consolidation.[36]

There are still many living today who were educated in the one-room schools of the early twentieth century. Their accounts and recollections of their experiences provide much that might be useful to the educational reformers of today. They reveal a world of "face-to-face, long-lasting relationships. There was no visible bureaucracy. The classroom teacher was engaged with the same children all day, except for a temporary respite when the students were at recess or lunch. Such teachers had the potential to have an enormous influence, especially if they stayed at the same school or taught in the same community for long careers."[37]

The one-room teacher taught a group of students ranging in age from 5 or 6 to 14 or 15. There were no other adults in the school other than the teacher—no administrators, principals, registrars, counselors, disciplinarians, teaching aides, custodians, or security personnel. Students were not just expected to passively sit back and watch. Rather great emphasis was placed on oral discussion and recitation of what the students had learned.

Larry Cuban's study of early 20th-century one-room schools reveals that teachers conducted an average of 26 recitations a day, suggesting "the rugged schedule a teacher in a one-room school followed, according to both expectations and self-reports."[38] These recitations constituted a method of daily individual testing of what each student had learned from reading and listening to the teacher. (Today there is heavy reliance on multiple-choice exams rather than recitation for testing.) Because students were required to listen to recitations of students studying at different levels, they often learned at a faster pace.

Historian Alice Rinehart has observed that students "heard the recitations of the other grades and learned from them. . . . A bright pupil could accelerate through the curriculum, as the teacher could assign the precocious student to the lesson where he or she was competent, not necessarily the one in which his or her age peers were involved."[39]

James Gerhart of Pennsylvania recalls his one-room experience as follows:

We went up front and stood up front there. (We learned much) from listening to the other classes reciting . . . their lessons. That is one thing I often appreciated, listening to the other grades. . . . We already had the basis for the lesson by listening to the other grades.[40]

Margaret Seylar has related to Robert Leight and Alice Rinehart how difficult it was to make the transition from the learning environment of her one-room school to that of her new consolidated school: "The year I started in the consolidated school I didn't have anything to do because I knew the lessons already. . . . In the one-room school you were learning two things at once. You were learning whatever it was in your grade and whatever they were doing in the next grade or beyond."[41]

Jesse Stuart, in his book *To Teach, To Love* recounts his experience and that of his brother James in a one-room school:

When I went from one grade to another in my scanty (one-room school) I could have skipped the grade ahead of me. I had already listened to others ahead of me in their recitations and discussions. My brother James (who also attended) learned so much so quickly that when he was 10 years old he entered (another school) and finished when he was 14.[42]

Hamlin Garland has written of his experience in a one-room school in which he "knew not only my own reader, the fourth, but all the selections in the fifth and sixth as well. I could follow almost word for word the recitations of the older pupils and at such times I forgot my squat little body and my mop of hair, and became imaginatively a page in the train of Ivanhoe, or a bowman in the army of Richard the Lion Hearted battling the Saracen in the Holy Land."[43]

In comparing the one-room curriculum with that of the consolidated school, Robert Leight has observed:

Now we have age-graded schools with teachers becoming specialists in teaching fourth grade, or eighth grade, or twelfth grade. Students spend most of their school time with peers who are essentially of the same age. In the typical one-room eight-grade school, their peers were individuals who exhibited a whole range of human development while participating in a variety of formal and informal activities for six hours or so over nine months. A younger child had a number of role models with whom he or she could identify both in the formal educational program within the classroom and during lunch and recess on the playground.[44]

It has been noted that "the one-room school was abandoned because graded classes were considered more efficient. . . . Elementary teachers like them because they needed to teach only three or four lessons a day for one grade only."[45]   But even teachers encountered difficulties in making the transition from one-room to consolidated schools. Carrie Horne, for example, has described her first experience in a consolidated school:

For the first time . . . I experienced a gang that would stick together. If you punished one you had difficulty with the whole gang. This was not true in the (one-room) schools . . . because if there were two or three who banded together you could get some of the good kids to help you disperse the gang and to back you up in disciplining them. This was not true when you had a larger gang in a larger set-up.[46]

The consolidation movement in public education was not accomplished without resistance. None fought harder against it than Jesse Stuart, who years later reflected; "This is what we must never forget. There was a day and time when education was considered a priceless gift. . . . We've lost something we've got to get back. Not the one-room schoolhouse, but the spirit of the one-room schoolhouse."[47]

Others have also reflected on the loss: "We have lost opportunities for applications of a distinctive pedagogy. Also gone is a particularly rich type of social system and environment for values for education that was, in a broad sense, educative."[48]   Former First Lady Barbara Bush has observed that the one-room school was representative of the pioneering families who "understood one of Thomas Jefferson's most deeply held convictions—that good education is the essential foundation of a strong democracy."[49]   The reformers of today give little credence to the idea of regaining the "spirit of the one-room schoolhouse." Like Elwood Cubberly, they view the one-room school as a symbol of rural backwardness[50], a romantic and quaint anachronism has no more place in modern American society than the ice-box, the corner soda fountain, or the horse and buggy. In taking this view, however, such reformers have mistaken bricks and mortar, empires of administration and bureaucracy, for an educational spirit of learning. It is a view that has taken the reformers down the path of finding salvation in ever greater expenditures of tax dollars rather than applying the lessons of our own heritage and experience.

It has been suggested that consolidation of one-room schools was as inevitable as the demise of corner drugstores and the rise of giant supermarket chains. Quaintness, community, and inefficiency inevitably had to give way to modern methods of achieving efficiency and productivity. But the analogy is not apt. Supermarkets used economies of scale and more efficient production methods to offer better products at lower prices to consumers. Consolidated schools, on the other hand, have offered an inferior product at grossly inflated prices, in contrast to their one-room predecessors, which offered a disciplined and successful learning environment at very low cost. As documented in Chapter One, the achievement of students in consolidated schools continues its inexorable decline and violence accelerates at an alarming rate at the same time that educational expenditures, teacher training, and salaries continue to rise. Indeed, had the supermarkets performed in the marketplace like the consolidated schools have performed, they would doubtless have gone out of business long ago. Like the inefficient industries of today's dying communist societies, today's public schools are propped up and survive only because of the application of raw political power and the infusion of massive taxpayer support.

The foregoing observations are not meant to suggest that our present school systems should be broken down in to one-room schoolhouses. Rather it suggests that reformers have much to learn from the teaching environment that was created in the one-room school houses.

The one-room schools provided not only a learning environment, but a learning community in which students of all ages and backgrounds supported each other in a learning experience. The lack of indoor plumbing or even running water were not substantial impediments to learning. As in today's Japanese schools, "teachers and students were expected to keep the classrooms clean and warm, thus saving janitorial fees."[51] Costs were kept to an absolute minimum, the only major expenses being "salary for a teacher, the purchase of wood and coal to heat the buildings, and for maintenance and instructional materials."[52]

It has been documented that the one-room schools "spent far less per student and per classroom than the [consolidated] schools during the first half of the twentieth century."[53] One comparative study has revealed that in some states the tax revenues per student were twice as much in school districts with consolidated schools as those with one-room schools."[54]

As at the English Brockhurst School, one-room schools did not segregate students by age. To be sure, the combined class was born of necessity since the one-room school had only one teacher and the room was too small to be divided into separate classes for each age group. But as the personal experiences of the one-room school students reflect, combined classes created an environment in which students of different ages could help and support one another, and in which cliques and exclusive peer groups were less likely to interfere with the learning process. Combined classes not only offered the opportunity for fast learners to advance rapidly by listening to the recitations of students at higher levels, but also permitted slower students to advance at their own pace without stigmatization or humiliation.

THE ADOPTION OF THE PRUSSIAN MODEL
OF EDUCATION

School consolidation did make combined classes possible. However, combined classes could still have been conducted in consolidated schools. During the period of consolidation, however, the new administrators came to look with admiration at the Prussian model of schools in which students were rigidly separated by age. As early as 1843, Horace Mann wrote in an annual report that "the first element of superiority in a Prussian school, and one whose influence extends through the whole subsequent course of instruction, consists in the proper classification of the scholars."[55] Mann went on to speak with admiration of the Prussian model and its rigid segregation of students by age.

Most appreciated by the new educational bureaucrats of the consolidated schools was that age segregation created an additional layer of educational organization, which in turn created new career opportunities for educational administrators. It also provided the opportunity to create an educational hierarchy with a leader at the top and the teacher at the bottom taking orders. Historian Joel Spring has noted that when American public schools adopted the "Prussian method of classification . . . [they] incorporated not only graded (age-segregated) classrooms, but also what Tyack refers to as the 'pedagogical' harem of a male principle and female teachers."[56]

Even today, combined classes of the American one-room model could offer advantages in educating slow learners and learning disabled students. No longer would these students be faced with the dilemma of either attending segregated special classes or mainstreaming in classes in which they can not keep up or in which they are rejected or stigmatized by the other students for holding back the rest of the class.

Many public school teachers today have gotten so used to teaching only one grade level at a time, that they can not conceive of simultaneously teaching students at different grade levels in accordance with the traditional American model. Many even claim that they can not even teach one or two extra learning disabled students in their class. Yet the one-room teachers did so, and by all accounts did it well.

Nevertheless, the public school teacher of today has a valid point in claiming that it would be impossible to teach students of different levels in the present disciplinary environment of the public schools. It is this very point that should bring the reformers to the most important lesson to be learned from the one-room school experience—namely, that a learning environment is best created by making the teacher the focus of the educational experience.

There were no principals in the one-room schools, no administrators to tell the teacher how to teach, and no chain of command along the lines of the Prussian model. Rather the teacher was given not only the authority to control the classroom, but in most cases given the flexibility and freedom to develop a teaching method and style suitable for that classroom. If the teacher's performance did not meet the expectations of the community that hired her, she could be discharged. But she did not have to answer to an army of administrators looking over her shoulder.

It is perhaps ironic that the lessons of America's one-room school experience have been learned and adopted by schools in many foreign countries, but not in the United States. It will be recalled that the Japanese public schools, like America's one-room schools, are also spartan and place far more emphasis on the learning experience itself than on considerations of bricks and mortar. Also like the one-room schools, Japanese schools expect students to scrub floors and maintain the school premises.[57] But most important, administrative overhead is reduced to a minimum and teachers are given the authority to control their classroom.

That the American educational establishment has other matters in mind than applying such lessons to today's public schools is reflected in the topics of doctoral dissertations in educational administration. A survey of over 290 such dissertations revealed that almost half were on such subjects as "fiscal administration . . . business administration . . . pupil personnel . . . personnel management . . . and legal provisions."[58] Many of the others were on topics such as "school plumbing, the school janitor, fire insurance, and the cafeteria."[59]

It is not surprising that along with school consolidation and the adoption of the Prussian model has come the cult of administration for its own sake. Along the way some very basic lessons about the nature of education have been lost.

SEXISM IN AMERICAN EDUCATION

By 1920 the Prussian model of education had been adopted in most urban areas of the United States. Students were rigidly segregated by age into grades, and an administrative chain of command had been established in which a male leader, known as a principal controlled and supervised female teachers. Philbrick has described the typical hierarchical arrangement of the Prussian model as adopted in the urban American schools: "Let the Principal or superintendent have the general supervision and control of the whole, and let him have one male assistant or sub-principal, and ten female assistants, one for each room."[60]

The Prussian leadership principle in education found fertile ground in an American society in which the role of women was strictly stereotyped and in which women were not permitted to vote. Sociologist Rosabeth Moss Kanter has described the typical stereotypical view that "the 'masculine ethic' elevates the traits assumed to belong to men with educational advantages to necessities for effective organizations . . . and a cognitive superiority in problem solving and decision making."[61] Such views provided the rationale for the creation of an extensive administrative superstructure in which male administrators could supervise female teachers—the "pedagogical harem" described by David Tyack.

Women, on the other hand, as described in a *Harper's* magazine article in 1878, were "preferred by (male) superintendents because they are more willing to comply with (orders) and less likely to ride headstrong hobbies."[62]   According to *Harper's*, it was the view of male superintendents that female teachers were to teach as ordered by their male superiors; any advice female teachers wished to give to their male superiors "is to be given as the good daughter talks with the father."[63]

History reveals that the two basic principles of the Prussian model (age segregation and male dominance) were inextricably intertwined. Before students were segregated by age into separate classrooms and grades, the female teacher's authority in the classroom was paramount. There was no need for a chain of command or an administrative apparatus in which male authority could be asserted. The creation of consolidated schools, however, provided the perfect opportunity for the imposition of the Prussian model of segregated classrooms, and the creation of a complex organizational structure. This in turn gave professional male administrators the opportunity to fill leadership positions at the top of the organizational hierarchy.

At the height of the American one-room school system in the early 1800s there were a significant number of male teachers. It was no coincidence, however, that after the Civil War, and particularly after the beginning of the consolidation movement and the imposition of the Prussian model in urban schools, that women came to predominate in teaching positions.[64] The creation of administration and bureaucracy provided the perfect vehicle for the assertion of male dominance in education and the reduction in authority of the female classroom teacher. That the creation of bureaucracy and administration could be justified on grounds of efficiency and modernity made it all the more desirable as an educational policy. (Even today, 72% of primary and secondary school teachers are women.)

As early as 1911 a link was recognized between the imposition of male domination in American public schools and the increase in the number of female classroom teachers. A study of teachers in that year revealed that the increased number of female classroom teachers was due to

the changed character of the management of the public schools, to the specialization of labor within the school, to the narrowing of the intellectual range or versatility required of teachers, and to the willingness to work for less than men. . . . all of the graded school positions have been preempted by women [while] men work as "managing" or "executive" officers.[65]

Historical analysis thus reveals that the top-heavy and bloated administrative superstructure that so plagues today's public schools has its origins in the sexism of 19th and early 20th century American society. It is a testament to the overwhelming triumph of Prussian male authoritarianism that age segregation and administrative predominance in public schools is now justified not on the basis of sexist stereotypes but on the basis of efficiency and the need for conformity and uniformity in the classroom. Reformers, however, should not overlook the sexist origins of the system they seek to save through such reforms as spending even greater sums of money on administration, extravagant facilities, teacher training and multiple-choice testing.

THE LEGACY OF SEXISM IN THE PUBLIC SCHOOLS

Sexism in the public schools has diminished during the past 20 years, but it has not been eliminated. Although there are now a significant number of male teachers in elementary and secondary public education, females continue to predominate as classroom teachers, particularly at the elementary level. Although females have broken into the ranks of administration, males continue to dominate supervisory positions. And while the application of principles of equal protection have served to promote equal opportunity for the sexes in education, there continues to exist a legacy of sexism in public education.

Providing equal opportunity for employment in the educational establishment is important as a matter of law and social policy. However, sexism's legacy in public education is not limited to denial of equal opportunity in the educational establishment. The very hierarchical and administrative structure of public education today is a legacy of 19th-century sexism and Prussian male authoritarianism. Simply providing equal opportunity to the sexes to participate in positions of power in the educational establishment does nothing to alter the nature of the structure itself, which is still based on the Prussian model of age segregation and the administrative leadership principle.

Real reform must involve a reexamination of the conceptual underpinnings of today's educational establishment. Real reform can never take place as long as the course of reform is controlled and directed by those within the educational establishment who have an interest in preserving their own prerogatives and powers.

An analogy might be found in the deregulation of transportation in the late 1970s. In 1975, congressional hearings revealed that airline regulation was notoriously inefficient, and in fact constituted government collaboration in the practice of price-fixing—a practice already made illegal in the private sector. The hearings revealed that the cost of airline travel in regulated markets was 40-100% higher than in deregulated markets, costing consumers $3.5 billion in excess fares.[66] After deregulation, air traffic and productivity doubled, and fares declined dramatically.[67]

The lawyers and government bureaucrats who had a vested interest in continued regulation fiercely resisted the deregulation of transportation. Indeed, had regulation been left to the regulators, government price-fixing would still be the order of the day.[68] It took an act of Congress to overcome the bureaucratic resistance and to deregulate transportation.[69]

As a former counsel of the Civil Aeronautics Board remarked after deregulation, "It is understandably painful for one involved in economic regulation over a professional lifetime to consider his life's work outdated, or even worse, misdirected." In the same manner, as in the area of economic reform educational reform will never take place if it is left to those who now have a vested interest in the current educational establishment.

THE UNIONIZATION OF TEACHERS

In an age when women lacked the vote and their roles were strictly stereotyped, the female teachers who found themselves at the lowest rung of the administrative ladder in a Prussianized school system found that there was little they could do to reestablish the prerogatives and authority they had once enjoyed in the classroom.

Many female teachers placed their hopes in the creation of the National Teachers Association (changed to the National Education Association [NEA] in 1870), which was formed to further the interests of education and teaching. Although every member was originally given a vote at annual meetings, administrators and educational bureaucrats found their own votes diluted by votes of the large number of teachers. Voting at meetings was subsequently changed to a representative system in which each state association would elect delegates. As a result, delegates elected to attend the conventions tended to be administrators and bureaucrats. A typical delegation was that of Illinois in the 1920s. Of 167 delegates to an NEA meeting, 135 were administrators, principals, and superintendents, and 14 were elementary school teachers.[70]

Not surprisingly, the female teachers on the lowest rung of the educational hierarchy found it difficult to assert their interests and those of their students in such an organization. Typical of the attitude of the organization's leaders was that of William Harris at the 1901 meeting of the NEA. After Harris made a speech extolling the exemplary state of the Prussianized educational establishment, teacher Margaret Haley rose to question his conclusions and to make a case on behalf of the classroom teacher. Harris responded to an audience that no doubted nodded its approval:

Pay no attention to what that teacher down there has said, for I take it she is a great teacher, just out of her school room at the end of the year, worn out, tired and hysterical . . . if there are any more hysterical outbursts, after this I shall insist that these meetings be held at some other time."[71]

Faced with such obtuseness and condescension in the administrative hierarchy, it is not surprising that many teachers turned to organized labor for redress. In 1916, Ella Young explained why many teachers were turning to such organizations as the American Federation of Teachers. (which later became affiliated with the American Federation of Labor.) "These female (teachers)," Young explained, "were realizing that they had not the freedom, the power, which people should have who are to train the minds of the children."[72]

Young also provided the reason why a labor union for teachers was needed: "college-bred men were not ready to do anything for them; therefore they were compelled to go in with those who had felt the oppression and the grind of the power of riches."[73]

The unionization of teachers marked a turning point in the history of public school education in America. The Prussianization of schools and the establishment of a male-dominated administrative hierarchy insensitive to the needs of teachers drove teachers to the only institutions in society that had the power to take on the educational establishment.

Although the teachers' unions were at first content to engage in collective bargaining, by 1947 teachers' unions had begun to use the strike weapon to enforce their demands. In 1960, a strike by the United Federation of Teachers resulted in a collective bargaining agreement with the New York City school system, and set the example for other teachers' unions and affiliates throughout the country. Thereafter union membership increased substantially. At the beginning of the 1970s over half of all teachers belonged to unions,[74] and by the 1980s membership in the American Federation of Teachers exceeded half a million. Teachers strikes soon became an "annual rite of fall."[75]

That teachers turned to unions to protect their interests is understandable, considering their treatment by an insensitive and Prussianized male-dominated bureaucracy. However, the unionization movement has had several unfortunate consequences. In many respects unionization served to further entrench the administrative hierarchy and solidify the barrier between the "professional" administrator, and the teacher "worker." In short, it served to deprofessionalize the teacher by creating the perception that the administrator was analogous to the manager in private industry, and the teacher was analogous to the factory worker. As a consequence, both administrators and teachers slipped comfortably into the roles created by this perception. Like the factory worker performing routine tasks for an hourly wage, teachers in unions began to see their interest primarily in achieving marginally higher pay, benefits, and working conditions. And like the managers of a factory, administrators saw their role as one of resisting union demands while preserving their own prerogatives.

In fact, these roles suited perfectly the power brokers in the educational establishment who welcomed the new siege mentality. Administrators now had yet another justification for their exis-tence—namely, keeping unions under control, resisting their demands, and engaging in almost continuous negotiations. In addition, their own professional status was enhanced, while that of the teachers was commensurately reduced. This in turn justified even greater salary increases for administrators who could earn their pay by resisting union demands and thereby further expand their administrative empire.

Unionization in itself might not have caused this result, but by making pay, benefits, and working conditions their primary focus, many unions were putting the cart before the horse. Union leaders failed to recognize that pay, benefits, and status flow naturally from professional status. Once that professional status is undermined by assuming the role of a wage laborer, there is little left to which to aspire except a marginally higher wage and better working conditions.

In the pursuit of such goals, teachers lost the opportunity to regain that status and authority that they had previously enjoyed before the adoption of the Prussian system and the creation of the administrative empire that placed them on the lowest rung of the educational ladder. In the one-room school, each teacher had been her own administrator. She adopted a teaching method that worked for her students and for her class, planned the lessons, and formulated her own educational policy. After unionization, the teacher became the mere executor of policy formulated and dictated by the professional male leaders in the administration and bureaucracy. In short, the teacher lost the authority "which people should have who are to train the minds of the children."[76]

This point may be illustrated by comparing public school teachers with teachers in higher education. Law professors, for example, come from the ranks of licensed attorneys.[77] Despite the large number and oversupply of lawyers in the United States, however, law professors teaching at law schools in the United States enjoy generous pay, benefits, and working conditions. (A typical professor of law earns between $75,000 and $140,000 a year and teaches an average of 4-8 hours a week.)[78] In public schools, only administrators can hope to achieve such levels of pay. Law teachers did not achieve this level of pay and benefits through unionization, however. Rather, law teachers have carefully worked to protect and enhance their professional status.

It is true that lawyers must take three years of postgraduate education to earn a law degree, while some public school teachers have only a college education or a master's degree. But a difference of one or two years of schooling can not account for the entire difference in pay between public school teachers and law professors. Rather, the main difference between public school teachers and law professors is that the latter have preserved their professional status and are compensated commensurately with that status. (It is perhaps also not a coincidence that law schools have not been Prussianized by age segregation and administrative control of classroom teaching.)

The Prussian system of administrative authority is now so entrenched in the educational establishment that the notion that schools can function without hierarchical administrative control is inconceivable even to many teachers. Ironically, it was the recent experiment at the Koln-Holweide school district in Germany that revealed that student performance rose dramatically after the teachers were freed from administrative control.[79] It will be recalled that at Koln-Holweide "teachers, rather than administrators make all instructional decisions"[80] (see Chapter One).

By unionizing, teachers have in fact become part of the very educational establishment that imposed the Prussian model and began the process of deprofessionalizing the teacher. It is not surprising, therefore, that teachers have joined other members of the educational establishment in resisting educational reform, particularly any reform that might have even a short-term effect on teacher pay and benefits. It has been noted, for example, that "union-style security is not compatible with flexibility in replacing mediocre or poor teachers,"[81] and teachers' unions, not surprisingly, have resisted most reforms that might affect the civil-service brand of security enjoyed by many unionized teachers.

Although educator Nancy Perry has noted that "in many cities the teachers' unions fight reforms,"[82] Michael Massarotti, a school superintendent in Westminster, Colorado, has warned that "the unions are at a crossroads. Either they will change or they won't survive."[83] Of course, the same might also be said of public school administrators as well.

Had the consequences of unionization fallen only on teachers, there might be less cause for concern. However, one researcher has examined the "political factors in public school decline" and tested the "connection between two commonly used indices of social breakdown . . . the rising crime rate . . . and student performance."[84] This study concluded:

In the 1965-1980 period, SAT scores were declining by five points a year in the average state. . . . The growth of teacher unionization has contributed to the student test score decline. Before 1960, hardly any teachers were unionized. In the 1960s the growth of teacher unionization was very rapid. . . . I have looked at what happened to student achievement in those places where the push for teacher organization was most successful most quickly. In those areas, student achievement tended to deteriorate more than average. This should not be too surprising . . . union concerns and education concerns aren't always compatible."[85]

Although there may be a statistical correlation between the rise of unionization and the deterioration of student achievement, unionization is almost certainly more of a symptom than a cause of the decline of public education. It should be recalled that unionization was the response of teachers to an authoritarian system that was insensitive not only to the needs of teachers but to the needs of public education. It would be far more fair to attribute the cause of decline to an educational ideology that deprived teachers of their educational authority in the classroom.

PRESCHOOLS

It will be recalled that a 1994 report by the Carnegie Institute revealed that the learning environment provided to children under the age of three "determine(s) their brain structure and ability to learn," and that "children's experiences in their early years can influence how many brain cells, or neurons, are formed between them."[86] The report also found that "underused synapses are naturally pruned from the infant brain."[87]

The belief that the early earliest stages of a child's educational development are the most critical is not a new one. Without the benefit of the latest scientific advances in molecular biology and neurology, Jean-Jacques Rousseau wrote in his 1762 work *Emile* his belief that a child's senses were most active in the first few years of life, and that education should be used to stimulate those senses at the very earliest opportunity.[88] John Locke's *Treatise on Education* also urged, for similar reasons, that children should be educated at the very earliest opportunity.[89]

During the latter part of the 18th century, Swiss educator Heinrich Pestalozzi further developed these ideas of early education, stating his belief that early childhood education would be the most effective means of improving society. He recognized that many children of poor families did not receive the intellectual training and mental stimulation in their own homes that would enable them to become useful and productive members of society when they became adults.[90] Pestalozzi set forth the educational principle that later provided the pedagogic foundation for preschools: "All instruction of man is then only the Art of helping Nature develop in her own way; and this Art rests essentially on the relation and harmony between the impressions received by the (young) child and the exact degree of his developed powers."[91]

In 1828 a group of civic-minded women in Boston, formed the Society for Infant Children to put into practice the ideas of Pestalozzi and others who espoused the early education of children aged between 18 months and four years. The avowed purpose of the society was to provide intellectual stimulation to the very young children, particularly the children of the poor who were deprived of a loving and nurturing home environment in which they could receive such stimulation. The Society's charter stated: "Infants, taken from the most unfavorable situations in which they are ever placed. . . . are capable of learning at least a hundred times as much, a hundred times as well, and of being a hundred times as happy, by the system adopted in infant schools."[92]

Community approval of the new movement was widespread. An 1829 editorial in the *Boston Recorder and Scriptural Transcript* endorsed the new movement and declared that "a ray of millennial hope has shone upon us, and reveals a way in which poverty, with all its attendant evils—moral, physical, and intellectual—may be banished from the world."[93]

The *American Annals of Education* and *Ladies' Magazine* helped to draw financial support for the movement, and promoted it as a means of breaking the "cycle of poverty."[94] An 1829 article in *Ladies' Magazine* observed that it was "nearly, if not quite impossible to teach such little ones at home, with the facility they are taught at an infant school. And if a convenient room is prepared, and faithful and discreet agents employed, parents may feel secure that their darlings are not only safe but improving."[95]

By the early 1830s the infant school movement had spread across the country, and infant schools for children between the ages of 18 months to four years were established in such diverse cities as New York, Charleston, Philadelphia, Providence, and, of course, in many of the large towns in Massachusetts. It even spread to many rural areas, particularly in Connecticut and Massachusetts.[96] In Massachusetts, 40-50 percent of all three year olds were attending infant school.[97]

Had this movement taken the course that had been expected and hoped for by its advocates and supporters, it would have gone far toward curing the social evils of poverty, discrimination, and injustice that were to inflict themselves on American society as poor immigrants flocked to the cities, society became more urbanized, and the plight of the cities began to take on its modern form. Had they been permitted to take root, the infant schools that provided intellectual stimulation to children as young as 18 months would have been the true equalizer of opportunity in society. No longer would the children of the poor have entered the public schools at such a disadvantage in development that they had little hope of breaking the cycle of poverty from which they were born. No longer would educationists and administrators have been able to use disparities in intellectual development upon entering public school as excuses for tracking the poor and underprivileged in dead-end programs from which they had little opportunity to escape. But it was not to be. The list of developments that have so plagued and ruined American public education is long indeed: the emasculation and usurpation of the authority of the classroom teacher in order to establish a bureaucratic hierarchy in which male dominance could be asserted; the Prussianization and age segregation of the classroom, and the abandonment of the successful and proven American model of education; the "psychologicalization" of the public schools and the adoption of courses in self-esteem, multi-culturalism and table manners; the invidious segregation of students on the basis of race, bilingualism, learning disability, or intellectual capacity as determined by multiple-choice tests administered by the educational establishment; and the mindless and inappropriate imposition of judicial standards of due process in ways that both disregard the Constitution and prevent schools from maintaining a safe learning environment for students who want to learn.

But perhaps the most unfortunate and sad development in American education was the destruction of the infant schools by a group of self-proclaimed "physiologists" in the mid-1830s. The leader of this group was a "doctor" named Amariah Brigham, who in 1832 wrote a book entitled *Remarks on the Influence of Mental Cultivation and Mental Excitement Upon Health*.[98] In this influential and widely disseminated book (which went through four printings), Brigham listed the causes of insanity. The primary cause, he proclaimed, was "the predominance given to the nervous system, by too early cultivating the mind and exciting the feelings of children."[99]

It is true that the late 1700s and early 1800s were the golden age of quackery. George Washington's physicians literally bled him to death on the theory that by bleeding their patient they would cure him. "Doctors" declared that masturbation caused blindness and insanity. It is therefore perhaps not surprising that the pseudo-theories of psychologists such as Brigham found a receptive audience for the theory that early intellectual development of children caused insanity.

Magazines and journals that had previously supported the infant schools now turned on them, citing the scientific physiological theories of Brigham and his disciples. Magazines such as *Ladies' Magazine* and the *Christian Examiner and General Reviewer* "trumpeted the ill effects of intellectual precocity with increasing physiological precision,"[100] predicting that education of young children would cause "future imbecility or premature old age" as well as "epilepsy and insanity."[101] Even the *American Journal of Education* now took the view that infant schools "furnish occasion for remissness in the discharge of parental duties by devolving the care of infancy on teachers."[102]

The "wealthy and socially conscious women who prided themselves on their knowledge of the latest intellectual trends, and whose donations and contributions at annual fund-raisers helped to finance the infant schools"[103] were dismayed and mortified by such attacks on the whole idea of early educational development. By 1833, contributions to the infant schools had dried up, and by 1835 most of these schools had closed.[104]

Not for the last time had a psychological theory served to influence and alter the course of public education. Today, the successors to Brigham continue a process of psycologicalization that has resulted in more modern times to courses in self-esteem multiculturalism, and segregation by race and language.

PRIMARY SCHOOLS AND KINDERGARTENS

So total was the repudiation of the whole idea of early educational development that even today there are few schools for children aged 18 months to three years. Rather, most children of this age group are either kept at home (in the declining number of homes in which there is a mother at home during the day and where the children may or may not receive intellectual stimulation) or else parked in child care centers. The primary purpose of most such centers is not to educate, teach, or stimulate the child, but rather to baby-sit the child so that both parents can work. In many ways, such children now experience the worst of both worlds that the Society for Infant Children sought to avoid by creating the infant schools. Such children are denied not only a nurturing and learning environment at home but also the opportunity to attend an institution that exists for the intellectual development of the child rather than the convenience of the parents.

Thus despite such reports as that released by the Carnegie Institute in 1994, the public schools continue to ignore that phase of children's educational development that is most critical to their later success. Education is even denied to a large number of children between the age of three and five. The *Digest of Education Statistics* released in 1993 by the U.S. Department of Education revealed that in 1992 only

39.4% of the nation's three and four year olds received any education whatsoever,[105] and most of the children who did receive such education were from families wealthy enough to pay for it at private schools.

What remains today is but a vestige of the Pestalozzian philosophy of early educational development. It is called kindergarten, but it seeks to begin development of a child's mind long after the critical phase of learning development has passed. The American kindergarten was founded on the ideas set forth by German educator Friedrich Froebel, who believed that by employing women to teach young children, "the female sex (would be rescued) from its hitherto passive and instinctive situation, and through its nurturing mission raise it to the same level as the male sex."[106]

The first kindergartens were established in the United States in the late 1850s, and by the late 1800s they had spread to Chicago, Philadelphia, and Boston.[107] That the kindergartens succeeded where the infant schools had failed was remarkable in light of the fact that the prevailing view of physiologists was still in accord with Amariah Brigham. Brigham, who had gone on to manage a lunatic asylum in New York and found the *American Journal of Insanity*, had continued to develop his theory that the child's brain was "almost liquid" and was therefore "particularly susceptible to damaging influences."[108] At the 1873 meeting of the National Education Association, for example, a follower of Brigham's theories declared that "the most competent men protest more earnestly, from year to year, against subjecting the pupil to the discipline of serious schooling before he has reached his seventh year."[109]

That kindergartens succeeded at all was due to two factors. First, they excluded all children under the age of five, and thus avoided the wrath of the most fervent advocates of avoiding over stimulation of children's liquid brains. Second, the kindergartens vehemently denied any intent to educate children in any way, stressing that kindergartens were "not schools, taught nothing 'schoolish' and that play, rather than study, was the core of their activity." Educational historian Caroline Winterer has observed that "while these arguments were certainly directed in part against the bureaucracy and hierarchy of the public school system as a whole, they also succeeded in isolating the kindergarten from some of the criticisms that had felled the infant schools."[110]

An early kindergarten pioneer, Elizabeth Peabody, stated that "reading and writing properly belong to a second stage of education after kindergarten" and referred to the "American insanity" of teaching children to read in kindergarten.[111] "Precocious knowledge," she warned, "and the consequent morbid intellectual excitement (were) quite out of harmonious relation with moral and aesthetic growth."[112]

The persistence and longevity of such theories no doubt account, at least in part, for the small percentage of three and four year olds who attend school today in the United States. Another explanation, however, can be found in the tendency to view kindergarten as an expendable frill that can be cut when budgets are tight. During the depression, for example, "kindergartens were singled out as areas that could be eliminated."[113]

Although infant schools have never been adopted by the American public school systems, the infant schools in Britain may offer some lessons for educational reformers in the United States. The British Infant School combines elements of the early American infant school, and the American one-room school. The British Infant School has been described as "three years of a child's life, uninterrupted by arbitrary promotions (or failures). Beginning at age (four or) five . . . children move along comfortably and steadily, never encountering the rigid categories of kindergarten, grade one, or grade two."[114]

Like in the American one-room school, the teacher in the British Infant School works with a group of children of mixed ages (4-8), and the children and the teacher spend most of the school day working together. Robert and Donna Shannon have described the typical experience in the Infant School:

Everywhere in the Infant School rooms there are books, books of all shapes and sizes. And children are reading them. Some of the children are reading to themselves, while others are reading to the teacher or to classmates. Children are reading books by writers from all over the world, and many of those writers are the children themselves. Their stories are on the walls, in the bookshelves, on the tables, always ready for everyone to enjoy. . . . Infant School teachers know that when they follow certain educational procedures almost all children become readers who love to read. It is a reading scheme far different from the endless pre-test, post-test, lock step reading group situations so common in the schools of the U.S.[115]

One visitor to a British Infant School heard a child ask the headmistress: "Miss, have you got a paper and pencil? I feel a poem coming on."[116]   In the Infant School the headmistress is not an administrator or manager as in American public schools, but an educational leader who relates daily with the students.

Holidays are short, but more frequent, making for a longer school year. Most important, however, teachers and the headmistress are given both autonomy and authority to develop their own teaching programs without having to answer to an administrative hierarchy. The schools are generally small (usually less than 250 children). "Because the schools are small, the head can know each child and spend time with children."[117]

The Shannons have suggested that public schools can learn much from the example of the British Infant School: "In the United States big schools are facts of life. Therefore, the task is to figure out how to make small schools out of big schools. Although the idea of schools within a school has long been advocated, not much has been accomplished in implementing the idea."[118]

The Shannons made one final observation about the measurement of achievement in the British Infant School: "In a typical American primary school children are grouped according to reading achievement, or mathematics achievement, or other measures of achievement based

on test scores—a misleading and frequently harmful practice. ...
Children are grouped, chased and raced from specialist to specialist."[119] In the British Infant School, however, there is ample information opportunity for a teacher to evaluate student performance. Like in
the American one-room school, the teacher is "constantly studying
what and how each child is doing, using subjective, professional
judgment based on observation and common sense."[120]

COMPENSATORY EDUCATION

Brigham's legacy can be found even in the prevailing assumptions
underlying the implementation of experimental compensatory
education programs in the United States in the 1950s and 1960s. Such
programs were based not on the premise, revealed by the Carnegie
Institute Study, that a child's ability to learn is developed prior to the
age of three, but rather on the Brighamian assumption that learning
skills are developed after the age of three. These programs therefore
focused on the perceived cultural deprivation of children aged four, five
and six, and attempted to compensate for such deprivation.

The theory of cultural deprivation was essentially that the
cultural background of certain racial and socioeconomic groups was
inferior to the perceived cultural background of white middle-class
families, and that programs could be created that provided an institutional and functional equivalent of a white, middle-class cultural
background. One of the first such programs was New York City's
Higher Horizons program in 1956.[121] This program was followed by
a project implemented in 1962 called the Early Childhood Project, the
curriculum of which purported to concentrate on the development of
"conceptual, and perceptual skills, as well as 'self-image.'"[122]

Another project implemented in 1962 as part of the Great Cities
Project was Baltimore's Early School Admissions Project. The program,
which selected only children who had reached the age of four or five,
purported to compensate for the "limited education of the parents" and
the "limited social and economic circumstances" of children from
"culturally deprived" home environments.[123]

Philadelphia's Experimental Nursery School Program in the early
1960s came the closest to accepting children of an age young enough to
obtain significant developmental training. They accepted a few children
as young as 3 1/2, although even children of this age were beyond the
age determined by the Carnegie study to be of significant potential for
brain development.[124]

By the mid-1960s, there were numerous such programs, many
financed under Title I of the Elementary and Secondary Education Act
of 1965.[125] There followed even more massive spending authorized by
the Economic Opportunity Act. Such funds enabled the federal Office
of Economic Education to initiate the Head Start Program in 1965 and
1966.[126]

Not surprisingly, the results of such massive programs were
disappointing. Although studies revealed that children in such programs

gained as much as six points on the Stanford-Binet IQ Test compared to other children not in the programs, "in almost every case, follow-up studies show(ed) that the gains in IQ scores the children made during their participation in the preschool projects faded out during the first few years of their careers in elementary school."[127]

Other studies have concluded that these programs revealed that "extra spending on educational services cannot erase the results of cultural differences between the poor and middle class."[128]   Robert Church, Associate Dean of Education at Northwestern University, who previously taught education at Harvard University, has concluded that "it was a hard lesson to learn, partly because Americans were habituated to the belief that money could solve any problem, partly because educators wanted desperately to believe that the traditional tools of their trade, if used profusely enough, would succeed in effacing the effects of poverty."[129]

The real lesson to be learned from the experimental compensatory education programs is not so much to prove the point that schools are not the place for politicized social programs (although it may be argued that such is the case here); rather, it is that political motives and preconceptions may be obstacles in the search for effective educational programs. In the case of compensatory education programs, a political preconception about the inferiority of certain cultures and the superiority of a white, middle-class culture led to government programs focused on compensating for the perceived deprivations encountered by children of a disfavored culture, rather than on programs focused on providing children with a learning environment during the most critical years of their intellectual development.

This is not to say, however, that preschool and kindergarten programs are educationally unsound. On the contrary, the increase in IQ for children attending such programs is reason enough to provide a learning environment for children aged 4-6. To deny educational opportunity to students of such an age would be a severe deprivation indeed. Indeed, the fact that IQ, which is supposed to measure innate intellectual capacity, can be altered at all by a kindergarten education casts severe doubt on the very notion that intellectual capacity is determined primarily by genetic factors. (Controversial educational researcher Arthur Jensen, for example, claims that 80% of intelligence is inherited.)[130]

But neither political preconceptions about inferior cultures, nor Brighamian and psychological theories about children's liquid brains, can not be permitted to obscure the such scientific findings as revealed in the Carnegie report—namely, that the critical period of intellectual development occurs before the age of three. No education program can hope to achieve true compensation for learning deprivation without providing a learning environment for children aged one to three.

MEASUREMENT MADNESS

Contrary to popular perception, the idea of testing for purposes of classification did not originate in education but in the military. Faced with a Prussian military machine in World War I, the American army employed psychologists to draft intelligence tests and then test draftees in order to properly classify them and assign them to their proper duties. These army intelligence tests were modeled after the French intelligence tests developed by French Psychologist Alfred Binet. After the war was over, the government released thousands of unused test booklets onto the open market, where educators were able to obtain them at very low cost.

The army's head psychologist, Robert Yerkes, was delighted that his test booklets were to receive such wide distribution, and proclaimed that "before the war mental engineering was a dream; today it exists and its effective development is amply assured."[131] Soon these tests were being used to prove that certain ethnic groups had higher intelligence than others.[132] For the members of the educational establishment, however, the tests provided the opportunity to further expand the Prussian model of education, as well as expand their own administrative powers and authority.

The army's intelligence tests were used to avoid what educators feared would be an inundation of the public schools by the poor in the aftermath of the compulsory education laws. The tests were used to classify students and assign them to special classes. In 1922, for example, the Baltimore school system set up classes entitled "Crippled," "Subnormal," "Prevocational," and "Mentally Handicapped."[133] The army tests were then used to determine which students would attend such classes.

Educational historian Joseph Tropea has observed that "compulsory attendance laws did not eliminate exclusionary practices; they merely changed the form of exclusion to in school segregation."[134] The underlying assumption behind the use of such tests to classify students was that intelligence was almost exclusively genetic and unalterably related to ethnic and racial background. Education could not appreciably alter these intelligence quotients, and therefore the primary goal of the schools should be to "build correct social attitudes, select individuals for their place in society, and educate them for those places."[135]

In fact, the perceived need to classify students was but one tragic result of the educational system's failure, and remains so to this day. Now as then, students from disadvantaged backgrounds are denied an education and intellectual stimulation during the very stage of their lives when their intellectual capacity is being formed (that is, before age three). This educational failure is then used to rationalize the adoption of the Prussian model in order to classify children at the very beginning of their public school careers and to select them for their predetermined place in society.

American children from all backgrounds continue to suffer on the altar of the liquid brain theories of Amariah Brigham. It has been observed that "measurement madness has a stranglehold on education in America."[136] Government policymakers and politicians continue to advocate increased testing as the way to raise public schools standards. The 1994 Goals 2000: Educate America Act has been characterized as based on the premise of "let's prove we have standards by giving a national test."[137]

Multiple-choice testing has now become an integral part of the Prussianized administrative hierarchy of the public schools. The mindless administration of multiple choice tests prepared by bureaucrats now performs two functions. First, it enhances the administrative power of those in the educational establishment to control the lives and destinies of children. Second, it relieves teachers of the responsibility for hands-on teaching and evaluation. The rugged schedule of the one-room schoolteachers who evaluated children by conducting "an average of 26 recitations a day"[138] bears little resemblance to today's public school classroom in which the teacher, stripped of her authority, is ordered to distribute countless volumes of multiple-choice tests to her numbed students.

There exists a valid role for standardized tests. They can help to monitor the progress of students in specialized areas, particularly in comparison to students in foreign schools. (For example, it will be recalled that standardized tests revealed that American children were virtually equal in science achievement to their Asian counterparts in the early grades, and only lost ground in the upper grades when the deleterious effects of American education kicked in.)[139] When evaluated in proper perspective and in combination with graded classroom achievement, standardized tests can provide a useful common denominator for college admission committees. But the salvation of the public schools does not rest on standardized testing. Rather it rests in the creation of a learning environment in which testing is secondary to achievement.

MODERN TRENDS IN POLITICIZATION

In recent years, politicians and other leaders have found the public schools to be fertile ground for politics. The Vietnam War created a environment in which political tension increased between government and the educational establishment. Much of the resistance to the war appeared to come from so-called pampered students who pursued their studies while enjoying protection from the draft. President Nixon proposed the creation of a National Institute of Education, through which tax money could be directed toward basic research in education rather than toward education itself.

Daniel Moynihan spoke for the Nixon administration in advocating more emphasis on "placement of the school graduate in the job market,"[140] rather than "spending more money on early educa-tion."[141] As a result of such priorities, Joel Spring has observed that a shift occurred in financial support from early education to "providing financial support for white-collar research workers."[142]

The political controversy ignited by such policies soon led to further political involvement by public schoolteachers and their unions. In 1976 the National Education Association formally entered the political arena by endorsing Jimmy Carter for president. In return, Carter promised to deepen federal involvement in the formulation of public school policy and established the U.S. Department of Education.

Not willing to relinquish the votes of an education constituency, the Reagan administration cultivated the votes of those opposed to teachers' unions and the educational establishment by proposing vouchers and tax credits, which the parents of middle-class children could use to subsidize private education. Republicans also exploited the issues of busing and school prayer in their political campaigns. Civil rights groups flocked to support or resist legislation in the area of bilingual education, education for the disabled, and federal aid and control of public education.

That politics of the most virulent variety have found a home in public education is not surprising. There are few issues more important to voters than the well-being and education of their children. Much of America's vitality has its roots in the spirit and hope of Americans that the succeeding generation will have opportunities they never had. But in this process of politicization the most important principle of Jefferson's original vision of public education—that a free a democratic society rests on the education of the citizenry—has been consumed by its ill-fated corollary that public education can be the political repository for failed social reforms.

Chapter Five

The Legacy of Racial Discrimination

The practice of separating groups within society is as old as civilization itself. Although one of the most invidious types of segregation is that based on race, throughout history segregation has also been based on alienage, language, sex, wealth, perceived intelligence, and membership in a caste or socioeconomic group. Although the rationale for each type of separation may differ, all types of segregation have one common denominator. They are all based on the power of the dominant group to enforce a separation from others who, because they possess characteristics that differ from those of the dominant group, are either feared, despised, or deemed to be inferior as members of the human race.

Humans have shown an instinctive tendency to favor those who are most like themselves. In a competitive world, humans' quest for status, power, and dignity has often come at the expense of others over whom power is gained. Indeed, the very nature of power, is superiority and control. The very fact that such power has been achieved has often served as the basis for claims superiority in matters unrelated to those characteristics manifested by the dominant group in achieving its power (such as the superior application of physical or military force).

The most extreme example of the assertion of power by one group over another—that of slavery—was certainly not unique to America. Indeed slavery has existed since the beginning of civilization and persists even today in the isolated backwaters of global society. But slavery is only the most extreme application of raw power over fellow human beings. There exist a variety of intermediate levels of domination that may manifest themselves by the enforcement of segregation.

There are two kinds of segregation in American public education today—de facto and de jure. De jure segregation is imposed by force of law, and is therefore most easily dealt with through application of the law. De facto segregation, on the other hand, is more intractable since it results from individual choices and from economic and social forces beyond the immediate control of the courts.

De jure racial segregation in the public schools was first declared unconstitutional in the case of *Brown v. Board of Education* in 1954.[1]

However, de jure segregation based on such characteristics as primary language and perceived intelligence and socioeconomic status continue to exist in the form of such official programs as bilingual and special education.

Ideology now plays an overpowering role in the administration of programs within the public schools. Considerations related to providing a high quality of education have become secondary to ideological considerations—or, more accurately, perceptions of how one's ideology will be perceived. Thus, even policies of blatant racial discrimination are acceptable if they purport to achieve some ideologically desirable social result. In the doublespeak of the educational establishment, an abhorrent means (racial discrimination) may be used to achieve a bureaucrat's claimed ideological goal.

For example, it will be recalled that in Kansas City the exclusion of students from the best magnet schools on grounds of their race was found to be acceptable because the bureaucrats who sought to implement the policy claimed that they had an ideologically correct goal in mind. In 1884 the public schools in San Francisco excluded Chinese Americans on the social grounds of protecting society from "Mongolian barbarism." In the 1980s, prestigious universities in California excluded qualified Asian Americans and set racial quotas in order to promote a perceived ideologically correct social agenda. Public schools continue to exclude students from certain classes based on their perceived low levels of ability and who allegedly come from an inferior culture.

Thus, despite developments in the law, actual policies have not changed as much as the rationales given to justify them. Not surprisingly, given the use of such abhorrent means, the goals set forth to justify those means are rarely achieved. In most cases segregation has intensified when policies of "benign" racial discrimination have been imposed. (Patrons of political correctness have even coined a euphemism—"reverse discrimination"—to justify policies of racial discrimination.) For example, the percentage of African Americans attending predominately African American schools in 1992 was higher than in 1972.[2]

In short, the legacy of policies of exclusion and segregation pervades public education today and constitutes one of the most significant obstacles to providing educational opportunity for all Americans.

THE ORIGINS OF RACIAL SEGREGATION

Although the Constitution of the United States is now a hallowed and enshrined document of the American Republic, it very nearly did not come into being. After the American Revolution, the former colonies entered into a very loose confederation described as a "firm league of friendship," under which each participating state was assured that it would retain its "sovereignty, freedom, and independence."[3] Like the Holy Roman Empire, however, which Voltaire observed to be neither Holy, Roman, nor an Empire, the "firm league of friendship" turned out to be neither firm, a league, or very friendly. Internal rebellions broke out, each state began quarreling and passing punitive tariffs on each other, and the Confederation Congress had neither the resources nor the power to raise revenues, pass national laws, or enforce them.

By 1785 several states had sought to form their own amalgamation and quasi-states. Maryland invited Delaware, Virginia, and Pennsylvania to form a commercial alliance, and several states south of Virginia were negotiating to form a counterweight to that of Maryland's four-state "nation." It was assumed that states north of Pennsylvania would form their own nation-state.[4]

In was in the midst of such political flux and uncertainty that James Madison and Alexander Hamilton in 1786 at Annapolis prevailed upon the Confederation Congress to authorize a "convention of all the states to be held in Philadelphia . . . to take in consideration the situation in the United States, to devise such further provisions as shall appear to them necessary to render the Constitution of the Federal Government adequate to the exigencies of the union."[5]

However, the Confederation Congress, wary of what might be a hidden agenda of such a convention, specifically directed that the convention be for the "sole and express purpose of revising the Articles of Confederation." In other words, the convention was not legally authorized to consider any drastic restructuring of the government and was to confine its attention to moderate revisions of the existing political structure of confederation in which each state retained its "sovereignty, freedom, and independence." Indeed, the Confederation Congress authorized even this limited purpose with much trepidation. It has been suggested that one might "imagine the discomfiture of the Confederation Congress by considering how Congress might feel today if delegates outside Congress began holding a meeting to consider the formation of a new form of government."[6]

Given the tame and even boring agenda authorized for the Philadelphia Convention by the Confederation Congress, it was not surprising that only a handful of delegates from the states bothered to show up on its opening day in Philadelphia on May 14, 1787. Even George Washington, who had despaired about the state of "thirteen sovereignties pulling against each other" debated whether to attend the Philadelphia Convention or the Convention of the Society of the Cincinnati (a fraternity of Revolutionary War army officers), which had invited him first. Others of the Revolution, like Patrick Henry, refused to attend the Convention. Henry declared that he "smelt a rat."[7]

It was not until May 25 that there was even a bare quorum of 29 delegates from seven states, and there was only one delegate from all of New England. Some 19 delegates failed to appear at all, and during the entire convention average attendance never exceeded 29. New Hampshire failed to even provide a travel allowance for its two delegates, who had to hitchhike at their own expense, and arrived two months late, after most important business had been conducted.

When it became clear that Madison and Hamilton had in mind an agenda that went far beyond that authorized by the Confederation Congress, many delegates became dismayed and claimed that the convention was acting beyond its legal authority. John Lansing of New York asked whether is was "probable that the states will adopt and ratify a scheme which they have never authorized us to propose?" and protested that "New York would never have concurred in sending deputies to the convention if she supposed the deliberations were to turn on a consolidation of the states and a national government."[8]

Two major issues threatened to prevent any agreement by the delegates on a national constitution: whether there would be equal representation of each state in a national legislature, or whether representation would be according to population; and slavery.

The two issues were connected. Delegates from the Southern states insisted that if states were to be represented according to their population, slaves should be counted for purposes of determining the number of representatives to which a state would be entitled in the legislature. Northern delegates protested that since slaves had no rights of citizenship in the Southern states, and could not vote, they should not be counted at all for purposes of determining the number of representatives to which a state would be entitled. The resulting compromise was that slaves and untaxed Indians would count as three-fifths of a person for purposes of determining the number of representatives in Congress to which a state would be entitled.

This "three-fifths of a person" provision of the Constitution[9] has often been criticized as reflecting the racism and prejudice of the Founding Fathers. In fact, however, this provision was the best Northern delegates could obtain. Had slaves been counted as a whole person, the Southern states would have had more representatives in Congress to protect the institution of slavery.

The issues of state representation and slavery came close to preventing any agreement on union. The small states insisted upon equal representation because they feared that the large states might overwhelm the smaller states in Congress if representation were based on population. Delaware, for example, specifically limited the authority of it delegates to voting for the "one state, one vote" principle and directed them to immediately depart from the convention if there were any suggestion that this principle would not be accepted. For the same reason, Rhode Island refused to participate in the convention at all.

Hugh Williamson of South Carolina warned ominously that "if no compromise should take place, what would be the consequence? A secession, I foresee, will take place."[10] Luther Martin observed that at the convention "we were on the verge of dissolution, scarce held together by the strength of a hair".[11] Gouvernor Morris of Pennsylvania opposed any compromise and thundered that "this country must be united, and if persuasion does not unite it, the sword will. The scene of horror attending civil commotion can not be described. The stronger party will then make traitors of the weaker, and the gallows and halter will finish the work of the sword."[12] When the convention seemed irretrievably deadlocked over the issue, even George Washington despaired of "seeing a favorable issue to the proceedings of the convention and do therefore repent having had any agency in the business."[13] Eventually calmer heads prevailed, and a compromise was reached whereby each state would be represented equally in the upper chamber (the Senate), and according to population in the lower chamber (the House of Representatives).

Although Madison was instrumental in mediating a compromise between the large and small states over the issue of representation in Congress, he saw that the more important issue was slavery. "The great danger to our general government is the great southern and northern interests of the continent being opposed to each other," he observed, and the "states are divided into different interests not by their difference in size . . . but from the effects of their having, or not having, slaves."[14]

But on the issue of slavery the delegates of the Southern states were as intractable as the delegates of the small states had been on the issue of congressional representation. When some Northern delegates began referring to the immorality of slavery and suggesting its abolition, an enraged John Rutledge of South Carolina spoke for his fellow Southern delegates when he thundered that "religion and humanity have nothing to do with this question. Interest alone is the governing principle with nations."[15] He then got down to the nub of the matter: "The true question at present is whether the Southern states shall or shall not be parties to the union. . . . If the convention thinks that North Carolina, South Carolina, and Georgia will ever agree to [the Constitution] unless their right to import slaves is untouched, that expectation is in vain."[16]

The delegates from the Northern states have since been criticized for not taking a firmer stand on the issue of slavery. But the Southern states had made it very clear that they would not participate in a union that would interfere with the institution of slavery within a state; and forming a union without the Southern states would have done little to promote the abolition of slavery. Indeed, slavery would doubtless have continued for much longer than it did in the South had the Northern states formed their own separate union.

The most the Northern states were able to extract by way of concession on the slavery issue was a provision permitting Congress to abolish the slave trade after the year 1808.[17] However, the compromise included a provision that implicitly recognized a state's power to protect the institution of slavery within its borders. That provision, set forth in Article IV, states that "no person held to service or labor in one state, under the laws thereof, escaping into another, shall, in consequence of any law or Regulation therein, be discharged from such service or labor, but shall be delivered up on Claim of the Party to whom such Service or Labor may be due."

One final concession was made to the sensibilities of the Northern delegates. There would be no use of the word "slave" or "slavery" in the Constitution. Instead such phrases as "persons held to service" or "persons held to labor" would be used. As delegate Roger Sherman later explained, the use of the term "slave" was not "pleasing to some (delegates)."[18]

Even with such concessions, the Constitution was a hard sell in the state legislatures, and was ratified only by the thinnest of margins in many of the states. The Confederation Congress refused to indorse it, and antifederalists argued vehemently that the Philadelphia Convention had exceeded the authority granted to it by the Confederation Congress.

Pennsylvania ratified only after boycotting antifederalists were physically dragged to the State House to provide a quorum. New York ratified only after Hamilton threatened to join the union with New York's southern counties (leaving the northern ones on their own), and even then the New York legislature only voted to ratify by a three-vote margin. North Carolina held out and refused to join the union until after Washington was elected president, and Rhode Island was induced to ratify only after the newly constituted U.S. Senate voted to cut off all relations with it. Even then, the Rhode Island legislature voted to ratify and join the union by only a two vote margin.

Although there could certainly have been no union in 1787 had the Northern states insisted upon the abolition of slavery, many Northern delegates did not believe slavery would survive much longer anyway and that it would therefore be futile to make it an overriding issue. Many states in the North had already abolished slavery, and even in the South its days appeared numbered. A French visitor of the day observed that "[Americans] are constantly talking of abolishing slavery, and of contriving some other means of cultivating their estates."[19]

At the time of the American Revolution, long-staple cotton was grown in only a few isolated areas of the South. Most plantations cultivated tobacco, indigo, and rice, and slavery was slowly but surely dying out. In 1793, however, an event occurred that the Founding Fathers could not have anticipated. Eli Whitney invented the cotton gin. This meant that short-staple cotton could now be profitably cultivated by slave labor on a large scale. The value of prime slaves increased to over $1,800 by the 1850s, thereby making slaves a significant percentage of the property in the Southern economy.

As a result, not only did slavery not die out in the South, it soon became the foundation of the Southern economy based on cotton. However, the slave trade was abolished in 1808, in accordance with the provision in the Constitution that permitted Congress to do this, and even some of the Southern states considered emancipation. As late as the 1820s, there were more abolitionist societies in the South than in the North,[20] and many prominent Southerners were freeing their slaves and supporting colonization efforts. In 1832 the Virginia Legislature seriously considered a proposal to emancipate the slaves and compensate the owners.[21] However, none of these proposals were enacted into law in the Southern states, and by 1819 the country had become evenly divided between 11 slave states and 11 free states.

Despite growing abolitionist sentiment in the North, however, there existed political parity between the two regions on the slavery issue — until new territories applied for admission to the union. Both North and South realized that these new states could upset the delicate balance of power on the slavery issue in the Congress. Southern planters also realized that if the institution of slavery was to survive, it was imperative that the cultivation of cotton be extended west as the eastern lands became depleted and eroded.

Despite growing abolitionist sentiment in the North, a series of political compromises, such as the Missouri Compromise and the Compromise of 1850, served to maintain political parity and keep the slavery issue from igniting. When California applied for admission to the union as a free state in 1849, however, many Southern leaders began to see what they feared was the handwriting on the wall, and a threat to the institution of slavery. Under the provisions of the Compromise of 1850, the price of the admission of California as a free state was the enactment of the Fugitive Slave Law, which put the force of federal law behind the recovery of runaway slaves in the North.

RACIAL LAWS PRIOR TO THE CIVIL WAR

Although African Americans enslaved in the South had virtually no rights whatsoever, even in the free states there existed no legal concept of equal protection of the laws. In 1850 the Massachusetts Supreme Court adopted the doctrine of "separate but equal" in upholding segregated schools for African Americans.[22] In 1859, when a Wisconsin Court released from jail a man charged with assisting a fugitive slave to escape from custody, the Supreme Court reversed the Wisconsin Court's attempt to nullify federal law and held the Fugitive Slave Law to be constitutional.[23]

It was a misguided spirit of compromise, however, that led the United States Supreme Court to render the most thoroughly repudiated judicial decision in American history. In 1857 an African American slave named Dred Scott, who had been brought into the free state of Illinois, but was later returned to Missouri, sued for his freedom in federal court. Although there were a number of technical legal avenues the Supreme Court might have pursued in resolving the case, the Court chose instead to modify Southern interests by using the case as a platform to establish the principle of white supremacy and declare that the constitution forbade both Congress and the states from extending rights of citizenship to African Americans. Chief Justice Taney's opinion sought even to preclude the emancipation of slaves by legislative action, holding that emancipation of a slave would violate the right of a slaveowner not to be deprived of his slaves without due process under the Fifth Amendment.[24]

The case did little to modify the South, but enraged many in the North. The decision has been explained on the theory that the Supreme Court believed that its "effective existence depended upon acceptance of the principle of national authority," and that "there was no hope this principle would be entertained in the South one minute after an antislavery opinion was rendered."[25]   However, it has also been observed that "the monumental indiscretion of the *Dred Scott* decision had forfeited Northern allegiance. For the first time in its history, the Court seemed almost friendless (for the fair-weather friendship of the South provided very cold comfort)."[26]

The spirit of compromise on the issue of slavery finally collapsed in 1860, when the Democratic party split over the issue of extending slavery into the new territories, and allowed the Republican Abraham Lincoln to be elected with but 39% of the popular vote.[27]   Although Lincoln was opposed to slavery, the Constitution he was sworn to defend implicitly enshrined (in Article IV, Paragraph 3) the right of a state to protect the institution of slavery within its borders. Lincoln did not therefore propose to meddle with the institution of slavery in those states where it existed. (Some abolitionists, however, argued that since Article IV was only implicit rather than explicit in protecting slavery, Congress had the power to abolish slavery in all the states.) Lincoln was, however, prepared to draw a line in the sand over the issue of the extension of slavery into new territories where it had not previously existed, and he rejected a last-minute compromise proposed by John Crittendon of Kentucky (which would have banned slavery in territories north of the old Missouri compromise line) because it would have permitted slavery in new territories south of that line. Some critics of Lincoln point out that had Lincoln supported Crittendon's compromise, war might have been avoided and the loss of the lives of over 600,000 Americans. However, Crittendon's compromise was also unacceptable to Lincoln because it would also have pledged strong federal enforcement of the Fugitive Slave Law and required amending the Constitution in such a way that it could never be amended in the future to give Congress the power to interfere with slavery within the states.

Neither the *Dred Scott* decision nor Lincoln's promise not to meddle with the institution of slavery in states where it existed satisfied Southern secessionists, who believed that the only real way to assure the long-term survival of slavery was to leave the union and form their own independent confederacy of Southern states.

The Civil War that followed was long and bitter. Had the North been able to mobilize is superior resources in both manpower and material, the war might have ended quickly with no significant change in the status of the institution of slavery. Reunion would almost certainly have been established on the basis of an agreement to limit the extension of slavery in return for guarantees of noninterference with slavery where it existed. Indeed the war had begun not as a crusade to abolish slavery, but as one to save the union. Lincoln himself declared that if he could save the union by either freeing the slaves, not freeing the slaves, or freeing some of them, he would do it.

The brilliant military leadership of the Southern armies succeeded in defeating time and again superior federal armies. By the middle of 1862 the succession of Union defeats had come close to bringing the

Confederacy recognition, and military assistance, from the major countries of Europe. France was urging recognition of the Confederacy, and Great Britain was on the verge of granting recognition. Had it done so, the Union cause would almost certainly have been irretrievably lost. In 1862, the Chancellor of the Exchequer, William Gladstone, gave an official speech in which he proclaimed that "there is no doubt that Jefferson Davis and other leaders of the South have made an army; they are making, it appears, a Navy; and they have made what is more than either—they have made a nation." Gladstone concluded that "we may anticipate with certainty the success for the Southern States so far as regards their independence from the North."[28]

However, the British cabinet hesitated, and decided to await the outcome of General Robert E. Lee's invasion of Maryland in September 1862. Lincoln by now had given up all hope of reconciliation and peace without the abolition of slavery and realized that freeing the slaves would be necessary to win the war and save the Union. However, Lincoln knew that any emancipation of the slaves prior to a union victory would appear as a last desperate gesture of a defeated country, so he waited until after a Union victory to issue the Emancipation Proclamation.

Several days before the Confederate invasion had begun, the Confederate battle plans had been carelessly used to wrap a cigar. It had then been carelessly discarded and subsequently found by a Union soldier. Armed with precise knowledge of the Confederate battle plans, even Union General McClellan managed to fight the Confederates to a standstill at Antietam and turn back the invasion. Five days later, on September 22, 1862, Lincoln issued the Emancipation Proclamation. This one act changed the character of the war into a crusade for freedom. Even the British working classes, many of whom had been put out of work by the Union blockade, supported the Union as the champion of emancipation. No civilized nation in the world now wished to support the enemy of a nation fighting to abolish slavery.

However, the Emancipation Proclamation was not a permanent legal document. It only freed the slaves in the states controlled by the Confederacy, and was issued only as a temporary measure pursuant to the president's wartime emergency powers—for there was no other basis in the Constitution for issuing such a decree. After he issued the proclamation, however, Lincoln refused ever to consider any peace with the Southern states that did not include the abolition of slavery. Having freed the slaves, Lincoln would under no circumstances return them to bondage.   Had the Southern generals not been so brilliant, and the Union generals so incompetent, the war might have ended in early 1862 with slavery preserved in the South and border states. Ironically, emancipation owes a great debt to both this brilliance and incompetence. Had either quality been lacking, slavery might well have continued for many, many years. Most ironic of all, however, was that the greatest threat to the preservation of slavery had been the South's own secession. Had the Southern states not seceded, they could have continued to find absolute protection for slavery in the very Constitution from which they were seeking to sever all ties.

Had it not been for a carelessly wrapped cigar, Confederate independence might have been won. After 1862, however, the struggle could end only with the permanent abolition of slavery. It continued for three bloody years, until all power of resistance by the South was crushed. One of the most important spoils of victory was the North's political empowerment to amend the Constitution to remove the blight of slavery without the need for Southern cooperation or support.

THE CIVIL WAR AMENDMENTS

In the same year that General Ulysses Grant accepted the surrender of General Robert E. Lee at Appomattox in 1865, Congress passed, and the Northern states ratified, the Thirteenth Amendment to the Constitution, which abolished slavery. With the South under military occupation and Reconstruction, Congress passed two additional constitutional amendments that would serve as the foundation stones for all subsequent civil rights legislation and judicial decisions—the Fourteenth and Fifteenth Amendments. Ratification of the necessary three-quarters of the states was procured, however, only after Congress passed the Reconstruction Act of 1867, which forbade the Southern states to send representatives to Congress until they passed the amendments.[29]

The Fourteenth Amendment provides that any person born or naturalized in the United States is a citizen of the United States, and forbids any state to "abridge the privileges and immunities of citizens," to "deprive any person of life, liberty, or property, without due process of law," or to "deny to any person within its jurisdiction the equal protection of the laws." The Fifteenth Amendment provides that the "right of citizens to vote shall not be denied or abridged . . . on account of race, color, or previous condition of servitude."

These amendments were fundamentally different from previous constitutional amendments. The first ten amendments were enacted primarily to provide a check on the exercise of federal power, which it was feared could be abused by a strong national government. The enslavement of persons by certain states, however, revealed that state power, as well as federal power, required legal limitations. The Fourteenth and Fifteenth Amendments were enacted to provide legal limitations on the exercise of state power.

RACIAL DISCRIMINATION AFTER THE CIVIL WAR

The North did not enter the Civil War with the purpose of abolishing slavery. The Emancipation Proclamation was an exercise of military emergency powers during a period when the North faced the very real possibility of international recognition of the Confederacy. Many Northerners did not support the abolition of slavery, and racial prejudice was by no means limited to the South. In 1863, draft riots broke out in New York City in which African Americans were attacked, beaten, and blamed as the cause of the war. Many protested a war they now perceived as a war to abolish slavery.

Despite the passage of the Civil Rights Act of 1871, which set forth civil and criminal penalties for those depriving citizens of their civil rights,[30] lynchings and other atrocities against African Americans were a common occurrence.

Supreme Court decisions in the period after the Civil War did not always serve to deter racial discrimination. Although the Court struck down a West Virginia Law in 1879 that excluded African Americans from sitting on juries on grounds that it violated the Fourteenth Amendment,[31] the Court also declared several parts of the Civil Rights Law to be unconstitutional, including the provisions that purported to impose sanctions on private citizens who violated the civil rights of other citizens.[32] And it was not until 1967 that the Supreme Court finally struck down as unconstitutional state laws interracial marriage.[33]

Nor were many state legislatures or courts more sympathetic to the cause of racial equality. Many states passed "black codes" limiting the legal rights of African Americans. Not untypical was a Texas law passed in 1866, which decreed that schools for African Americans could only be supported by taxes collected from African Americans.[34]

THE DOCTRINE OF SEPARATE BUT EQUAL

The principle of "separate but equal," first set forth in the Massachusetts pre-Civil War decision of *Roberts v. City of Boston*,[35] was adopted by states across the country. Many states declared that the only purpose of educating African Americans was to train them for occupations that white society had set aside for them.

A typical view was that expressed by William Baldwin, a wealthy industrialist and prominent member of the Southern Education Board, that African Americans should "willingly fill the more menial positions and do the heavy work at less wages," reserving to whites the task of "more expert labor."[36] His advice to African Americans seeking an education was to "avoid social questions; leave politics alone; live moral lives; live simply; learn to work . . . know that it is a crime for any teacher, black or white, to educate the negro for positions which are not open to him."[37]

Education for African Americans in the South was "tailored to produce a black person who adapted well to the tenant system, who was 'neither too illiterate to take advantage of his surroundings, nor more educated than is demanded by his dependent economic situation.'"[38] Except for a relatively short period during Reconstruction in the South, most separate schools for African Americans not in fact equal. A study of separate schools in the South in 1930 revealed that "the amount of money spent on black public school education represented only 37% of their proportionate share of the school funds.

The remaining 63% of the funds for black schools was diverted to support white education."[39]

There were many other instances of separate but unequal. For example, the student/teacher ratio in separate African American schools in 1912 was 67 to 1.[40] A study of the segregated schools in Nashville revealed that schools for whites spent almost twice as much as did African American schools.[41] In Georgia, South Carolina, North Carolina, and Virginia, the average salary in 1911-1913 was $127.88 for teachers in the separate African American schools, and $287.29 for teachers in the white schools.[42] The rationale given by General S. C. Armstrong for such disparities was typical—that the "mental processes" of African Americans was different than that of whites, and that the purpose of education for African Americans should be to "train blacks for their already ascribed roles in . . . agriculture, domestic and personal service, common labor, and the like."[43]

THE EFFECTS OF IMMIGRATION ON EDUCATIONAL POLICY

After the Civil War, immigration policies played an important role in making possible the perpetuation of the "separate but equal doctrine" in the public schools. Although the Fourteenth Amendment in theory required that states provide equal public educational opportunities, the prevailing view among many educators that African Americans were unsuited for certain occupations provided a rationale for providing education that was not really "unequal" in their view, but was rather merely adapted to the requirements of each race. According to the advocates of the separate but equal doctrine, it would be a wasteful exercise in futility to provide African Americans with an education and training for occupations they could not realistically hope to enter, and for which they were not suited.

Such a view of educational opportunity was made credible, however, only because African Americans were in fact excluded from many of the more desirable occupations. Although the rationale for exclusion was often that African Americans were unsuited for desirable occupations, in most instances the reason for exclusion was racial prejudice and the fear that jobs for whites would be lost. However, such exclusion would not have been economically practical had it not been for the immigration policies of the United States.

After the end of the Civil War, the abolition of slavery resulted in the release of hundreds of thousands of African Americans into the labor market. As the nation turned its attention and energies from war to domestic production, however, America's industrial revolution began to require the infusion of vast numbers of workers to work in the new factories and assembly lines. Indeed, if anything, a severe labor shortage loomed. It therefore appeared that there would be employment opportunities for the newly freed slaves.

But it was not to be.   The prospect of a labor shortage alarmed the industrialists, for such a shortage would have given the workers greater bargaining power and resulted in the rise of wages. Worst of all, however, it might have necessitated the hiring of African Americans against whom many employers were racially prejudiced and whom they considered inferior. It was therefore imperative that another source of labor be found. The industrialists turned to the teeming throngs of white immigrants from Europe to staff the factories and assembly lines of the new industrial revolution. They had no problem in convincing Congress to pass laws allowing the importation of millions of unskilled workers. That an immigration policy founded on the premise that an alternative source of labor must be found in order to avoid hiring African Americans and to keep wages low could be implemented under the guise of "promoting the American dream as set forth on the Statue of Liberty made it all the more desirable as a policy."[44]

Between 1870 and 1900, over 1.5 million Scandinavians immigrated to the United States.[45] Between 1880 and 1920, 8 million workers from Italy, Czechoslovakia, and Austria, and 2.5 million from Eastern Europe immigrated to the United States.[46]

Not all Americans failed to see what was happening, however, or discern the driving motive behind the immigration policies. Booker T. Washington, the great African American educator, tried desperately to "alter the course of this policy, which he knew was so disastrous to the aspirations of African Americans."[47]

In 1895 Washington was given the opportunity to express his concerns about the catastrophic effects of U.S. immigration policy on the economic aspirations of African Americans. On September 18 he was invited to address not only American industrialist leaders, but the president of the United States at the Atlanta International Exposition.

That an African American had been invited to deliver one of the opening addresses at the Exposition was itself an extraordinary event. Washington himself was apprehensive about giving the address, later writing that "this was the first time in the entire history of the Negro that a member of my race had been asked to speak on the same platform with (white men) on any important national occasion. I was asked now to speak to an audience composed of the wealth and culture of the white south, yet there would be present a large number of northern whites."[48]

In his autobiography, Washington recalled his determination to "say nothing that I did not feel from the bottom of my heart to be true and right. I felt the directors [of the Exposition] had paid a tribute to me. They knew that by one sentence I could have blasted, in a large degree the success of the exposition. . . . Not a few of the Southern white papers were unfriendly to the idea of my speaking."[49]

To a vast assemblage that included President Grover Cleveland, Washington delivered one of the most famous and courageous speeches ever delivered by an African American in the United States. In his address, Washington told the story of a ship lost at sea:

Suddenly the ship sighted a friendly vessel. From the mast of the unfortunate vessel was seen a signal, "water, water; we die of thirst!" The answer from the friendly vessel at once came back, "cast down your bucket where you are." A second time the "water, water send us water" ran up from the distressed vessel, and was answered "cast down your bucket where you are." The captain of the distressed vessel, at last heeding the injunction, cast down his bucket, and it came up full of fresh sparkling water from the mouth of the Amazon river.[50]

Washington then turned to the African American members of his audience, many of whom he knew were contemplating emigration from the United States as a means of escaping the burdens and suffering of racial prejudice. "To those of my race who depend on bettering their condition in a foreign land, I would say, "cast down your bucket where you are," he told them, his voice rising to a dramatic pitch. "Cast it down in agriculture, mechanics, in commerce."[51]

But then he turned to the powerful white titans of industry and the politicians in Congress, without whom he knew the aspirations of African Americans could never be realized. "To those of you who look to the incoming of those of foreign birth, 'cast down your bucket where you are,'" he cried. If they would only do so, Washington promised, "we shall stand by you with a devotion that no foreigner can approach, ready to interlac[e] our industrial, commercial, civil and religious life with yours."[52]

The speech itself was well received. The *Boston Transcript* editorialized that "the speech dwarfed all other proceedings and the Exposition itself. The sensation that it has caused in the press has never been equalled."[53] The editor of the *Atlanta Constitution* wrote that "I do not exaggerate when I say that Professor Booker T. Washington's address yesterday was one of the most notable speeches. The whole speech is a platform upon which blacks and whites can stand with full justice to each other."[54]

However well the speech was received, it was totally ignored by the white industrialists and politicians in Congress who remained as determined as ever to "cast their bucket" with foreign immigrants to fulfill America's labor needs. It was not necessary of course to completely cut off all immigration. It was only necessary to moderate immigration policies so that industrial demand for the employment of African Americans might outweigh the forces of prejudice. But it was not to be.

Were the concerns of Booker T. Washington justified? Several recent reports have studied the correlation between immigration policies and domestic unemployment during the period 1940-1986. During the period 1940-1951, only 1 million immigrants entered the United States, and the unemployment rate averaged 4.6%. When immigration rose to 2.5 million during the 1960s, the average unemployment rate also rose—to 4.9%. When the number of immigrants increased to 4.5 million in the 1970s, average unemployment also increased to 5.8%. When immigration rose to 7.3 million in the 1980s, average unemployment increased to 8.9%. [55]

A statistical correlation does not by itself prove cause and effect, of course; and a number of other political and economic factors doubtless played a part in the unemployment figures during the studied periods. But there is much additional empirical data that reveals the effects of immigration on employment—particularly the employment of African Americans who have historically suffered the highest rates of unemployment.

For example, in 1887, at a time when the unemployment rate among teenage male African Americans approached 80%, garment factory owners in Los Angeles were petitioning the Immigration and Naturalization Service to increase the number of unskilled immigrants on grounds that there was an "skilled labor shortage."[56]

Other studies have revealed that racial prejudice still plays an important role in why employers prefer to hire immigrants instead of African Americans if it is possible to do so. The *Chicago Tribune* conducted a survey of employers in Chicago who chose to hire white immigrants instead of African Americans. Reasons given by employers for preferring immigrants over African Americans included: "I don't think black people want to work in Chicago"; "the blacks are the most unreliable help you can get, whereas the illegal immigrants are reliable"; "the black people we've got here are uneducated and unskilled."[57]

Such examples of racial prejudice explain current immigration policies in the United States. Employers favor lax immigration laws because it permits them to exploit immigrants rather than hire African Americans. For similar reasons, other rich Americans also favor lax immigration. As one major study has revealed, "if an influx of illegal professionals could lower the wages of the overpaid, of doctors and lawyers, rather than the wages of the poor, then there might be some economic benefit to their coming to this country. But doctors and lawyers would not allow that to happen. Instead, it is low-wage markets, the wages at the bottom that are being depressed."[58] The study concludes that immigration "widens the differences between classes in the United States; it keeps down the price of hiring a maid or a gardener for the rich while it makes things worse for the poor."[59]

Indeed, a continuing influx of immigrants protects employers from having to pay higher wages, and can even reduce labor costs substantially. Ironically, however, the ones who suffer most from such policies are the immigrants themselves. For example, in 1989 in New York City, Chinese immigrants were earning an average of $1,200 a month washing dishes in fancy restaurants. This was apparently higher than many employers wanted to pay. The solution? Simply import even more Chinese immigrants. The result was that four years labor the average wage for Chinese dishwashers in New York fell to $700 a month within two years. The beneficiaries were the employers (who made higher profits), and the rich (who got fancy meals at reduced prices). The immigrants of course, suffered the most.[60]

A similar example can be found in the laying off of African American janitorial workers in Los Angeles office buildings during the 1970s. At that time the janitorial workers (predominately African American) were earning $9 an hour plus generous benefits. However, these wages were apparently higher than the office building owners wanted to pay, so they farmed out the janitorial jobs to independent contractors who hired desperate immigrants willing to work for slave wages. Thousands of African Americans lost their jobs and were thrown back into the streets.

It is sometimes argued that immigrants are of benefit to the American middle class as well because, by working for slave wages, immigrants help to reduce the price of products used by the middle class. While this might be true, the same could be said of products produced in China by slave labor. Most Americans would be willing to pay a little more in order to achieve social, economic, and racial justice.

It is sometimes argued that immigrants take only jobs that others do not want. This is clearly not true. Employers have no problem finding Americans willing to work at the very dirtiest of jobs if the wages paid are fair. For example, there is no dearth of applicants to be municipal garbage workers when the wages and benefits paid are sufficient to enable a worker to feed and raise a family in dignity. Likewise, Americans are willing to work as coal miners (one of the dirtiest and most dangerous jobs) if they are paid a high wage. It is the willingness of desperate immigrants to work at low pay, not at undesirable jobs that pay fairly, that makes them subject to exploitation by the rich and powerful and that hurt minorities.

Although the rich and powerful are rarely willing to concede their motives for supporting lax immigration policies, they are sometimes caught in situations that reveal them. When the wealthy and successful Zoe Baird was considered for the position of U.S. Attorney General in 1993, for example, it was revealed that she had chosen to hire an immigrant as a nanny and pay a below-market wage (and no Social Security) rather than hire one of America's many African American unemployed.

Even the legal entry of 800,000 immigrants into the United States in 1992 was not enough to satisfy the rich and powerful interests; as a result there has been little action to disrupt the annual flow of a quarter of a million illegal immigrants, whom the U.S. border patrol can (or will) not even protect from marauding muggers along the border. Business interests have resisted any measures that might put teeth in the employer sanctions bill, which was supposed to have imposed sanctions on those exploiting illegal immigrants. As a result, there is only a pretense of enforcing the law.

In short, the fears that Booker T. Washington expressed in 1895 have been vindicated, and the conditions that led to his desperate pleas for justice exist today. Despite the fact that a 1992 Harris poll revealed that 63% of African Americans were aware that illegal immigrants were taking jobs from them,[61] their pleas for economic justice have not been answered any more than the pleas of Booker T. Washington in 1985. A 1992 Roper poll revealed that a majority of Americans, including Hispanics and African Americans, want stricter immigration laws and enforcement.[62] It remains to be seen, however, whether racial prejudice can be overcome, and the most powerful political and business interests can be persuaded to take some action.

In 1965 Congress passed the Civil Rights Act, which raised the hopes of many African Americans. At the same time, however, Congress passed an immigration law that permitted millions of immigrants to enter the country. "Over 25 million immigrants were added to the U.S. population between 1970 and 1990, dashing the hopes of African Americans."[63]

A 1992 study by the Center for Immigration Studies revealed the reasons why the "economic plight of [African Americans] has not improved since the Civil Rights Act took effect in 1965; [the answer] is that the Immigration Act passed the same year. Since then the importation of millions of foreign workers into U.S. inner cities has done two things: it has provided an alternative supply of labor so that urban employees have not had to hire available black job seekers, and the foreign workers have oversupplied labor to low-skill markets."[64] The study concluded that recent American immigration policy has "kept the jobs in a seemingly perpetual state of declining real wages which are incapable of lifting unskilled black workers out of poverty."[65]   Finally, the immigration study confirmed that little had changed since Booker T. Washington delivered his "cast down your bucket" address in 1895: "Whether intended or not, present immigration policy is a revived instrument of institutional racism."[66]

Although such policies may appear to have only a direct effect on the economic status of minorities in the United States, they also have a very important effect on public education. As will be documented in the remainder of this chapter, the primary cause of continued segregation in the public schools is the low socioeconomic status of minorities, and in particular the inability of minorities to breach the economic barriers to living in integrated neighborhoods and thereby break the pattern of de facto segregation upon which the public school system is at present based.

The failure to acknowledge this ultimate cause of segregation has led to educational policies that are not only hypocritical and misguided but, worst of all, counterproductive to the cause of quality education and equal educational opportunity in the public schools for all Americans.

THE DEVELOPMENT OF THE LAW OF DE JURE SEGREGATION

The 1954 Supreme Court case of *Brown v. Board of Education* is often pointed to by legal scholars as the classic case justifying judicial activism and the overturning of legal precedent.[67]   It is cited as reversing the "separate but equal" legal doctrine of de jure segregation in the public schools first set forth in the 1896 case of *Plessy v. Ferguson*.[68]

In fact, however, the Court in *Brown* did not overrule *Plessy* at all, but instead observed that in its decisions since *Plessy* it had "expressly reserved decision on the question of whether Plessy should be held [applicable] to public education."[69]   In other words, the issue of whether the "separate but equal" doctrine was applicable to public schools was a case of first impression and had not ever been previously addressed by the Supreme Court.

The case of *Plessy v. Ferguson* dealt with a matter quite unrelated to public education—namely, whether a state law requiring "equal but separate accommodation for the white, and colored races"[70] on railway passenger cars was a violation of the Equal Protection Clause of the Fourteenth Amendment. The Supreme Court held that there was no denial of equal protection to African Americans and rejected the argument that "the enforced separation of the two races stamps the colored race with a badge of inferiority. If this be so, it is not by reason of anything found in the act, but solely because the colored race chooses to put that construction on it."[71] The Court concluded that such an argument assumes that "equal rights can not be secured to the negro except by the enforced commingling of the two races. We cannot accept this proposition."[72]

In a vigorous dissent, Justice John Harlan accurately foresaw how the *Plessy* decision would be viewed by future generations: " In my opinion, the judgment this day rendered will, in time, prove to be quite as pernicious as the decision made by this tribunal in the *Dred Scott* case that the descendants of Africans were not included under the words 'citizens' in the constitution . . . and that they were subordinate and inferior beings who had been subjugated by the dominant race [and] remained subject to their authority." Harlan concluded by asking "[What] can more certainly arouse race hate . . . than state enactments which proceed on the ground that colored citizens are so inferior and degraded that they cannot be allowed to sit in public coaches occupied by white citizens?"[73]

Although the holding in *Plessy* would later be reversed by legislation and other court decisions, *Brown v. Board of Education* distinguished rather than reversed *Plessy* and relied on substantial legal precedent holding that separate but equal facilities in education was a violation of the Fourteenth Amendment.

In the case of *McLaurin v. Oklahoma Board of Regents*, decided in 1950, a state university admitted an African American student, but required him to eat and study alone in designated areas and to sit in class behind a railing with a sign which read "for colored's only."[74] Although this case was similar to one decided two years earlier in which the Court upheld a university policy that established an entirely separate law school to teach just one African American,[75] the Court in *McLaurin* held the school policy to be unconstitutional. The Court did not specifically strike the separate but equal doctrine, but it did strike the substantial legal equivalent by recognizing that enforced separation was inherently unequal. Separation restricted the African American student's "ability to study, to engage in discussions, and exchange views with other students, and in general, to learn his profession."[76]

Nor was the Court in *Brown* faced with any directly contrary legal precedent. In *Gong Lum v. Rice*, decided in 1927, a Chinese student was denied admittance to a public "whites only" school, but the only issue specifically addressed by the Supreme Court was whether a Chinese child should be classified as "colored."[77]

In *Cummings v. Board of Education*, the Court permitted an all-white school to stay open until a separate school for African Americans was built, but again did not specifically address the constitutionality of the separate but equal doctrine.[78]

In *Berea College v. Kentucky*, the Court upheld a separate but equal doctrine as applied to private schools, but did not address the constitutionality of the doctrine as applied to public schools.[79]

In addition, there were a number of state court decisions upholding the separate but equal doctrine as applied to public schools, but these decisions were not binding upon the Supreme Court.[80]

There was one decision decided prior to 1954 that, although it did not directly relate to public education, nevertheless did provide a conceptual basis for *Brown v. Board of Education*. In *Buchanan v. Warley*, decided in 1917, the Court struck down as violative of the Fourteenth Amendment a city ordinance forbidding African Americans from moving into a white neighborhood.[81] Law Professors Benno Schmidt and Ronald Rotunda have since suggested that this case, decided during a period when property rights were strictly protected, in fact "provided the foundation for the equal protection decisions that came later in the century."[82]

BROWN V. BOARD OF EDUCATION

Brown v. Board of Education is the most important case relating to public education decided by the Supreme Court. It established principles of equal protection based on foundations of morality, justice, common decency, and not least, the law as set forth in the Constitution. Had these principles been honestly followed by the decisions that followed, much of what is wrong with public education today might have been avoided.

Ironically, the plaintiffs in *Brown* did not originally plan to challenge the separate but equal doctrine, but rather sought to obtain the equal facilities and opportunities that the doctrine purportedly was required to provide them.[83] Indeed, had the facilities for African Americans been equal in terms of facilities, student-faculty ratios, teacher pay, and per capita expenditures, school districts might have been able to perpetuate their policies of segregation for many more years. But, as the plaintiffs in *Brown* showed, the facilities were not equal in terms of physical or human resources.

By the time the case reached the courts, the decision had been made by the lawyers representing the plaintiffs in *Brown* (and four companion cases) to argue that segregation was inherently unequal in violation of the equal protection clause of the Fourteenth Amendment. In any case, the evidence was clear that the physical, human, and financial resources allocated to the all African American schools were not in fact equal.[84]

At the trial, a number of psychologists and social scientists testified concerning the effects of racial segregation. Kenneth Clark testified that "segregation is prejudice concertized in the society; segregation is a mist, like a wall, which society erects, of stone and steel . . . constantly telling the [African Americans] that they are inferior and constantly telling them that they cannot escape prejudice."[85]

Helen Trager testified that African Americans in segregated schools "showed a tendency to expect rejection. . . . [I]f we are to diminish the amount of hostility and fear that children of all groups have toward each other [the place to do it] is the school."[86]

Professor Hugh Speer testified that "colored children are denied the experience in school of associating with White children, who represent 90% of our national society in which these colored children must live."[87]

These conclusions were buttressed by the results of a survey of 253 African American children who were asked their reactions to white and black dolls. Some 67% of the children responded that they would prefer to play with the white doll, and 59% said the black doll "looks bad."[88]

Perhaps the most insightful observation of segregation was later given by Charles Black: "the social meaning of segregation is the putting of the Negro in a position of being walled-off; such treatment is hurtful to human beings."[89]

Although a number of other studies were submitted purporting to show the effects of segregation on the motivation to learn,[90] it was clearly sufficient to show that segregation was inherently unequal in order to establish a violation of the equal protection clause.[91] Who could honestly claim, for example, that the African American student in *McLaurin* who was required to sit at the back of the class behind a railing with a sign reading "for coloreds only" was being treated "equally"?

The Supreme Court declared that the "separa[tion] of negro children from others of similar age and qualifications solely because of their race generates a feeling of inferiority as to their status in the community that may affect their hearts and minds in a way unlikely ever to be undone."[92] The Court concluded with perhaps the most famous words it has ever uttered: "in the field of public education the doctrine 'separate but equal' has no place. Separate educational facilities are inherently unequal."[93]

RESPONSE, REACTION, AND FOLLOW-UP TO THE *BROWN* DECISION

The *Brown* case represents the high-water mark of the Supreme Court's participation in the development of standards of justice and fairness in the law of public education. Unfortunately its decisions since *Brown* have not lived up to the lofty principles set forth in that case. The Court's first betrayal of its own principles came almost immediately. In the face of opposition to its decision, the Court was soon to reveal a lack of conviction.

It is true, of course, that the opposition was fierce and in many cases almost overwhelming. In 1956, for example, 101 U.S. senators and congresspersons took the unprecedented action of declaring that Supreme Court's integration decisions were "contrary to established law."[94] (Apparently none of these legislators had taken a course in constitutional law, or read *Marbury v. Madison*, in which it is explained that the Supreme Court, not Congress, has the power under the Constitution to declare what the law is.)

In Arkansas, the legislature amended the state constitution to require the General Assembly to oppose "in every constitutional manner the unconstitutional desegregation decisions of May 17, 1954 . . . of the United States Supreme Court,"[95] and passed a law relieving children from the requirement of compulsory attendance at any integrated school."[96] In Virginia, the Prince Edward County School Board simply closed down the public schools, and supported segregated private schools with aid in the form of indirect grants and tuition aids.[97] Virginia also enacted a law requiring the disbarment of any civil rights attorney who represented organizations that had no "pecuniary interest" in the litigation.[98]

Many states resurrected the pre-Civil War state's right doctrine of state nullification of federal laws deemed unconstitutional,[99] and in Little Rock, Arkansas, the state governor dispatched state military troops to prevent African American children from entering an all-white school.[100] When a federal court enjoined the Governor from further military interference, it required federal troops to enforce its injunction.[101] It many ways it appeared to be the start of Civil War II. Although some of these responses took place after the Court's next school integration decision in *Brown II*,[102] they were reflective of the prevailing mood in much of the country prior to *Brown II*.

In *Brown II*, decided in 1955, the Supreme Court addressed the question of how its decision in *Brown I* would actually be enforced. After paying lip service to its determination that "the vitality of the [constitutional principles set forth in *Brown II* cannot be allowed to yield simply because of disagreement with them," the Court proceeded to effectively retract the relief it had appeared to grant in *Brown I* to the African American plaintiffs who had been denied admittance to an all-white school. It was not necessary, the Court declared, to immediately implement a nonracial policy in assigning students to schools; rather, because schools would need first need to solve "varied local school problems," it was necessary only that they make a "prompt and reasonable start" toward obeying the ruling of *Brown I*, and that they move with "deliberate" speed.[103]

All that any school district had to do to implement *Brown I* was to cease making school assignments according to race. Indeed, the biggest logistical problem encountered under segregation was transporting students long distances (usually African American students) in order to keep each school racially pure. Now that race need not and could not be taken into account, the assignment process should have been greatly simplified. It was therefore not clear what the "varied local school problems" were that justified delays in obeying the Court. Presumably the Court was referring to the need for allowing time for community attitudes to change and for administrators to adjust "mentally" to the change in the law. If so, the Court's purpose was not achieved, and the results were both unfortunate and enduring.

Not the least of the unfortunate results was that the African American plaintiffs in *Brown* did not obtain the relief they requested. By the time their school district had taken advantage of the permission by the Court to delay implementation of desegregated schools, the plaintiffs were long graduated. The Court is not a quasi-legislative body authorized to issue grand legal pronouncements. Its duty under the constitution is to decide particular "cases and controversies" — and any law of interpretation that flows from that decision is a by-product of deciding a particular case. In this case, the plaintiffs who had originally sought relief were lost in the judicial process that recognized their rights but then failed to enforce those rights in a manner that would actually benefit them.

More significant for the development of constitutional law and the law of public education was the fact that school districts took advantage of the reprieve offered by the Court to develop strategies for entrenching policies of segregation so that it would be more difficult to dismantle them. As one observer has noted, the most unfortunate effect of *Brown II* was that it "enormously confused and complicated the issue of just what the school districts were required to do. For the relatively clear and simple issue of whether racial assignment had ended there was substituted the almost totally unmanageable issue of whether . . . the time for ending it had come and whether a partial ending would suffice."[104] As a result, a school's desegregation "plan" became more important than simply ceasing the policy of racial assignments.

After *Brown II*, the Court did not issue a single signed opinion on the issue of segregation for nine long years,[105] giving hope to many school districts that desegregation might be delayed indefinitely (especially in the North), and giving them time to develop strategies to resist any future desegregation orders. Indeed, had Congress not gotten into the act at this critical stage, de jure segregation might have persisted for much longer than it did.

THE 1964 CIVIL RIGHTS ACT

The Civil Rights Act of 1964 prohibited racial segregation as a matter of national public policy. A number of representatives in Congress opposed the act on grounds that it would inevitably result in the forced assignment of students to overcome racial imbalance, and would not merely outlaw official racial discrimination. Proponents of the act, however, vigorously denied such an intent and pointed to the language of the act, which stated that 'desegregation' means the assignment of students to public schools . . . without regard to race."[106]

Senator Hubert Humphrey of Minnesota, the leading liberal proponent of the act, criticized opponents of the act who stated publicly their fears that it might be applied in such a way as to assign students based on their race as a way to overcome racial imbalance. "This bill cannot be attacked on its merits," Humphrey responded. "Instead bogeymen and hobgoblins have been raised to frighten well-meaning Americans."[107]

Humphrey assured his fellow senators that "while the Constitution [as interpreted by *Brown*] prohibits segregation, it does not require integration. The busing of children to achieve racial balance would be an act to effect the integration of schools. In fact, if the bill were to compel it, it would be a violation, because it would be handling the matter on a basis of race and we would be transporting children because of their race."[108]

Liberal Senator Jacob Javits of New York asserted that anyone who attempted to use the Civil Rights Act to require racial balance would be "making a fool of himself," and that any such action by a court or public official would give a school district an "open and shut" defense.[109]

In supporting the act, many representatives in Congress no doubt relied on the Supreme Court's decision in *Brown* that it was unlawful to assign or separate students "solely because of their race." Some of them may also have relied on the statement of Thurgood Marshall, the counsel for the NAACP in *Brown* (and later became the first African American Supreme Court Justice), who asserted that "the only thing the court is dealing with . . . [is] whether or not race can be used. . . . What we want from the court is a striking down of race."[110]

Although such assertions were very effective in creating support for the act and its eventual passage, there was no way to insure that the Supreme Court would rely on the legislative history of the act, or even follow its own principles as set forth in *Brown*. The stage was set for the Court's next great retreat from the principles set forth in *Brown*.

THE RESURRECTION OF RACISM AS A FACTOR IN STUDENT ASSIGNMENT

In 1968 the New Kent County School District in Virginia adopted a plan whereby any student in the county could choose which school to attend. When such a plan did not result in a racial balance in the schools that approximated the racial balance of the population in the county, the Court held the plan unconstitutional on grounds that it did not in fact create racial balance in the schools. The Court declared that any district operating a state-compelled "dual" system was charged with the "affirmative duty to take whatever steps might be necessary to convert to a unitary system."[111]

There were a number of possible grounds on which the Court might have based its finding of unconstitutionality, but did not. For example, there appeared to be ample evidence in the record to support a conclusion that the prior racial identification of the schools rendered the free-choice plan practically ineffective, and that the plan was therefore a disguised plan for the continuance of de jure segregation.

Had the Court found the plan to be the result of official race discrimination, its finding of unconstitutionality would have been faithful to the principle in *Brown* that assignment of students by race is a violation of equal protection. However, the Court did not base its ruling on the existence of official racial discrimination, but rather on the fact there happened to exist a racial imbalance in the schools. Thus the Court concluded that the plan was not a "sufficient step to 'effectuate a transition' to a unitary system."[112]

Nevertheless, the decision did not arouse much excitement, perhaps because there was at least some language in the decision that suggested that since the New Kent County school system had once been officially segregated by race, the county plan was a disguised strategy to continue the old policy. Whatever benefit of the doubt observers gave to this interpretation of the decision were shattered by the case of *Swann v. Charlotte Mecklenburg Board of Education*, which came before the Supreme Court in 1971.

SWANN V. CHARLOTTE MECKLENBURG BOARD OF EDUCATION

The *Swann* case involved the Charlotte-Mecklenburg school district in North Carolina.[113] In 1966 its school system had been certified to be constitutional and not racially discriminatory by the Fourth Circuit Court of Appeals. As a result of residential patterns and a large increase in the district's African American population, however, by 1968 some of the schools had African American student percentages that exceeded the 29% African American population in the district.

In 1968 a federal district judge ordered massive busing in the district in order to insure that "each of the 107 schools in the district's 550 square miles are be made approximately 71% White."[114] Although, the Supreme Court did find some express discomfort with the District Court judge's forthright objective of a quota, stating that it could not uphold the district judge's decision solely on that basis,[115] it nevertheless upheld the district judge's decision on grounds that the "limited use of mathematical ratios was within the equitable remedial discretion of the District Court."[116]

In deciding the case, the Supreme Court was faced with the clear command of Section 2000(c) of Title IV of the Civil Rights Act of 1964, which stated:

"Desegregation" means the assignment of students to public schools . . . without regard to their race, color, religion, or national origin, but *"desegregation" shall not mean the assignment of students to public schools in order to overcome racial imbalance*. . . . Nothing herein shall empower any official or court of the United States to issue any order seeking to achieve a racial balance in any school by requiring the transforation of pupils or students from one school to another (emphasis added).

This provision had been inserted in the Civil Rights Act to insure that the principles of *Brown v. Board of Education* would be followed, and that no court would attempt to resurrect the use of racial criteria as a means of assigning students to school. In *Swann*, however, the Court chose to completely ignore this express provision on grounds that it was not intended to pertain to situations in which there had been any prior racial discrimination that caused the racial imbalance—a proposition for which it could cite no legislative history whatsoever.

Nevertheless, this rationale for ignoring the Civil Rights Act might have carried some weight had it not been for the fact that, as noted by one observer, the record revealed that "most, if not all of the existing school partial separation was plainly the result, not of the former dual system, but as in the North of residential racial concentration."[117] Indeed, the Fourth Circuit had declared as early as 1965 that the school district did not use racial criteria as a means of student assignment, and that the school system was in compliance with the Constitution.

Thus the Court in *Swann* approved a plan whereby school officials would take note of a student's race, and then assign that student to a school according to that race. Somehow Thurgood Marshall's plea that "what we want from the Court is a striking down of race"[118] had been lost, as well as the principle set forth in *Brown I* that assignments "solely because of [a student's race]" are a violation of the equal protection clause of the Constitution.

Although Congress attempted to redress this new resurrection of race as a factor in student assignment, and numerous bills and over 55 constitutional amendments were introduced in the years following *Swann*,[119] there was little that could be done. The Supreme Court had not only declared that under the Fourteenth Amendment race could be considered as a factor in assigning students; it had declared that the Fourteenth Amendment *required* that the race be considered as a factor in assigning students. Although the Court had avoided an explicit finding that the Civil Rights Act was unconstitutional by rationalizing its reasons for ignoring Section 2000(c), the Civil Rights Act had in fact been gutted with almost surgical judicial precision. Those who had hesitated to support the Civil Rights Act for this very reason were thus vindicated in their fears.

Nor was outrage over the case limited to Congress. Law Professor Lino Graglia condemned the *Swann* case as a decision "that historians may someday rank with *Dred Scott* in terms of gratuitous infliction of injury on the country by the court in matters of race."[120] Professor Graglia observed that while the Court's stated objective was to "ensure that 'school authorities exclude no pupil of a racial minority from any school on account of race,' the order the Court approved required the pupils of the minority race be excluded from their neighborhood schools on account of their race."[121]

Criticism of the *Swann* opinion was not based on doubts of the Supreme Court's sincerity in seeking to redress the evils of past official race discrimination in the public schools. Rather it was based on a perceived judicial hypocrisy, and the Court's sacrifice of principle to expediency in its analysis of the Civil Rights Act and the Constitution. As in the case of so many sacrifices of principle to expediency (of which the *Dred Scott* case is but one example), the results of *Swann* were tragic and counter-productive to the cause of eliminating the evils of racial discrimination in the public schools.

RESEGREGATION IN THE AFTERMATH OF *SWANN*

Once *Swann* became established as the law of the land, a series of unfortunate decisions followed in its wake.[122] In *Keyes v. School District No. 1 (Denver)*,[123] Denver implemented a busing plan to achieve a greater balance of races in its public schools. When it became apparent to Denver voters that such a plan in fact involved consideration of a student's race in assigning a student to a particular school, it elected a new school board that attempted the plan in order to reestablish a race-neutral policy of student assignment. Even though the original busing plan had not been ordered by a court, the Supreme Court held that the revocation of the busing plan was unconstitutional. There was, however, vigorous dissent on the Court.

Justice Lewis Powell observed that the majority had required Denver to "alleviate conditions which in large part did not result from historic, state imposed de jure segregation" and had ignored the root cause of the racial imbalance—namely, "segregated residential and migratory patterns the impact of which on the racial composition of the schools [is] is often perpetuated and rarely ameliorated by action of public school authorities."[124] Justice Powell's observations and predictions about the pernicious effects of court-ordered plans to assign students according to their race soon proved to be sadly accurate.

The resegregative effects of *Keyes* were tragic indeed. Prior to that case, the percentage of whites in the Denver Public Schools was 64%. Today, after years of white flight, whites constitute only 31% percent, while African Americans and Hispanics constitute 65% of the students. Thus, the Denver schools have, in effect, been resegregated by a perhaps well-meaning, but ultimately self-defeating, Supreme Court decisions.

In 1975 James Coleman, S. D. Kelley, and J. A. Moore released their study for the Urban Institute, which concluded that "desegregation was a significant cause of declining White enrollment in the public schools."[125] Although this study sparked an acrimonious debate about the existence and nature of "white flight," the study itself was misinterpreted and misused by many opponents of "forced busing."

Indeed the whole issue of school busing in the 1970s and 1980s came to fan not only the prejudices and fears of parents (both white and minority) but to attract a seemingly endless number of political diatribes and demagogues. It soon became apparent, however, that busing itself was not the real issue. Many of the same white parents who opposed busing as part of a desegregation plan had had no problem with busing when it was used to bus African American children across town to a segregated all African American school. Indeed, the primary cause of busing was not the desegregation movement of the 1970s and 1980s, but the Prussianization of the American school system and the conversion to consolidated schools, which necessitated busing on a massive scale.

Typical of the political dilemma posed by busing to achieve integration was that faced by Senator Joseph Biden in 1976. Senator Biden, considered to be of the liberal wing of the Democratic party, had cast the deciding vote in the Senate to defeat a 1974 antibusing amendment.[126] In 1976, however, Biden became the first Senator to support Jimmy Carter (who opposed busing) and later became Carter's confidential campaign chairman. Citing Coleman's findings, Biden was soon calling busing a "bankrupt concept" contrary to the "cardinal rule of common sense," and a "domestic Vietnam."[127] He later stated proudly that "no one has done more to stop forced busing than Joe Biden."[128]

News media coverage of Coleman's findings were misleading and sensational. A *National Observer* headline read "A Scholar Who Inspired It Saying Busing Backfired,"[129] and the *State Journal* of Lansing, Michigan, screeched "Court Ordered Integration Rapped by Sociologist Who Started It All."[130] A bitter scholarly exchange followed between Coleman and sociologists who challenged his findings.

Sociologists Thomas Pettigrew and Robert Green wrote a rebuttal to Coleman in the *Harvard Educational Review*, claiming that there were "serious methodological and conceptual problems in Coleman's work on so-called 'white flight,'" and challenging Coleman's use of statistics, subsets, and "regression co-efficients."[131] They also reviewed political scientist Christine Rossell's analysis of white flight.[132] Although Rossell's 1976 study of white flight had originally concluded that "school desegregation has little or no effect on white flight," her 1978 Postscript to her original work conceded that "school desegregation does significantly increase the decline in white public school enrollment in the year of implementation, if (certain factors are present)."[133]

Although Pettigrew and Green disputed many of Coleman's conclusions, in the end they conceded that all the studies supported, and none contradicted, the generalization that "extensive school desegregation in the largest metropolitan school district, particularly in the South, may hasten 'white flight' in the first year of the process, but at least part of this effect may disappear in later years."[134]

In 1978 Sociologist David Armor conducted a comprehensive analysis of the conclusions of studies of white flight conducted up to that time, including studies conducted by Reynolds Farley, Rossell, and Pettigrew and Green.[135] Although Armor noted significant differences in the conclusions of each study, he noted that Farley concluded that "the effect of desegregation on white loss will be strongest in larger, central city school districts that have a substantial proportion of blacks and that show preexisting white enrollment declines."[136]

As a result of examining all these studies, Armor concluded that "the findings of Coleman, the latest Farley and Rossell studies, and the present study all agree on one important fact: desegregation can cause accelerated white flight, particularly in larger school districts with substantial minority enrollments (over 20% or so) and in districts with accessible white suburbs. This conclusion is robust, based on a consensus from four different studies employing different conceptual and analytic strategies."[137]

However, Armor went beyond the previous studies and examined the reasons for white flight. At first, he considered the opinion of some commentators that white flight is simply another form of "old fashioned racism." However, after examining polls of racial attitudes around the country, Arnold concluded that "it is not racial intolerance itself that causes white flight, but something else about mandatory busing." He identified one important component to be "belief in the neighborhood school."[138]

A Gallup poll conducted in 1976 appeared to confirm Armor's conclusions that racial prejudice was not the primary cause of white flight. The Gallup poll revealed that only 3% of white parents in the North and 15% of white parents in the South objected to sending their children to integrated schools (although these percentages rose to 24% and 38%, respectively, when the integrated schools had African American enrollments exceeding 50%).[139]

Opposition to busing has not been confined to one racial group. Although Gallup polls conducted in 1974, 1975, and 1978 revealed that between 70 and 85% of whites opposed busing,[140] a study by Andrew Greeley of the Center for the Study of American Pluralism revealed that "half of the American Black population now opposes busing."[141] A Los Angeles survey conducted by the local school board in 1977 revealed that a majority of Mexican Americans also opposed busing.[142] In July 1994 the Hispanic community of Denver threatened a public school boycott over such issues as forced school busing and the ignoring of Hispanic interests in the school.[143]

Although belief in the neighborhood school is often cited as a reason for opposing busing, Thomas Sowell, the renowned African American economist at the University of California, has offered another perspective. He has disparaged the notion of quotas in racial integration as "the noble lie of our time"[144] and decried those who advocate forced integration while "their own children are safely tucked away in private schools . . . away from the storm they creat[e] for others."[145]

In his book *Race and Economics*, Sowell observes: "The very real educational problems of Black children, and the early hopes that desegregation would solve them, provided the impetus and the support for a crusade that has now degenerated into a numerical fetish and a judicial unwillingness to lose face. What actually happens to black children, or white children, has been openly relegated to a secondary consideration in principle, and less than that in practice."[146]

Sowell maintains that numerical approaches to integration have been "futile," and that the "message that comes through loud and clear is that minorities are losers who will never have anything unless someone gives it to them. The destructiveness of this message—on society in general and minority youth in particular—outweighs any trivial gains that may occur here and there. The falseness of the message is shown by the great achievements of minorities during the period of equal-rights-legislation before numerical goals and timetables muddled the waters."[147]

Finally, Sowell expresses his resentment at the insensitivity and arrogant treatment of minorities by bureaucrats and judges who have discarded the principles of *Brown* in favor of considerations of expediency:

Underlying the attempt to move people around and treat them like chess pieces on a board is a profound contempt for other human beings. To ignore or resent people's resistance—on behalf of their children or their livelihoods—is to deny our common humanity. To persist dogmatically in pursuit of some abstract goal, without regard to how it is reached, is to despise freedom and reduce three-dimensional life to cardboard pictures of numerical results. The false practicality of results-oriented people ignores the fact that the ultimate results are in the hearts and minds of human beings. Once personal choice becomes a mere inconvenience to be brushed aside by bureaucrats and judges, somethings precious will have been lost by all people from all back-grounds.[148]

Sowell's views are clearly not those of militant Black separatists (such as Malcolm X, who declared in his *Autobiography* that "the word 'integration' was invented by Northern liberals . . . the word has no real meaning . . . the black masses prefer the company of their own kind").[149] Indeed, this separatist approach has been "rejected by 90% of African Americans."[150] As Andrew Greeley has suggested, "what counts for Black Americans is not mathematical integration but improvement of the quality of their children's education."[151]

But a high-quality education is precisely what the public schools have failed to provide to minorities. Once the sacred principles of race neutrality set forth in *Brown* were sacrificed on *Swann*'s altar of judicial expediency, it was inevitable that what Sowell described as a "judicial unwillingness to lose face" would lead to results totally contrary to those that would have followed from the application of principle. Evidence of the abandonment of inner-city schools and the denial of quality education for minorities was arrogantly brushed aside, and even declared inconsistent with the predictions of theory and ideology. What so many bureaucrats failed to understand was the underlying evil of racial segregation so accurately described by Charles Black—that the meaning of segregation is the "putting of the [minority] in a position of a walled-off inferiority . . . and such treatment is hurtful to human beings."[152] The white establishment finally came to accept the elimination of segregation because it was evil; and most minorities welcomed it because it signaled the dismantlement of the walls that denied their equality, humanity, and dignity—and not because they accepted the premise posited by some well-meaning but condescending whites who insisted that minority children's ability to learn was determined by the proximity of a certain number of white students. As one black parent explained why she welcomed desegregation: "Sitting next to a white child is no guarantee that my child will learn, but it does guarantee that he will be taught."[153]

Although sociologists and political scientists disagree on the dimension and causes of white flight and the abandonment of inner-city schools, the data are clear that abandonment has occurred. In Pasadena, California, the public schools lost 18,000 white students during desegregation between 1969 and 1973.[154] The percentage of whites in the Denver school system dropped from 62% to 47% between 1970 and 1977.[155] In Jackson, Mississippi, white enrollment dropped from 55% to 36% the year following a busing order.[156]

Not all of the flight was to public schools in the suburbs. Much of it was directed toward private schools. The year after busing was ordered in Memphis, private schools gained 14,000 of the 30,000 students who abandoned the city public schools.[157] The percentage of white children attending private schools in Boston increased from 34% to 50% between 1970 and 1980, while private school enrollment in Los Angeles increased from 22% to 43% during the same period.[158]

Nevertheless, when entire counties were desegregated rather than just inner-city school districts, white flight was greatly diminished, since parents who could not afford private schools had no place to go but out of state.[159] However, metropolitan desegregation plans were no guarantee that white flight would not occurred, as in the Nashville-Davidson County (Tennessee) schools, where 10,000 students fled to private schools after a metropolitan desegregation order.[160]

The fact that such policies have resulted in the tragic resegregation of the American public schools does not seem to have acted as a deterrent to bureaucrats and judges determined to pursue remedies that have time and again proven ineffective and counter productive. Indeed, the *Swann* case proved to be a turning point in the quest to end segregation. Between 1968 and 1972, the percentage of African Americans attending predominately minority schools was on a healthy decline, falling from 76.6% to 63.6%.[161]

In the aftermath of the 1971 *Swann v. Charlotte Mecklenburg* decision, however, and the subsequent abandonment of inner-city schools, the percentage of African Americans attending predominately minority schools began an inexorable rise from 63.6% in 1972 to 66% in 1992.[162] For Hispanics the rise was even more dramatic, rising from 56.6% in 1972, to 68.1% in 1980, 71.5% in 1986, and finally to 73.4% in 1992.[163] In states with large urban populations where the effects of white flight were felt most severely, the extent of resegregation in 1992 reached staggering proportions: in New York, 84.6% of African American students attended predominately minority schools, in Illinois 80.2% did so, and in California, 80%.[164]

No doubt related to these developments was a decline in the number of Hispanics and African Americans finishing high school and going on to college. In 1976, 36% of Hispanics and 33% of African Americans who graduated from high school went to college. By 1986 the figure for both groups was down to 29%.[165]

Not surprisingly these developments have alarmed African American parents. In 1994, *Time* magazine reported that "many black parents insist their children are still victims, targets of discrimination more subtle but just as pernicious as that practiced in the days before the Supreme Court outlawed desegregated schools. In their view their school district cares more about the course arithmetic of integration goals than about meeting the needs of inner-city kids."[166]

Perhaps one of the worst effects of *Swann* was the breeding of cynicism among parents of all races. Among parents who could not afford to send their children to private schools or participate in flight, Journalist Judith Bentley has described the typical practice of "bus-dodging":

A blue-collar worker in Richmond, Virginia, had two school-age daughters and a married daughter who was living in the suburbs. The two families simply switched homes, so the worker's two youngest daughters could go to suburban schools and avoid busing. A family may give a false address for a home in a nonbused neighborhood in the same city. In San Francisco, some Chinese doctors routinely write medical excuses for students who claim they get motion sickness and so cannot travel by bus outside their neighborhood. Qualifying one's child for an alternative class in cities that have them or in a program for the gifted is another way of avoiding forced busing. . . . [E]vasion is widespread.[167]

Despite the departure from the principles of *Brown* and the resurrection of assignment by race as approved in *Swann*, however, white flight and the subsequent resegregation of the public schools might have been minimized if the Supreme Court had at least shown conviction in pursuing the remedies it had ordered in *Swann*. Such conviction could have been shown by extending busing across school district lines. Although such an order would not have retarded the flight to private schools, it would at least have retarded the flight to suburban public schools and the abandonment of inner-city public schools. However, in what would no doubt be described by Professor Sowell as a classic example of "judicial unwillingness to lose face," the Court in the 1974 case of *Milliken v. Bradley* confirmed its decision in *Swann* while at the same time declining to order busing across school district lines.[168]

In *Milliken*, white flight had created a Detroit school system that was 64% African American and a surrounding suburban school system that was almost all white. It was obvious to the District Court judge that no meaningful integration by busing could occur without busing children across district lines, and he so ordered. The Supreme Court reversed the order, however, holding that such interdistrict busing was not constitutionally required absent a showing that there was racial discrimination within each district or that the district boundary lines were created with "the purpose of fostering racial segregation."[169] Given that the suburban district was virtually all white (and there were few if any African Americans in the suburban district against whom discrimination could even be practiced), no such facts could possibly be proved, and the District Court order was reversed. Imposing coercive remedies on inner-city residents was one thing; but imposing them on politically powerful white suburban interests was apparently quite another.

Justice Thurgood Marshall dissented vigorously, acknowledging the reality of white flight and suggesting that "the State is responsible for the fact that many whites will react to the dismantling of the segregated system by attempting to flee to the suburbs."[170] Marshall stated his belief that the Court's refusal to grant an interdistrict remedy was a virtual guarantee that "the Negro children in Detroit will receive the same separate and inherently unequal education in the future as they have been unconstitutionally afforded in the past."[171]

Nevertheless interdistrict remedies would at least reduce white flight, and the Court's refusal to order it reflects a lack of commitment to its original remedy. Of course, even interdistrict busing would not eliminate white flight, since parents who could afford to do so could still send their children to private schools. There is reason to believe that interdistrict busing might simply reinforce resegregation by economic status in addition to resegregation by race. Indeed white flight could only totally be eliminated by reversing the 1925 Supreme Court case of *Pierce v. Society of Sisters* (which upheld on Fourteen Amendment liberty grounds the right of parents to send their children to private schools—a right few Americans would wish to deny).

In the end, *Milliken* exposed the total bankruptcy of the desegregation policies that had first been adopted when the Court abandoned the race-neutral principles of *Brown* and instead pursued the racial assignment policies of *Swann*. Together, the two cases imposed on African American children the worst of two worlds: a coercive remedy that uprooted them from their own communities, but which was not pursued with enough conviction to even retard white flight and the resegregation of the schools.

A few decisions rendered subsequent to *Milliken* recognized some limits to the *Swann* doctrine,[172] relying less on the often insupportable assumption that racial imbalance must be the result of prior de jure discrimination, and more on the reality of existing residential patterns. In *Pasadena City Board of Education v. Spangler*, for example, the Supreme Court reviewed a district judge's order to annually readjust attendance zones. The order had been issued to guarantee that "there would not be a majority of any minority in any Pasadena school."[173]

In reversing the order, the Supreme Court acknowledged the "quite normal pattern of human migration result[ing] in some changes in the demographics of Pasadena's residential patterns, with resultant shifts in the racial makeup of some of the schools." The Court further acknowledged that "these shifts were not attributed to any segregative

actions on the part of the defendants," and that "having once implemented a racially neutral attendance pattern in order to remedy the
perceived constitutional violations on the part of the defendants, the
District Court had fully performed its function of providing the
appropriate remedy for previous racially discriminatory attendance
patterns."[174]

In 1992 the Supreme Court finally began to recognize that the
policy of assigning students according to their race was not only of
questionable constitutionality, but a significant factor in the resegregation of the schools. In the case of *Freeman v. Pitts* the Court addressed
the question of how long judicial supervision of a school district should
continue after that district has achieved "unitary status with regard to
student assignments."[175]   Some 25 years after the *Green* case, the
Court in *Freeman* recognized that "as the de jure violation becomes
more remote in time and demographic changes intervene, it becomes
less likely that a current racial imbalance in a school district is a vestige
of the prior de jure system. The causal link between current conditions
and the prior violation is even more attenuated if the school district has
demonstrated good faith. . . . There was no showing that racial balance
[in student assignment] was an appropriate mechanism."[176]

Several of the concurring justices were even more explicit, one of
whom recognized that "a multitude of private factors has shaped school
systems in the years after the abandonment of de jure segregation—normal migration, population growth, 'white flight' from the
inner cities. . . . [T]he percentage of current make-up of schools systems
attributable to [prior *de jure* discrimination] has diminished to the
point . . . where it cannot realistically be assumed to be a significant
factor."[177]   After years of pursuing a racially based remedy that had
resulted only in resegregation, one justice was even willing to set aside
the traditional judicial tendency to save face: "We should consider
laying aside the extraordinary and increasingly counterfactual presump-
tion of *Green*."[178]

Unfortunately, the Court's belated recognition of the evils of
racial assignment has come much too late. The worst damage had
already been done by the late 1970s—most of the white exodus had
already occurred, the inner-city schools were abandoned, new private
schools were established and patronized, and the trend toward
resegregation had gained the momentum it would retain entering the
1990s.

Much of that damage can not be easily undone. While the
contrition of the Court may be reassuring, it does little to reverse the
trend toward resegregation. Policies can be implemented, however, that
attack the root cause of racial imbalance in the public schools —namely,
segregated residential patterns. It is true that not all segregated housing
patterns can be attributed to economic barriers. A study by Reynolds
Farley, for example, concludes that if income and housing costs "were
the governing factor, levels of residential segregation would be
low."[179] Racial prejudice, community hostility, and, of course, white
flight from the cities has severely affected residential patterns. But

economic barriers nevertheless remain formidable. Perhaps the most important factor in segregated residential patterns has been almost totally ignored—namely, access to jobs, many of the most desirable of which are located in the suburbs.

As already noted, the immigration policies of the United States have had a catastrophic effect on the job market for African Americans. It will be recalled from the Chicago survey of employers (discussed earlier in this chapter in the section "The Effects of Immigration on Educational Policy.") that many of the reasons given by employers for hiring immigrants instead of African Americans carried racist overtones. In light of such facts, the question must be asked as to what employers would do if deprived of a steady supply of immigrant labor to exploit. Would they just go out of business for lack of applicants to fill their needed positions, or would they put aside their racist predilections and hire African Americans, train them, and prepare them for the jobs that are now denied them?

It is not to late to heed the pleas of Booker T. Washington and implement policies that will lead to full African American and minority integration in American society. It will not be easy to undo the damage caused by the judicial policies of the 1970s and to reverse the trend toward resegregation caused by those policies. But a focus on community and providing a high-quality education, combined with reforms that respond to the root causes rather than the symptoms of racial segregation, can begin the long road back to achieving equality of opportunity in American education.

Chapter Six

Alternative Methods of Segregation: Bilingual and Special Education

It is beyond the scope of this book to review all the law relating to public education, although there are a number of texts that do so.[1] Instead, this chapter considers the important landmark decisions of the American judicial system and evaluates the effects of those decisions on public education in the area of bilingual and, special education. Although these areas have been briefly mentioned in earlier chapters discussing the reform of public education, they are considered here in the legal context of judicial application of the due process and equal protection clauses of the Fourteenth Amendment. More specifically, this chapter considers the effects of such judicial intervention on the quality of public education.

One legal scholar has observed the surprising frequency with which "the Constitution has provided the law that directly controls an educational issue. Moreover, it always provides the fundamental legal framework within which every educational issue must be resolved."[2] In the early case of *Marbury v. Madison*,[3] it was determined that the Constitution gives to the Supreme Court the power to determine whether laws or government policies are constitutional.

In the previous chapter, the role of racial discrimination in the segregation of the public schools was discussed. However, racial considerations are but one of the factors used by schools to segregate students. It will be recalled that segregation by age was the basis for the Prussianization of the American schools during the period following the Civil War.[4] Theories of male superiority and domination resulted in the segregation of sexes in the educational establishment, with females predominating as teachers, and males predominating under the Prussian "male leadership" principle as supervisors and administrators.[5]

Other methods of segregating students according to perceived differences in characteristics persist today in the public schools. Special education and programs of bilingual education continue to segregate students according to primary language, national origin, and socioeconomic status. It is to the Supreme Court's intervention in these areas that we now turn.

BILINGUAL EDUCATION

In the 1974 case of *Lau v. Nichols*,[6] the Supreme Court considered a class lawsuit brought by non-English-speaking Chinese students against the San Francisco School District, alleging that the lack of English instruction in the public schools denied them equal educational opportunity in violation of the Fourteenth Amendment. The Federal District Court found that of 2,856 non-English-speaking Chinese, 1,000 were being given courses in English, while the remainder were receiving no instruction in English. On appeal to the Supreme Court, the petitioners asked only that the Board of Education be directed to address the problem.

The Court did not reach the equal protection issue, since it determined that the case could be decided by application of Section 601 of the Civil Rights Act, which bans discrimination "on the ground of race, color, or national origin."[7] Clarifying regulations later issued by the Department of Health, Education and Welfare stated that "when ability to speak and understand the English language excludes national origin-minority group children from effective participation in the educational program offered by the district, the district must take affirmative action to rectify the language deficiency in order to open its instructional program to these students."[8]

The Court held that these provisions gave the petitioners the right to the relief they requested, and remanded the case for the fashioning of specific appropriate relief. However, the Court was careful not to direct that any specific method of teaching English be employed, acknowledging that "no specific remedy is urged upon us. Teaching English to the students of Chinese ancestry who do not speak the language is one choice. Giving instruction to the group in Chinese is another. There may be others."[9]

Although the Court had made it very clear that it was not mandating any particular method of providing equal educational opportunity to non-English-speaking students, in 1974 the Republican administration then in power issued the "Lau Remedies," which "mandate[d] programs that relied heavily on native-language instruction."[10] According to one educator, these "remedies" were issued after "little academic input."[11] Despite the fact that these requirements for bilingual education were never enacted into law, the administration was able to coerce many school districts into adopting bilingual education by threatening to cut off federal funds if they did not adopt the bilingual method of teaching limited-English-proficient children.[12]

In 1974 Congress amended the Bilingual Education Act of 1974 (which had been enacted in 1968) to provide that any school district that dared to use any method other than transitional bilingual education was to be "rendered ineligible to apply for federal funds to develop their bilingual programs."[13] In short, the act "requir[ed] that local education agencies follow one and only one method of instruction—transition bilingual education."[14] Subsequent federal subsidies for bilingual education reached staggering sums—$169 million in 1981, $173 million in 1984, and rising to over $174 million in 1984.[15]

Schools that tried to establish effective English programs were deprived of funds. One of the most successful English programs was that of Fairfax County, Virginia, which provided an acclaimed program of special English instruction to over 3,800 limited English students in 75 different languages. Because the program did not segregate students by language, however, and conform to the government's rigid policy of bilingual education, "in 1985 Fairfax County could not receive any federal title VII funds from the Office of Bilingual Education."[16]

Schools districts that agreed to segregate their students by language and abandon their other English programs were showered with subsidies that soon required massive bureaucracies just to absorb them. Typical of such districts was the Los Angeles Unified School District, which "created a permanent transitional bilingual bureaucracy that has mandated and controlled the education of limited-English proficient students."[17]

A master teacher in that district, Sally Peterson, struggled for many years to teach limited English students under the mandated bilingual plan. Aware that the vast majority of studies had shown bilingual education to be ineffective (one recent review revealed that 71% of all bilingual studies had shown it to be ineffective),[18] Peterson finally formed the Learning English Advocates Drive to demand attention from an entrenched bureaucracy. "We all echoed a common concern: it doesn't work!" she later wrote. "However, because of the political pressure that has been exerted to support [bilingual education], few bilingual educators, politicians, or community leaders have been willing to criticize the programs. The educational establishment has turned a deaf ear to the experience of rank-and-file teachers. Never before in the history of education has a program that has been such a failure received so many accolades."[19]

If these bilingual programs had only wasted taxpayer money to no positive effect, they could be dismissed as just another example of the politicization of an entrenched and unresponsive educational bureaucracy. Unfortunately, however, as Peterson and her fellow teachers soon recognized, "by perpetuating the misguided notion that [bilingual education] is a success, the Los Angeles Unified School District has caused more damage to limited-English-proficiency students than has any other single group in the country. The bureaucracy of the bilingual education program has been impossible to penetrate."[20]

Sally Peterson has described how the bilingual program is administered in the Los Angeles School District. Parents are surveyed to determine if any family member speaks a language other than English at home. If the answer is positive, any child from that family is targeted for the bilingual program, whether the child is fluent in English or not.[21] The child's parents are then presented with a bilingual permission form, which represents that the child will be taught all subjects in her or his native language and then gradually taught in English. Although most parents willingly sign such a form, they soon find that "most students will be locked into their native language, and little emphasis at all will be placed on English-language development."[22]

If parents dare to refuse to choose the bilingual program in favor of alternatives that would permit the teacher to use other methods of teaching English, they are called in by school officials, lectured on the great benefits of bilingual education, and then shown a film depicting a "happy, well-dressed child who is learning in his native language, and a sad, downtrodden, miserable child who is learning English. The film continually repeats that learning in English is harmful."[23]

Parents who persist in resisting bilingual education for their children become the "target of repeated phone calls" from bilingual bureaucrats. Master teacher Peterson has described "bilingual permission forms that have been mistakenly filled out by parents in both the 'yes' and 'no' columns. When these forms eventually reach the classroom teachers, the 'no's have been scratched out and the 'yes's have been left in place. It is also not uncommon for the [alternative] permission forms to 'disappear' and for parents to be required to come to the school to sign additional forms."[24]

Parents who initially sign a permission form to have their child enter a bilingual program, only to discover that their children are falling behind, soon find that it is almost impossible to get their children out. At first, parents had only to sign a new form. When many parents began demanding release of their children, however, the procedures were tightened "first to require parents to obtain the permission form from the office of the bilingual coordinator. Then it was changed to require parents to make an appointment to see the bilingual coordinator to obtain the form. As a matter of practice, the bilingual coordinator is not readily available to parents who wish to sign their children out of the program. Parents who drop in to get a form are turned away and told to set up an appointment, regardless of whether the bilingual coordinator was available at that time."[25]

At parental meetings, bilingual bureaucrats "describe wonderful successes of bilingual education that are not actually occurring and at which those who are critical of bilingual education are forbidden to speak one word."[26] Children targeted for bilingual education are given a test called "Basic Inventory of Native Languages," which consists primarily of describing some pictures. Frightened or inhibited children who do not "pass" the test are labeled as "LEPs" (limited-English-proficient) and channeled into segregated bilingual classrooms.

The absurdity of these tests was revealed at a meeting of the Los Angeles Board of Education in June 1988. At that meeting, the president of the board was shown a picture from the test, which the president described as a "picture of a boy sitting on a rock." The president was then informed that she had failed the test because the picture was actually one of a boy "sitting on the back of a water buffalo."[27] The embarrassed president was then informed that had she been a child in her school system, she would have been labeled an LEP and duly segregated into a bilingual classroom with other LEPs.

Once a child is labeled as LEP and segregated with other LEPs, she or he is "effectively locked into native-language or transitional classes. . . . Many of those who are able to make the transition to English classes find themselves so far behind their peers in vocabulary and English skills that they never catch up."[28] Locked into such classes, with little hope of escape, LEPs are "denied the right to develop fluency in English."[29]

Like so many federal programs, what began as a modest attempt to solve a particular problem has ballooned into a vast program that has spawned so many bureaucrats who have a vested interest in its prolongation that it now has little chance of dismantlement. Herbert Walberg, a former Harvard professor who is now research professor of education at the University of Illinois at Chicago, has described costly bilingual programs that "require for each subject such as physics and auto shop as many teachers as there are home languages such as Vietnamese and Swedish spoken in the district (as many as 130). Students themselves . . . pay a heavy penalty, since they [are] segregated from the mainstream of school life."[30] Walberg notes that once students become segregated in such a fashion, criteria are "set so high—higher, for example, than many monolingual English speaking children could attain—it is nearly impossible, once a child is classified for some programs, to enter regular school programs."[31] One can almost visualize a sign posted above LEP classrooms, reading "Abandon hope all ye who enter here."

Walberg concludes that "all this might be tolerated if it could be shown that bilingual programs teach English better."[32] Unfortunately, however, he notes that "nearly all reviews of rigorous controlled studies show no advantage of bilingual programs over other alternatives", and cites Rosell Ross's 1986 review of 36 separate studies that revealed that 71% of the language gain comparisons showed bilingual education to be no different or worse than submersion, that is, doing nothing. In mathematics, 93% of the comparisons showed bilingual education to be equal or worse than submersion."[33] He cites independent studies by Engle (1975),[34] Epstein (1977),[35] K. Baker and A. De Kanter (conducted by the U.S. Department of Education in 1981),[36] R. Venezky (1981), [37] and Rotberg (1982)[38]— all of which reached similar conclusions.[39]

But it is the inflexibility of most LEP programs that is perhaps most disturbing. Political pressures ensure that many other alternative methods of teaching English can not be employed. Education historian Diane Ravitch concluded in her study of educational crises that "there is no justification for mandating the use of bilingual education or any other single pedagogy. . . . Language instruction programs that are generally regarded as outstanding, such as those provided for foreign service officers or by the acclaimed center at Middlebury College, are immersion programs, in which students embark on a systematic program of intensive language learning without depending on their native tongue."[40] Ravitch adds charitably that "immersion programs may not be appropriate for all children, but then neither is any single pedagogical method. The method to be used should be determined by the school authorities and the professional staff, based on their resources and competence."[41]

Studies of alternative programs have shown "striking rates of [language] acquisition" in such immersion programs as that conducted by the Army language school, which has set 1,300 hours of instruction as an appropriate time to learn a foreign language, such as Vietnamese.[42]

Studies by J. K. Hase, S. P. Rasher and H. J. Walberg have concluded that "a child who spends about ten hours a day in school, in play, and with media in English might gain comparable, though seemingly natural effortless, experience in 130 days"—a far cry from the virtual life sentence imposed by bilingual LEP programs.[43]

An English immersion pilot project conducted in El Paso, Texas, divided students into a control group following a traditional bilingual program at 18 district schools, and an immersion program at 18 other schools in which English was used as the language of instruction from the first day of school. An evaluation of the project issued by the Office of Research and Evaluation in the late 1980s revealed that "the immersion project students outscored students in the traditional bilingual education program at every grade level on tests of English reading. . . . and scored above average on state tests in science and social studies."[44]   Of even greater embarrassment to the bilingual establishment, however, were the findings showing that in a special study of third graders, 90% of the students in the immersion group had "mastered reading and writing skills in Spanish on a par with the control group, even though the former had a minimum of instruction in Spanish."[45]

Although the findings showing that the immersion group had outperformed the bilingual group in every grade level of tests requiring English comprehension, such results came as no surprise to teachers surveyed in the study. Only one-third of the bilingual teachers believed there was any real chance that their students would "successfully transfer to reading in English." And every principal in the school district who had experience with both programs "expressed the opinion that the immersion program [was] a better approach to educating language minority students."[46] The findings that bilingual students did not even show greater skills in their own native language than the immersion group came as a sobering shock to most disinterested observers, however.

Although the most compelling and logical explanation for such results is that bilingual education simply doesn't work, there are some other contributing explanations as well. Rosalie Porter, a former fellow of the Bunting Institute of Radcliffe College and a member of the National Advisory Council on Bilingual Education, revealed some additional explanations in her widely acclaimed article "The Disabling Power of Ideology: Challenging the Basic Assumptions of Bilingual Education."[47]   For example, she notes shocking federal statistics that reveal that up to "60% of the children in bilingual programs are English dominant; that is, their basic English-language skills are stronger than their Spanish-language skills."[48] Thus for a large percentage of students consigned to segregated LEP classes, "teaching them to read in their 'mother tongue' [is to] teach them in a foreign language." — the very practice to which bilingual ideologists claim to be opposed.[49]

During her seven-year experience as the director for the Newton (Massachusetts) Public Schools Bilingual Program, Porter "observed no difference in achievement in the mastery of subject matter between the children who are provided some native-language help in Spanish, Italian, Chinese, and the children from 25 other language backgrounds who are given no native-language support at all."[50]

In light of such overwhelming data, it might be assumed that the government would resist the demands of the entrenched bilingual bureaucracy, reassess their bilingual policies, and permit more funds to be used for immersion and alternative programs. But the bilingual establishment has only grudgingly given up ground. In 1985, Secretary of Education William Bennett asked to amend the Bilingual Education Act to permit more than 4% of Title VII funds to be used on immersion and alternative programs. (At that time the act mandated that 96% of federal funds for English programs be allocated to transitional bilingual programs.)

Secretary Bennett was not asking for the elimination of bilingual programs, but only for a removal of the 4% cap on alternative programs. Such a cap had not only cut off funds to successful English language programs, but also effectively stifled research into the effectiveness of immersion programs. Major liberal publications welcomed Bennett's proposals. In September 1985 the *New York Times* editorialized that Secretary Bennett was "right: the Federal government should not limit funds to only one pedagogical method. It should be concerned with the ultimate goal, helping children become proficient in English as quickly as possible."[51] On the same day, the *Washington Post* declared in an editorial headline that "Secretary Bennett Makes Sense" and opined that "we do not need apologies, as Secretary Bennett points out, for offering assistance in a form that brings children more quickly into American language and culture and strengthens their ability to participate more fully in national life."[52] Despite fierce resistance from an entrenched bilingual establishment, Congress eventually adopted a modest amendments to the Bilingual Education Act in 1988, raising the 4% cap to 25%.[53]

Bilingual programs might conceivably be tolerated on ideological grounds if the results were not so tragic for minorities, and particularly for Hispanics. A report prepared for the Department of Education by the National Assessment for Progress in Education has reported that "80% of all Hispanic high school students can't read well enough to go to college. . . . [S]eventeen year old Hispanics are reading at the level of thirteen-year-old Anglos."[54] Predictably, these educational statistics have translated into equally discouraging statistics on the status of Hispanics in the economy and American society. The National

Commission on Secondary Education for Hispanics has reported that "Hispanics suffer from a lack of the language skills. . . . essential to success in competitive society. Presently, 28% of all Hispanics live below the poverty line. . . . Unemployment among Hispanics is 40 to 50% higher than the national rate."[55]

A study by W. McManus, W. Gould, and F. Welch, has concluded that "differences associated with English language skills explain virtually all of the Hispanic wage differentials usually attributed to ethnicity, national origin, and time in the United States."[56]

There are disturbing parallels between the post-*Brown* policies of racial assignment and the bilingual policies of segregation according to national origin and native language. Both were originally perceived as solutions, but they produced results that their originators claimed they did not intend. The most important common denominator of both policies, however, was that principle was sacrificed in favor of considerations of politics and expediency.

Although pedagogical methods might appear to be an inappropriate arena for political mischief, bilingual education soon became wrapped in a political cocoon. In recent years, it has become fashionable for bilingual education to be perceived as a "liberal" cause; however, it is now clear to many teachers that such labels as "conservative" and "liberal" have little meaning when discussing a failed policy that puts ideology and politics above the interests of children who have little hope of succeeding in American society without effective training in the English language. It must also be recalled that the most virulent forms of segregated bilingual education were initiated in the form of the "Lau Remedies" promulgated by a conservative Republican administration in 1974.

But is there another hidden agenda to be found in the controversy over bilingual education? Brian Weinstein, a professor at Howard University, recently reviewed language policies in history and around the world, and concluded that "states generally make choices of language to reach final political goals rather than for linguistic or communicative goals."[57] In particular, he has found in many state language policies a desire to maintain the status quo. "Maintaining the status quo means resisting change in qualification for state employment and voting, keeping the symbols of state and societal identities intact, guarding patterns of external relations, and preserving extant distributions of wealth."[58]

Weinstein cites the example of India, in which the "best-paying jobs in the most important private and most powerful public sectors go to those with good English language-skills."[59] As a result, there has been a "flourishing of new, private, hastily organized English-medium schools, to which lower-middle-class families send their children in emulation of middle-class families, who have long patronized English-medium schools."[60]

Thus language can be used as a means of perpetuating the economic status of the privileged while excluding those who might aspire to compete with people who have the most desirable jobs and occupations in society. In the ante-bellum South, slaveholders sought to keep their slaves from learning how to read and write for fear of what they might learn. Today, millions of Hispanic children and other minorities whose native language is other than English are denied access to economic opportunities because of their limited proficiency in English. Were they to be effectively taught English they would no doubt provide substantial competition in the marketplace and thereby "upset the status quo." But such concerns, if reflected into the law, are not only short-sighted but unfair and unjust. Bilingual policies today harm limited English minorities in the same way in which immigration policies serve to deny African Americans fair economic opportunities.

The problem is not a shortage of good intentions. Many educators are doubtless sincere in their support of bilingual segregation, just as many educators were sincere in supporting school assignment according to race, and many employers were sincere in rejecting the pleas of Booker T. Washington and supporting racist policies of immigration as the solution to an unskilled labor shortage. Nor in the case of bilingual segregation can any blame be assigned to the Supreme Court. Its decision in *Lau* rightly and fairly recognized the right of limited English children to learn English and thereby receive the benefits of equal educational opportunity. They left it to the educators to determine the method. Unfortunately, they also left it to the politicians.

SPECIAL EDUCATION

Before the Prussianization of American schools,[61] there was little need for special education or the segregation of students on the basis of a perceived lack of ability, mental capacity, or handicap. Slower learners and mentally disabled students were permitted to learn at their own pace with younger, faster learners. Indeed, some of the older but slower students often helped the teacher to provide guidance for the younger students.

After American schools adopted the leadership and age segregation principles of the Prussian education system, however, problems began to arise with regard to students who learned more slowly than their peers. In classes that were rigidly segregated according to age, all students were expected to learn at the same pace. Those who were unable to do so began to be labeled as "retarded," "handicapped," "subnormal," and the like. Often schools simply got rid of these "problem" students by refusing to provide them with any education whatsoever, and typically "state law denie[d] education to the most severely handicapped children."[62] For those considered less severely handicapped, many state school districts created "special" education classes which served to segregate these students from the other "normal" students.

In the case of *Smith v. Robinson*,[63] the Supreme Court held that handicapped children had the same right to an education as nonhandicapped children. The Education for All Handicapped Children Act,[64] and the Individuals with Disabilities Education Act of 1990 have confirmed this right.[65]

The Education of All Handicapped Children Act required that state school districts seeking federal aid must provide a "free appropriate education" for all handicapped children. In also set forth specific procedures for identifying handicapped children, and directs that handicapped and nonhandicapped children be taught together "to the maximum extent appropriate."

Unfortunately, the term "appropriate" has provided an enormous loophole for school districts determined to segregate students according to perceived handicaps. Jonathan Kozol has described a typical school district in which a special education program has resulted in two schools within a school—one of the two schools consists "of about 130 children, most of whom are Hispanic, Black, assigned to one of the 12 'special' classes; the other of 700 mainstream students, almost all of whom are White or Asian."[66]

The abuse of this loophole as a means of segregating children inevitably invited judicial intervention. In the landmark case of *Hobson v. Hansen*,[67] Federal Judge J. Skelly Wright held the District of Columbia's student tracking system to be unconstitutional as a violation of the Fourteenth Amendment. In that case, the D.C. schools had employed a system of ability grouping under which students were placed in tracks according to the school's assessment of each student's ability to learn. Students were assigned to one of three tracks: retarded, average/above average, and gifted. A scholastic aptitude test was given to each child, consisting of such questions as geometric symbols or drawings, as well as questions testing verbal skills. Once students were assigned to a particular track there was little opportunity for "cross-tracking"—that is, "at least 85% of those assigned to the special academic track [remained] at the lowest achievement level . . . of all the students in the two lower tracks, constituting almost 60% of the student body, only 4.8% advanced to the college preparatory curriculum."[68]

Judge Wright decided that "whether a test is verbal or nonverbal, the skills being measured are not innate or inherited traits. They are learned, acquired through experience." Citing anonymous "modern experts," the Judge determined that such tests do not "measure some stable, predetermined intellectual process that can be isolated and called intelligence," and that they necessarily measure only a "student's background, his environment, [and] the cumulative experiences in his home, his community and his school". The judge also cited such as factors that might explain poor performance on a test, such as "psychological condition," "apathy," and "poor attitude."

Based on these findings, the court concluded that the track system did not reflect "classifications according to ability, [but rather constituted] placements based on status, [and therefore] amount to an unlawful discrimination against those students whose educational opportunities are being limited on the erroneous assumption that they are capable of accepting no more."[69] The court did not, however, merely order that the track system be reformed to more accurately reflect classifications according to ability, but instead peremptorily ordered that "the track system simply must be abolished."[70]

There were indeed a number of problems with the D.C. schools' track system—not the least of which was that there was no track for students who were less than average but not retarded. (If, by definition, half of all students are below average, and so do not qualify for the average/above average track, too many students are consigned under such a system to the "retarded" track.) Moreover, there was evidence to suggest that school administrators did little to challenge or improve the performance of students in the lower track or encourage them to transfer to the higher track.

However, the judge's order to simply abolish the tracking system was surely as shortsighted as the *Swann* remedy of assignment by race. Many parents of high-achieving students who had not yet decided to abandon the public schools were doubtless pushed to do so by such an order, thereby contributing to the white flight (referred to by Justice Thurgood Marshall) and the subsequent resegregation of the D.C. schools. As a result of this and other such orders, the D.C. school system remains one of the most (de facto) segregated school systems in the country.

Judge Wright's unsupported conclusion that "an aptitude test is necessarily measuring a student's background" is simply one extreme end of the spectrum, at the other end of which is controversial educational researcher Arthur Jensen who claims that 80% of intelligence is inherited.[71] In fact, the overwhelming opinion of social scientists is that both heredity and environment play an important role in intelligence. Judge Wright would have been on far firmer (and more persuasive) ground if he had simply made the point later confirmed by the Carnegie Institute Report, that the learning environment provided to children prior to age three "determines their brain structure and ability to learn."[72] However, such a finding would only justify an order mandating preschool education in the public schools, not an order totally abolishing the track system.

Nor were Judge Wright's generalizations about test-taking well taken. If some students do not reflect their knowledge or ability on a test because of anxiety or "poor attitude," the solution is to help that student overcome those problems, and provide ample opportunity for retesting. To dismiss all tests as nonindicative of ability paints far too broad a stroke.

Likewise, if certain questions on a test are culturally biased, the solution is to excise such questions, not to abandon all tests. (One frequently cited example of a culturally biased question was one that asked for the definition of "regatta," an activity not frequently encountered in low socioeconomic regions of the country.) It is difficult to understand, however, how abstract geometric drawings, or problems in algebra, could be interpreted as culturally biased.

All of this is not to suggest that tests are not much overused and abused in the public schools. They should be used as but one tool in the arsenal of learning, particularly as a means of providing a student with feedback; and they should certainly not be relied upon as an infallible indicator of ability at any given point in time. In short, standardized tests are not adequate substitutes for classroom discussion and recitation or written essays.

Judge Wright's order also purported to abolished tracks for "gifted" students. The law clearly provides that it is a violation of equal protection to deny a child the right to an education according to one's ability. This is the basis for the Supreme Court's holding that learning disabled children have the right to be educated according their abilities. The question therefore arises as to whether gifted children also have the right to be educated according to their abilities. A report entitled "The Other Minority," by Dr. Harold Lyon of the U.S. Office of Education, has pointed out that "there is another minority that has as much right to special attention—a minority denoted not by race, socio-economic background, ethnic origin or impaired abilities, but by their exceptional ability."[73] From this minority, Dr. Lyon asserts, "are the future Beethovens; the Newtons, the Jeffersons, the Picassos, the Baldwins, the Ernesto Galarzas and the Martin Luther Kings."[74]

To the question as to "why children with the potential to achieve a similar eminence should require special attention from our educational system," Dr. Lyon responds that "the explanation is that for every Einstein or Martin Luther King who emerges, it is likely that a dozen or more do not." Another answer was offered in a 1968 investigation of the gifted: "[T]hose individuals who constitute the 'creative minority' in our society . . . have achieved their eminence in spite of, rather than because of, our school system."[75]

The Lyon Report cites numerous example of those fortunate children who were able to reach their potential despite, and not because of, their school's inability to recognize that potential. Thomas Edison, for example, was withdrawn from the first grade because his teacher had labeled him as "unable." Isaac Newton left school at the age of 14 because school authorities had labeled him as a "poor student." Based on examinations, Winston Churchill finished last in his class at Harrow. Einstein found his grammar school to be "boring" and his later interest in mathematics was triggered by his uncle (who showed him number tricks) rather than his school. Gregor Mendel, who conducted much of the pioneering work in genetics, gave up taking his teacher's examinations after flunking them four times. Charles Darwin couldn't make it through medical school.[76]

Lyon concedes that "for every genius who did poorly in school, one can cite another who did well." Nevertheless, "this random sampling of academic misfits indicates that traditional academic programs are sometimes poorly suited to humans of extraordinary potential. One is left to wonder how many Churchills, how many Whistlers did not survive educational disaster—how many hatchlings (called ugly ducklings) had the good luck and the persistence to continue seeking other ponds until they were recognized as swans."[77]

The report revealed that while the public schools are zealous in tracking down and labeling children as "disabled" (due in part, no doubt, to the fact that federal programs award additional subsidies for each student so identified), they are not nearly so diligent in identifying gifted students. A U.S. Office of Education survey conducted from 1960 to 1970 reported that 57.5% of all public school districts in the United States claimed that they did not have a single gifted student in their entire student population.[78]

Lyon's report concluded that many public school staffs view the gifted as a "favored elite who deserve less than normal consideration," and that "many staff resent them." One study revealed "significantly greater hostility toward the gifted among psychologists" than among regular school staff.[79] Such attitudes are reflected in the educational resources allocated for gifted programs. No more than 10 states assign a full-time professional to programs for the gifted, and "fewer than four percent of the Nation's gifted and talented students have access to special programs."[80]

Lyon attributes some of these attitudes to the fact that American public education is conducted as a "mass enterprise, geared by economic necessity as well as politics to the abilities of the majority."[81] That public education need not be so constructed, however, is revealed by the fact that private schools, which spend far less money per student, do a far better job in identifying and meeting the educational needs of gifted children.

Nor have the courts been very helpful in ensuring that public schools provide gifted students with an equal educational opportunity to develop their abilities. Typical of the courts' attitude toward equal educational opportunity in this area was the case of *Bennett v. City School District of New Rochelle*.[82] In that case a school district chose students for a gifted program from a pool of students identified as gifted by conducting a lottery. The court held that there was nothing arbitrary or capricious about choosing students for the gifted program by lottery and that such a system complied fully with the requirements of the equal protection clause of the Constitution. Assuming that gifted children are entitled to the same equal opportunity to develop their abilities as other children, one wonders whether the court's ruling would have been the same had the school district chosen to deny equal educational opportunity to disabled students who lost a lottery.

The results of such policies of mediocrity are reflected in the international studies of student achievement. In international tests American children representing the top 1% of students in the nation placed "13th out of 13 in biology, 11th out of 13 in chemistry, and 9th out 13 in physics."[83]

Ironically, present policies harm the gifted minority child more than any other. It has been suggested that "the superior student wastes half his time in the typical American school, the gifted child wastes it all, and that the upper five to ten percent of America's school-age children are the most underprivileged group."[84] Marian Scheifele has observed that "it is a shocking fact that many gifted children, in terms of [potential] achievement, are the most seriously retarded pupils in our schools today."[85] Lyon cites the documented case of the "troublesome seventh grader whose baffled teacher reported that, while the girl claimed she could not understand simple fractions, she delighted in working compound trigonometry fractions, the same week that she failed a [standardized] math test, the girl was caught in study hall "writing her own math textbook.'"[86] Professor Arval Morris has concluded that "there is reason to believe that the characteristics denoted as 'giftedness' are equally distributed in children throughout the 'racial' and socioeconomic spectrum. Thus, the minority or lower income class student who is 'gifted' may be doubly at a disadvantage."[87]

Such treatment of gifted students is not only a personal tragedy for the students deprived of the equal educational opportunity to develop their abilities. It is also a tragedy for a country deprived of what such students could offer in the fields of medicine, technology, and in social programs. One need only think of how American society might be different if it had been deprived of what Thomas Edison, Jonas Salk, Susan B. Anthony, and Martin Luther King contributed to American society.

Cases such as *Hobson v. Hansen* have been significant contributors to the resegregation and rising tide of mediocrity in the public schools. But the blame should not be placed solely on the courts. Had the D.C. school system not abused its tracking system by using it in a manner that resulted in the segregation of students according to race and socioeconomic status, there would have been no cause for judicial intervention.

In 1994, however, many American public schools were following the same discredited special education programs as those of the D.C. schools in 1967. New York City today provides perhaps the most discouraging example, spending more than $1.3 billion each year on a vast, bureaucratic program empire providing special education to 130,000 students.[88] This number is four times greater than just 19 years ago. Federal law provides an irresistible incentive to label and assign students to the special education courses, showering New York schools with a $10,000 "bounty" for each student so identified, stigmatized, and segregated. But how are those staggering taxpayer billions being spent? A recent study conducted by the *New York Times* documents the education of a typical special education student in the New York schools.

Radaheya, a special education student, attends classes that the *New York Times* describes as a "communication arts" class, and a "period where students play pool or go to a game room."[89] His mother, a day care worker, succumbed to school pressure to place him in a special education program after being told that her son would be in smaller classes and get special attention. Only later did she discover that students segregated in special education classes are "almost never decertified and allowed to return to regular education, and that . . . fewer than five percent graduate in four years."[90] Although Radaheya was labeled as having "mild to moderate learning disabilities," the *New York Times* reported that his mother has tried for years to "wrest him from what she sees as a Kafkaesque cul-de-sac."[91] However, with New York City having a $10,000 interest in keeping him in special education, there appeared little possibility of his escape.

Radaheya's mother even had her son independently tested by the Manhattan Eye and Ear Clinic, which specializes in the evaluation of students with learning disabilities. Despite the clinic's recommendation that Radaheya be placed in a regular classroom with some outside academic help, school bureaucrats were unmoved by all pleas, apparently unwilling to give up the $10,000 they earned by keeping him locked up in special education. His saddened mother soon became desperate, lamenting that "special education has affected his ability to even try."[92]

The case of Damon Kimber was even more compelling. As an eleventh grader, Damon delivered a lecture to a packed Mandela Cultural Center audience, describing his life in special education at a school of "graphic communications." He stated his hope to one day escape from special education, and proudly described his success in the one regular class in hygiene he had been permitted to attend. But in the audience, his weeping foster mother later described her child as "so ashamed at his diagnosis, he would barely hold up his face when he was placed in her care four years ago."[93] The boy's natural mother, a drug abuser, had placed him in special education at the age of five, where he had remained ever since. Damon himself begs only for the chance to succeed in a regular classroom. "It will help me more than special education. . . . It [would] make me move ahead. It's important because it makes me advance like a professional. In special education, it slows you down."[94]

A New York City crisis intervention counsellor, Ted Gustus, has described his desperate attempts to free children from the tragic fate that awaits them in special education. "It's like a kid being in prison. You are taken out of society."[95] Gustus feels fortunate that he himself was spared the humiliation of special education. Although he grew up without a father, his mother died of alcoholism when he was 9, and he was moved frequently from one relative's house to another, he believes that he was spared assignment to special education only because no such program existed when he was in school; and, of course, federal bureaucrats were not offering $10,000 taxpayer-funded bounties for each stigmatized student. "Instead", he states proudly that "I made it through school, stigma-free. . . . I didn't have a label."

One of Gustus' rescues from the system was Marquis Scott. Scott had been so embarrassed at his stigmatization as a special education student that he pleaded with his mother not to tell anyone. "The system is telling you that you have a disability and you can't learn at the same rate as other students."[96] Scott is now a successful and productive mental health worker at a New York City hospital.

Not all the public school systems around the country segregate their learning disabled students so intensively. While New York permits only 7% of the students to attend regular classrooms, Vermont places 87% of its learning disabled students in regular classrooms, and even California places 25% of its learning disabled students in regular classrooms.[97] Apparently there is something very significant about one's domicile and state of citizenship that determines a disabled student's ability to learn in a regular classroom.

One can only ponder what the results in educational achievement in the public schools might have been had the staggering billions of dollars spent on special education instead been spent on preschool education. It will be recalled that a 1994 report by the Carnegie Institute revealed that brain development prior to the age of one is the most critical:

Babies are born with billion of brain cells, many more than they have at age three, and nearly twice as many as they have as adults. . . . During the first months of life, connections between these cells, called synapses, multiply rapidly to 1,000 trillion, forming the structures that allow learning to occur. Nature acts like a sculptor throughout childhood . . . chiseling away the excessive cells and synapses so that the brain can function more efficiency in adulthood. In part it decides which synapses are superfluous by determining which ones never get used.[98]

Harry Chugani, a neuroscientist at the University of Michigan's children's hospital, states that the above analysis explains "why people who take piano lessons [at an early age] find it easier to play piano as adults than those who didn't start studying the instrument until later in life."[99] Thus, by the simple act of enrolling a student in a piano class, "you've changed the anatomy of the brain."[100]

The empirical evidence substantiating these finding are overwhelming to all except the educational bureaucrats who persist in lavishing bounties on schools that comply with federal policy by segregating older children into special educational classes. For example, animal studies reveal that "when rats spend their lives before sexual maturity in cages filled with toys, they develop more synapses than rats in empty cages."[101] William Greenough of the Beckman Institute at the University of Illinois explains that "these rats have 80% more capillary volume per brain cell, that is, bigger capillaries and more of them, allowing the brain to receive a better supply of nutrients and oxygen. Meanwhile, the neuroglia, which help keep the nervous system stable, show increases in metabolic rates and size in these rats."[102]

Other studies reveal that children raised in unstimulating environments "display cognitive deficits by 18 months that may be irreversible."[103] Other studies have revealed that "severe stress in monkeys and rats, has created serious problems too, resulting in hormonal changes that cause the death of brain cells involved in learning and memory."[104]

Edward Ziegler, director of the Yale University Center in Child Development and Social Policy, observes that "stimulating a child is simple, but it does take time. Putting children on your lap, letting them turn the pages when you read to them—normal everyday interactions.

. . . Drop the nonsense about quality time. It the quantity time that children need."[105]

Perhaps most revealing of the studies conducted to date is that of Craig Ramey, a development psychologist at the University of Alabama. His studies have shown that "when extremely high-risk children entered educational programs by six months of age, their incidence of mental retardation was cut by 80%."[106] Even more revealing is the data showing that "by age three, these children had IQ's that were 15 to 20 points higher than children of similar backgrounds who had not attended programs. . . . *Children who enter preschool at age three also show improvement, but they never appear to fully overcome what they lost in the first three years*." (emphasis added).[107]

Present educational policy thereby appears to be the classic example of locking the barnyard door after the horse has already escaped. Billions are spent on students for whom it is far too late to develop their minds to their true potential, and the education provided them has degenerated into the most expensive type of custodial care, the primary benefit of which appears to be to spare less deprived children of the burden of their proximity. Virtually no free education is provided for the purpose of stimulating and educating children prior to the age of one—the most critical period of child development. Instead, working parents, and parents of low socioeconomic backgrounds must fall back on their own private resources to dump their children in child care facilities, only 9% of which, according to a recent report of the Families and Work Institute, "provide good quality . . . family child care."[108] The educational establishment prefers to pick up later the staggering special education bill.

Although researchers show that even the most minimal kind of stimulation (holding a child while reading to her, having her turn the pages, etc.) are critical to intellectual development, the problem with such studies may be that teachers who provide such elementary developmental training do not require the high salaries of the armies of counselors, psychologists, and administrators to which public school systems have grown highly attached. Just one of the many thousands of $10,000 bounties paid to school districts to segregate and imprison one learning-disabled student might provide one full-time nurturing preschool teacher who could help develop the minds of many infant children deprived of intellectual stimulation in the home. But such a system might put a few of the most powerful educational bureaucrats out of work, and there is little likelihood that this will ever be permitted to happen in the public schools today. The Senate Education and Labor Committee in 1994 introduced a bill to include preschooling in the Head Start Program. If this modest bill is passed, it will at least be in step in the right direction.[109]

Had the educational establishment not decided to adopt the Prussian model of education by implementing policies of male dominance and age segregation, there would be very little justification for tracking. Older but slower learning students would be permitted to learn side by side with younger but faster learning students. By forcing students into the Prussian model of rigid age segregation, however, problems inevitably arise when some students within a particular age group learn at a faster pace than others. As Professor Arval Morris has asked, "Is uniformity of age in grades beginning with the first grade a worthy educational goal? A useful administrative device? If you were an instructor in a course of beginning foreign language for adults, would you first group them by age for instructional purposes? Can you think of any educational or training program apart from the common school where children are grouped according to age?"[110]

When Prussian pedagogical methods of age segregation are combined with pedagogical methods imposed by such judges as J. Skelly Wright, the results can border on the absurd. In the name of due process and equal protection, students struggling to learn basic concepts of arithmetic may be forced into a class with students studying advanced concepts of integral calculus. Students who have no previous training or experience in French may be forced to take a class with students who have already taken four years of French. Many parents would surely object, however, to having their child who is having difficulty grasping basic arithmetic concepts placed in a class studying advanced integral calculus. Most of all, parents object to having their child placed in a class where learning is prevented by other disruptive students protected by judicial notions of due process.

There are but two rational education bases for segregating children. First, children who want to learn and develop have the right to do so in an environment that is safe and free from intimidation and disruption. Wealthy children who can afford private schools obtain this right, but the vast majority of the nation's poor and underprivileged children in this country are deprived of that essential right. This right can be provided, however, without socioeconomic stereotyping and stigmatization. All public school students should be permitted to apply for a magnet classroom in which discipline is maintained by a teacher who is given full authority over the classroom, and in which due process rights are waived in the same way as they are waived in private schools. Once these classrooms teachers are restored to the full authority they enjoyed before American schools were Prussianized by bureaucrats seeking to impose a male-dominated hierarchy based on the leadership principle of Prussian society, they will be free to emulate their one-room school predecessors who taught children according to their ability rather than their age, and who provided feedback with daily recitations and essays rather than mindlessly administered multiple-choice tests.

Second, limited tracking should be made available in a select category of subjects in which some gifted students have already reached a level of achievement, the further development of which can not reasonably be accommodated in a combined class — for example, a class in advanced astrophysics or integral calculus, or a fourth year class in French or advanced Greek. Such classes as home-room that discuss current events, history, and geography classes, should be taught, and abilities accommodated, in the same way as they were accommodated in combined classes before the days of consolidation and Prussianization.

Courts must be persuaded to hold their heavy hand of intervention, which in the past has relied on political and ideological theories (rather than upon legitimate considerations of the quality of education) to justify racial assignments and the deprivation of true equal opportunity for all students, including the gifted students who have such great potential to enrich American life.

But any school policy that departs from the American model of ability accommodation in the context of a combined class must be guided by one overriding credo: the decision to apply for admission to a innovative program such as a magnet classroom by a child and that child's parents must always be based on free choice, and not a prior determination by an educational bureaucrat or other educational professional. And once a student decides to withdraw from such a class they must be permitted, within a reasonable time, to reapply for admission to the magnet classroom upon making a renewed and joint written commitment to abide by the stricter rules of behavior in that classroom. Those students and parents who choose not to do so, and prefer the lax disciplinary environment imposed by the courts on the regular classrooms, must be left absolutely free to male their own choices (decline to apply to the magnet classroom, or make a commitment to the stricter rules of behavior). Indeed it is constitutional right of all students to try to learn in the typical classroom of today's public schools. Until the law is changed, their right to do so can not be disturbed.

Chapter Seven

School Violence and the Crisis in Due Process

As documented in the previous chapters, the most important feature of quality education is a safe and disciplined learning environment. Without this essential feature, per capita expenditures, the quality of teaching, textbooks, and facilities amount to little. Unfortunately, however, it is in this most important area of education that American public schools have been deficient.

There are several explanations for their failure. First, the adoption of the Prussian system resulted in placing greater emphasis and reliance on administration and hierarchical control, and reducing the authority of the classroom teacher. Since it is in the classroom where learning actually takes place, the dissipation of classroom teacher authority has had disastrous consequences.

Second, courts having limited expertise in educational matters have applied constitutional principles in ways that have resulted in the denial of equal educational opportunity. The misapplication of constitutional principles is not, of course, only a recent judicial phenomenon. It will be recalled that in the *Dred Scott* decision, the Supreme Court called upon the sacred principle of due process to enshrine slavery as a constitutional right (on the theory that confiscation of a slaveowner's property was to take his property without due process of law in violation of the Fifth Amendment). This example of judicial perversion of sacred principles is recalled, however, only to make the point that the mere recitation of sacred words found in the Constitution can not serve as a substitute for sound constitutional analysis.

Nor in the judicial cases dealing with public education should use of the phrase due process be permitted to obscure the natural right of every child to an education that provides an opportunity to pursue success and happiness in society. There is a touch of irony in the fact that while the Supreme Court has applied the concept of due process to justify slavery as a constitutional right, the Constitution itself provides no citizen the right to an education.[1] Rather it has been incumbent on each individual state in the exercise of its police powers to provide such a right in its own internal laws or state constitutions.[2] Indeed, the Supreme Court suggested that "education is perhaps the most important function of state and local governments."[3]

Every state in the union has provided to its citizens the right to a free public education.[4] A typical state constitutional provision is that of California, which states that "the legislature shall provide for a system of common schools by which a free school shall be kept up and supported."[5] State courts have typically held that "[common schools] are free schools, open to all the children of the proper school age residing in the locality and . . . affording equal opportunity for all to acquire the learning taught in the various common school branches."[6] The inherent authority to provide for the right to a free public education resides in the state, although the state may delegate that authority to local governmental entities such as cities or counties.[7]

If one accepts the underlying premise that the most important feature of a good education is providing a safe and disciplined learning environment, the cases of judicial intervention in the educational process must be examined critically with regard to whether they have served to promote or to hinder the basic right of every child, regardless of race or socioeconomic status, to an adequate education. As in many areas of the law, rights may conflict, and a hierarchy of constitutional principles must be balanced and established as a matter of law. In the area of criminal justice, for example, the courts must constantly grapple with the inherent conflict between the rights of the citizenry and the press under the First Amendment, and the rights of a defendant to a fair trial, all the while striving to strike a fair balance between both rights as set forth in the Constitution.

In the law of public education, the case of *Goss v. Lopez* gave the Supreme Court its most important opportunity to balance the rights of students subject to school discipline with the rights of students to obtain an adequate education.[8] In that case, several students committed violent acts in the presence of the school principal, including a physical assault on a policeman called to quell a violent disturbance in the school auditorium. The student who conducted the assault was suspended for a period of less than 10 days, but was given no other punishment. Although the physical assault on the policeman had been committed in the presence of the school principal, the Supreme Court declared the suspension unconstitutional because the student accused of the assault had not been provided with due process by being given a hearing.

Since the Constitution only forbids deprivation of "life, liberty, or property" without due process, the question arose as to whether suspending a student denied him "liberty" or took away a "property right." Since freeing the student to go home could hardly be called a deprivation of "liberty," the Court was reduced to raising the issue of whether "going to school" was a "property right." In a feat of mental gymnastics that rivaled the *Dred Scott* decision's incisive analysis (which concluded that slavery was required by due process), the Supreme Court decided that going to school was a property right, triggering the application of the full panoply of rights of due process. Although the Court purported to stop short of holding that "hearings in connection with short suspensions must afford the student the right to secure counsel, to confront and cross-examine witnesses supporting the charge, or to call his own witnesses to verify his version of the incident,"[9] the Court warned that suspensions exceeding 10 days might require "more formal procedures."[10]

Four justices, including the chief justice, vainly attempted to interject a note of reason, writing in their dissent that "the Court's decision rests on the premise that . . . education is a property interest. . . . A student's interest in education is not infringed by a suspension within the limited period prescribed. . . . Moreover to the extent that there may be some arguable infringement, it is too speculative, transitory, and insubstantial to justify imposition of a constitutional rule."[11]

Other court decisions have required even more formal due process requirements. A New Jersey court, for example, reversed a suspension of a student accused of physical assault on female students because he was not afforded a hearing at which he was accorded the right to "cross-examination."[12] Although the female victims as well as a number of eyewitnesses submitted written eyewitness accounts of the attack, their statements were dismissed because the witnesses failed to appear in front of the accused student after having received threats of physical retaliation if they did so. The mother of one of the victims informed the principal that she had received "a telephone call from the mother of one of the accused students threatening the life of one of the prospective student witnesses. There was testimony that the student witnesses were in terror of retaliation if their identity was revealed to the accused students."[13] Nevertheless, the court was unmoved and reversed the expulsion of the alleged attackers. The female victims were presumably left to the mercies of their attackers who remained in school.

Such decisions have provided the basis for the Model School Disciplinary Code issued by Center for Law and Education of Harvard University[14] (see Chapter Two). It will be recalled that this code forbids the imposition of "any" serious discipline without providing the student with a hearing, the right to remain silent, the right to counsel, a formal written complaint, and a panoply of other procedural and formalistic rights.

The application of due process rights to disruptive students has resulted in reciprocal rights of disciplined students to sue their teachers in tort for violation of these rights. In the Supreme Court case of *Wood v. Strickland*, for example, a school principal dared to suspend a student who admitted "spiking" and contaminating with intoxicants the community punchbowl at a student affair. Because no "hearing" was provided to her, the student thereupon sued two school administrators and two members of the school board for "compensatory and punitive damages" for violating her constitutional rights to due process. The Supreme Court held that the school officials were not immune from suit, on grounds that "an act violating a student's constitutional rights" can not be justified by "ignorance or disregard" of the law.[15] The Court concluded that a school official was not immune from [monetary] damages [under Sec. 1983 of the Civil Rights Act] if he knew or should have known that the action he took . . . would violate the constitutional rights of the student affected."[16]   Although the Court purported to limit liability to situations in which the school officials action "cannot reasonably be characterized as being in good faith," the fact remains that any ultimate determination of what constitutes good faith is to be left up to a particular judge or jury, and any lawyer worth his or her salt will not fail to allege lack of good faith in any complaint lodged by a student against a school official.

The four horrified justices who dissented in *Strickland* observed that the court majority had imposed a higher standard for school officials "heretofore required of any other official," and raised the compelling question of whether any "qualified person will continue in the desired numbers to volunteer for service in public education" knowing that they might be subject to staggering financial liability for "ignorance of the law."[17]   Justice Powell observed that the Court's holding would "impose personal liability on a school official who acted sincerely and in the utmost good faith, but who was found—after the fact—to have acted in 'ignorance' of the settled, indisputable law. The Court's decision appears to rest on an unwarranted assumption as to what lay school officials know or can know about the law and constitutional rights. These officials will now act at the peril of some judge or jury subsequently finding that a good faith belief as the applicable law was mistaken and hence actionable."[18]

Scholarly criticism of the *Strickland* decision has not been uniformly kind. Professor William Hazard has observed that "the case stands for the sobering proposition that, in matters of discipline (matters, which according to Gallup polls, stand at or near the top of the list of parent concerns about schools), school board members face a good chance of being held personally liable for money damages at the suit of a student whose constitutional rights were violated by board action, taken in good faith."[19]

Hazard observes that "one need not be an alarmist to predict that school discipline decisions will be made cautiously, if at all."[20]   The *Strickland* case, Hazard warns, "does more than expand the remedies available to parents and pupils for deprivations of important personal liberties and rights; it exposes the barren, near primitive state of our understanding of human behavior and the limited response capabilities of existing institutional machinery."[21]   Hazard concludes that "schooling shorn of unreplaced discipline tools, though more palatable to some consumers, may be less acceptable to others for its failure to produce their versions of disciplined young adults. The inadequate machinery to reach workable consensus or acceptable public priorities for dysfunctional social organizations lays a heavy burden on the schools."[22]

Other court decisions have held that students have a right to counsel at expulsion hearings.[23] Although the Supreme Court has held that corporal punishment is not in and of itself cruel and unusual punishment under the Eighth Amendment, at least where state law permits reasonable application of corporal punishment,[24] this has not stopped students from suing their teachers for perceived "excessive punishment." In *Marlar v. Bill*[25] for example, a student sued his teacher for damages for having searched his person for missing money; and in *O'Rourke v. Walker*, a student sued his school principal for striking him "eight times on each hand with a flat stick [causing] no injury" (the proverbial "slap on the wrist") as punishment for what the court described as "the abuse of little girls by young bullies."[26]

Even verbal corrections of a student by a teacher may subject the teacher to a lawsuit. In *Wexell v. Scott*, an 11-year-old student sued his teacher for allegedly having made disparaging comments about him and the quality of his schoolwork, including having called him "undependable."[27] His complaint, which was later appealed to the Appellate Court of Illinois, alleged that he suffered "great mental anguish" as a result of his teacher's criticisms.

Although not all these cases actually resulted in awards of money damages against the teacher personally, the very fact that such lawsuits occur at all is indicative of the kind of environment in which teachers are expected to maintain a safe and disciplined learning environment for those students seeking an education. Under prevailing law, a teacher contemplating taking action to provide a safe learning environment for her or his students must consider the staggering financial consequences of a wrong decision that might be second-guessed later by a court applying due process.

Some teachers are fighting back. In May 1994, *Newsweek* magazine reported the case of a private religious school teacher who expounded in class on a Talmudic passage relating to adultery and carnal knowledge. According to *Newsweek*, the teacher "used [the passage] to illustrate how Jesus' well known dictum from the sermon on the mount . . . resembles the Talmudic doctrine of the importance of intention when judging sinful acts. But unlike [the teacher], neither Jesus nor the rabbis had to contend with a Sexual Harassment Task Force. . . . Based on a complaint from a former female student, [the teacher] was put on probation [and urged] to get therapy."[28] The teacher is now suing his own school for defamation of character.

Although public schools alleged to have practiced gender discrimination were previously subject only to injunctive relief, in 1992 the Supreme Court held that schools could be liable for money damage judgments in cases alleging gender discrimination.[29]

The common law doctrine of "in loco parentis" has suffered severely at the hands of the judiciary. Under that doctrine, first expounded by William Blackstone, a parent delegates "part of his parental authority, during his life, to the tutor or schoolmaster of his child; who is then in loco parentis [in "place of the parent"] and has such a portion of the power of the parent committed to his charge, viz.

that is restraint and correction, as may be necessary to answer for the purposes for which he is employed."[30]

Under this doctrine, a teacher would have the same right as a parent to, say, search a child's room for weapons, dangerous substances, or contraband. Certainly in the days of the one-room schoolhouse, before Prussianization of the schools and stripping the authority of the classroom teacher, no one doubted the vitality of this common law doctrine. When the public schools became consolidated, however, and the urban problems of drugs and violence found their way into the public schools, many hoped that the doctrine would continue to be adhered to and used as a conceptual tool for creating that kind of a safe and disciplined learning environment without which equal educational opportunity would be impossible.

The Courts soon dashed such hopes, however. In the 1985 case of *New Jersey v. T.L.O.*,[31] the Supreme Court held that "'the concept of parental delegation' as a source of school authority is not entirely consonant [with public education laws]"[32] and that school officials therefore "cannot claim the parents immunity from the strictures of the Fourth Amendment."[33] In the case of *T.L.O.*, the Court held that the Fourth Amendment's applies to searches conducted by school officials. The Fourth Amendment only forbids "unreasonable" searches and seizures. By holding the Fourth Amendment applicable to searches by school officials, the Court was, in effect, holding that searches conducted in accordance with the long-established common law doctrine of in loco parentis were "unreasonable."

It is true that the Court in *T.L.O.* did recognize a slightly lower Fourth Amendment standard for a public school search, only requiring "reasonable grounds for suspecting that the search will turn up evidence that the student has violated or is violating either the law or the rules of the school."[34] In fact, however, the Court's purported distinction between "reasonable suspicion" and "probable cause" has proved somewhat illusory in terms of actual application of the Fourth Amendment in the public schools. In *In Re Williams, G.*, for example, a California Court interpreted the *T.L.O.* standard to require "articulable facts [which] together with rational inferences from those facts, warran[t] an objectively reasonable suspicion that the student or students to be searched are violating or have violated a rule."[35] Under such a standard, a search of a student's small black bag furtively concealed from a school principal, which contained four bags of drugs, was held to be unconstitutional.

Such decisions have not been enough to satisfy many legal scholars, however. The dean of the University of Colorado Law School recently opined in the *Yale Law Journal* that "[in cases of in-school searches] there has not been enough judicial intrusion to protect the rights of individuals."[36]

The suppression of evidence and inability to provide students with a safe and drug-free environment is not the only consequence of such decisions. Teachers themselves become targets of civil lawsuits by students claiming that such searches are unconstitutional. In the federal case of *Cales v. Howell Public School*, a 15-year-old student sued the school official whose search revealed "readmittance slips" in violation of school rules. The Court held that "the burden is on the administrator to establish that the student's conduct is such that it creates a reasonable suspicion that a specific rule has been violated.[37]

A naive observer might be inclined to believe that in a public school system in which half a million incidents of violence take place each month,[38] 40% of high school students are crime victims during a given year,[39] school vandalism and arson exceeds half a billion dollars,[40] and malicious destruction of educational property takes place in 80% of school districts,[41] the paramount issue facing the courts would be the denial to millions of American children of their right to an education in a safe and disciplined learning environment.

When one examines the Supreme Court cases in the area of public education, however, one is more likely to find among its selected landmark cases such decisions as *Tinker v. Des Moines*,[42] in which the issue considered was whether students should be allowed to violate school regulations by wearing protest armbands. (The Court decided they have such a right under the First Amendment.)

With public schools in a state of virtual anarchy and collapse, the 1990 federal case of *Roberts v. Madigan*[43] addressed its attention to the vital constitutional question of whether it was a violation of the First Amendment for a fifth grade teacher to have a Bible on his desk. The Supreme Court "let stand the Tenth Circuit's ruling that the school principal could require the teacher to remove the Bible from his desk."[44] The Court of Appeals was concerned that the teacher's mere placing of a Bible on his desk "had the primary effect of passing on the teacher's religious views to his students."[45]

There are literally dozens of federal cases addressing the equally vital constitutional issue of whether students should be allowed to wear their hair anyway they want.[46] The federal circuit courts have split on the issue, and the Supreme Court has thus far mercifully (or mischievously) declined to resolve the question. In *Bannister v. Paradis*, however, a federal Court held that the Fourteenth Amendment "embrace[s] the right to wear clean blue jeans to school."[47]

The cliche of "rearranging the deck chairs on the Titanic" is much overused, but it seems appropriate in analyzing the due process cases relating to public education. The courts spend vast amounts of judicial energy rearranging such conceptual constitutional deck chairs as whether students can wear blue jeans or a teacher can have a Bible on his desk, while basic rights of educational opportunity are being denied to millions of American children because of the failure of the public schools to provide a safe and disciplined learning environment. Indeed, such an environment has now become available only to those children of families rich enough to purchase such an environment at private schools.

The question raised by judicial intervention in the educational process is not whether public school students are entitled to fair treatment in the administration of discipline. Indeed, fairness is an essential feature of any effective program of discipline. But the principal function of the public schools is to provide children with the educational rights to which they are entitled by law. As so eloquently stated by the chief justice of the United States in his dissent in *Goss*, the concept of due process should not be distorted in such a way as to interpret a right to an education as a property right, which triggers application of all the formalities and procedures of the criminal justice system. To do so is to create an unreasonable balance of constitutional interests in a way that deprives all public school children of their basic right to equal educational opportunity.

Chapter Eight

Public School Financing and the Issue of Inequality

No discussion of equal educational opportunity would be complete without reference to methods of public school financing. It will be recalled that the earliest state education laws   delegated to local communities the responsibility for providing free public education.[1] For local communities, property taxes provided the most feasible means of raising the revenues necessary to finance public schools. Traditionally, therefore, property taxes have provided the primary source of funding for public education.

This traditional American means of financing public education did not result from any one calculated legislative policy or scheme. Rather it evolved naturally from the complex federalist structure of government, and the reservation of local and state powers envisioned by the constitutional framers and enshrined in the Tenth Amendment of the Constitution.[2]

Nevertheless, by the mid-1970s it had become apparent that school financing systems based on local property taxes resulted in inequalities between school districts in per capita educational expenditures. Since actual property tax revenues depend not only on the rate of taxation, but also on the underlying valuation of the property taxed, many property-rich school districts can provide higher per capita educational expenditures with lower property tax rates than many poorer districts can provide with higher tax rates. For this reason disparities in per pupil expenditures between school districts within a state exist in most states. In 1989, for example, per pupil expenditures in the Chicago area varied from $9,371 in Niles Township to $5,265;[3] in New York disparities ranged from $11,372 to $5,885;[4] and in New Jersey from $7,725 to $3,538.[5]

Because of such disparities, there has been a temptation to simplistically apply concepts of equal protection to strike down school financing systems in which per pupil expenditures are based on the wealth of the school district. As early as 1971, for example, the California Supreme Court in *Serrano v. Priest*[6] held that education was a fundamentally protected right and that a financing system that made the quality of a child's education dependent on the wealth of the district in which she lived was unconstitutional.

When the issue came before the U.S. Supreme Court in the 1973 case of *San Antonio v. Rodriguez*, however, the Court carefully considered the problems inherent in such a simplistic analysis. The Court did not deny that disparities existed in the Texas school financing system. There was no dispute that in the Texas district of Edgewood (where the average assessed property per pupil was $5,960) the per pupil expenditure was $356 per pupil, while in the district of Alamo Heights (where the assessed value of property was $49,000 per pupil), the expenditure was $594 per pupil.[8] The Court could not, however, ascertain a particular class "susceptible of identification in traditional terms."[9]

For example, the Court noted that while the evidence revealed that the wealthiest districts did indeed spend the most on education, and the poorest spent the least, the evidence also revealed that "for the remainder of the districts—96 districts composing almost 90% of the sample—the correlation is inverted; i.e., the districts that spend next to the most money on education are populated by families having next to the lowest median family incomes while the districts spending the least have the highest median family incomes."[10] It also cited a Kansas study that revealed in that state "an inverse correlation: districts with the highest income per pupil have low assessed value per pupil, and districts with high assessed value per pupil have low income per pupil."[11] An explanation for such a reverse correlation was found in a report that revealed that in many areas, "the poor were clustered around commercial and industrial areas—those same areas that provide the most attractive sources of property tax income for school districts."[12]

Nor did the Court accept the assumption that greater expenditures per pupil necessarily resulted in greater educational benefits, noting that "disparities in expenditures appear to be explained by variations in teacher salaries"[13] and that there was little empirical data to "support the advantage of any particular pupil-student ratio or that document the existence of a dependable correlation between the level of public school teachers' salaries and quality of classroom instruction."[14]

Another factor considered by the court was the effect that the abolition of locally based financing would have on the local control of the public schools. The Court cited studies suggesting that "one of the most likely consequences of [abolishing locally based financing] would be an increase in the centralization of school finance,"[15] and that "unless a local community, through its school board, has some control over the purse, there can be little real feeling in the community that the schools are in fact local schools."[16]

In short, the Court simply found "no factual basis upon which to found a claim of comparative wealth discrimination," and that it could therefore not accept a challenge based on allegations that a school financing system allegedly "discriminates against a large, diverse, and amorphous class, unified only by the common factor of residence in districts that happen to have less taxable wealth than other districts."[17]

Despite the Supreme Court's decision in *Rodriguez*, however, at least ten states have held their state school financing systems to be unconstitutional, either on grounds that their state financing system violated the equal protection clauses of their own state constitution,[18] or failed to provide an "efficient system of public schools throughout the state" in violation of state constitutional mandate.[19] A West Virginia Court even criticized the Supreme Court for failing to recognize education as a "fundamental right" requiring strict scrutiny.[20] In 1994, Michigan lawmakers proposed a radical new school financing system calling for a statewide property tax, legalized Keno, and new telephone and cigarette taxes.[21]

The difficulty in imposing a flat requirement of statewide financing is revealed by the example of Hawaii. Until recently, Hawaii was the only state that attempted to finance public education on a statewide basis rather than on local property taxes. In 1968, however, Hawaii finally amended its law to permit local communities to supplement their educational expenditures with funds raised locally. The Hawaiian legislature made clear the public policy rationale of its amendment: "Under existing law, counties are precluded from doing anything in this area, even to spend their own funds if they so desire. This corrective legislation is urgently needed to allow counties to provide . . . educational facilities as good as the people of the counties want and are willing to pay for. Allowing local communities [to do this] encourages the best features of democratic government."[22]

In light of the problems revealed by the Supreme Court in *Rodriguez* in applying an equal protection analysis to an amorphous class spread across many school district boundaries, it was not surprising that many of the school financing remedies mandated by state courts themselves soon "came under attack as constitutionally deficient."[23] The result has been the considerable expenditure of judicial energy without appreciable result. Indeed, in some cases, as in the post-*Brown* desegregation cases, the results have been counter to the claimed purposes of those who have sought to have school financing systems declared unconstitutional.

Jonathan Kozol notes that although plaintiffs in California were successful in having the state's school financing system declared unconstitutional, it was "to some extent a victory of losers."[24] This was because Proposition 13 (a state referendum that effectively limited spending in all school districts) followed in the wake of the school financing cases. The result, according to Kozol, is that although California "ranks eighth in per capita income in the nation, the share of its income that now goes to public education is a meager 3.8%—placing California forty-sixth among the 50 states. Its average class size is the largest in the nation."[25] Thus the net result of having California's financing system declared unconstitutional appears to be a reduction in spending in all California school systems.

Many courts and legislatures that decided not to heed the admonitions of the Supreme Court in *Rodriguez* are only now beginning to realize that the underlying problem with public education is not disparities in per capita expenditures. Even public schools with the very lowest per capita expenditures still spend more than most private and parochial schools,[26] and far more than is spent in such industrialized countries as Japan.[27]

Despite the lack of any empirical evidence showing a correlation between per capita expenditures and the quality of public school education, however, there remains the question of the fundamental fairness of disparities in per capita expenditures. However, such unfairness can not be dealt with on a state-by-state basis. Even if disparities in per capita expenditure within a state could somehow be completely eliminated, disparities would still exist between states. In 1986, for example, Alaska had the highest per capita expenditures for public education ($8,044), while Utah had the very lowest ($2,297)[28]— yet Utah was regarded as providing among the best educational opportunities for its children. Are Utah's children the victims of a denial of equal protection of the laws?[29]

Nevertheless, the goal of equal per capita expenditures is a worthy one, and should be pursued on equitable grounds. The danger, however, is that the in the quest for equal per capita expenditures, sight will be lost of the truly essential features of a quality education for all American children.

Chapter Nine

Conclusion: Can Our Public Schools Be Saved?

The problems of American public schools are steeped in history. Without an understanding of that history—the origin and evolution of the American system of one-room schools; the Prussianization and consolidation of those schools and the creation of an administrative and bureaucratic empire built on sexism, age segregation; the leadership principle, and the stripping of the authority of the classroom teacher, the early application of Brighamian "liquid brain" theories, which resulted in the termination of early attempts to provide preschooling; the legacy of racism and the judicial development of theories of segregation based on administrative preconceptions of language disabilities, intelligence, and socioeconomic status; the politicization of the public schools and their use as ideological tools; and finally the clumsy judicial imposition of arbitrary principles of criminal procedure and due process—there can be no understanding of the failure of the public schools today, the tragic decline of student achievement, and the shameless denial of equal educational opportunity.

In light of such a history, the present plight of the public schools comes not as a surprise but as a logical outcome of historical forces. As the renowned African American economist Dr. Thomas Sowell recently observed, it is not "surprising that academic work is so readily abandoned for social experiments, ideological crusades and psychological manipulations by educators whose own academic performances have long been shown to be substandard." The average (SAT) score for aspiring teachers is 389 out of a possible 800."[1] In *The Teacher Who Couldn't Read*, an author relates his 17 years as a teacher who couldn't read or write.[2]

In the few instances where public schools have attempted to impose discipline, the results have been dramatic. *Time* magazine has reported the policies of civil rights activist George McKenna, who in the 1970s was appointed as principal of a public school in the Watts area of Los Angeles, which was described as a school that "had a serious drug and gang problem [and] where students were, in essence, in control."[3] McKenna imposed a very strict discipline code, which both students and parents had to sign, that provided for a strict dress code and suspension of disruptive students. As a result of such policies, however, not only discipline but also educational achievement improved dramatically. Suspensions soon dropped by 40%, and 80% of the senior class went to college (compared to only 43% in previous years those who even expressed an interest in college). One observer noted that "the school has been turned around, virtually nobody wants to be bused away, and in fact, the school has a waiting list of 200 students to get in."[4] Today, of course, judicial applications of due process make such success stories very rare indeed.

Nor is it surprising that the underlying agenda of recent educational reforms is the ultimate abandonment of the public schools. Such proposed reforms as school choice, vouchers, and the like are all premised on the assumption that the public schools can not be saved; that society must therefore provide an alternative within the present decaying system—at least to those with the energy, diligence, and foresight to pursue those alternatives. Judicial pressure has provided the final nudge toward abandonment, as its ideological policies of force and coercion have hastened white flight and the abandonment of inner-city schools to a self-perpetuating underclass. In July 1994, the threat by the Hispanic community in Denver of massive resistance to such policies of coercion, abandonment, and neglect was but one manifestation of the atmosphere of crisis such policies have fostered.[5]

As student achievement declines, and students and parents alike fear even to enter the violent abyss of our Prussianized public school system, Dr. Sowell has observed that "it is not uncommon for those few schools with traditional academic programs to have waiting lists of parents who want to get their children admitted. When admission is on a first-come, first-served basis, it is not uncommon for parents to camp overnight in hopes of getting their children into institutions that will teach them substance instead of fluff and politically correct propaganda."[6]

But is the only solution to abandon our public schools, and to create a system of alternative private education in which only families of wealth and high socioeconomic status can hope to obtain a quality education? The answer suggested here is a positive one—that it is not too late to save our public schools if we can track and isolate the mistakes of the past, relinquish educational theories that, though long entrenched in the national psyche, have proved time and again to have resulted in the degeneration of educational quality and the denial of equal educational opportunity. In doing so, we need only to listen to those who have the greatest vested interest in America's children—their parents.

First and foremost, we must reverse the process of Prussianization that has resulted in age segregation, sexism, adherence to the leadership principle, the stripping of the authority of the classroom teacher, and the creation of a wasteful educational administration and bureaucracy that promotes such a process. The first step in reversal would be to give back authority to the classroom teacher, eliminate the segregation of classes by age, and create magnet classrooms open to all children willing to abide by a code of discipline and conduct.

Age desegregation would permit students of different levels and abilities to learn together, as well as provide mutual support to their classmates. It would allow children to progress and advance as fast as their abilities permit, as well as put an end to the shameless stigmatization of children who need more time to learn or who have been handicapped by the lack of intellectual stimulation in the early years of their life. Although there will doubtless be those who find our Prussianized system of age segregation to be so entrenched that it is inconceivable that it could be changed, such skeptics need only look at the example of our own early American tradition in which the teachers in the one-room schoolhouses did exactly that—with educational results that promoted the most powerful and democratic nation on earth. They might look also at the successful examples in other countries (and documented in the preceding chapters) where classes have been desegregated by age.

Second, preschools for children under 18 months of age must be established within the public school system. Without such schools, there is little chance that children from deprived economic and cultural homes can be provided with equal educational opportunity. If this is not done, special education and tracking programs will continue to stigmatize children and prevent them from achieving success. Class authority must be given back to the teacher. This would permit the dismantlement of an entrenched administrative empire consisting of predominantly male bureaucrats telling female teachers how to teach. Like teachers in our best private and professional schools, teachers in the public schools must be hired based on their credentials and qualifications in the subject matter on which they are to teach, and not on whether they have taken some educational course or run the gauntlet or jumped through the certification hoops set up by the entrenched educational establishment. Most important, the public school teachers must be given back their professional status.

Teacher certification programs (which exclude so many qualified teachers) must be eliminated in favor of a policy of hiring teachers who are most qualified in their areas of expertise. Professional schools now provide an excellent model for such a policy.

The Prussian model of the pedagogical harem must simply be abolished, permitting the public schools to adopt the kind of leaner and less wasteful administration practiced by most private and parochial schools. Although the purely sexist elements of the Prussian model have diminished, the basic educational structure upon which it was based has remained. Again, successful models for such dismantlement can be found not only in our own history, but in many foreign countries as well.

The creation of magnet classrooms is proposed as an antidote to the crisis of due process generated by inappropriate judicial intervention in the educational process. In a perfect world in which all families were wealthy enough to send their children to private schools of their choice, such classrooms would not be necessary. But the whole concept of public education is based on the reality that many children can receive an education only if it is provided free by society. The concept of the magnet classroom is based on the premise that all children (and not just children wealthy enough to attend private schools), are entitled to the right to learn in a safe and disciplined learning environment.

Wealthy families can afford to send their children to private schools in which discipline can be established by teachers with classroom authority, and in which students are not forced to endure the disruptions and violence of other students protected by due process. Students intent on disruption can be expelled or reasonably disciplined. Public school children, however, are denied the right to a safe learning environment. The magnet classroom would provide them with this right so long denied.

Admission to a magnet classroom within a school would have only one requirement—that the applicant, and the applicant's parents, make a joint written commitment to abide by a strict code of conduct. That code would then be administered and enforced by the magnet classroom teacher given authority to administer and enforce that code of conduct, and to expel students who violated it. The written commitment would also include a waiver of such due process rights as a formal hearing, cross-examination, the right to counsel, the right against self-incrimination, and the like. Of course, in order to comply with the current law relating to waiver, such waiver must be entirely voluntary, and no stigma whatever attached to a student who declined to sign the waiver. Students not willing to waive such rights would simply attend the regular classrooms in which the entire panoply of due process rights would continue to be accorded. For them, nothing in the public school would change from current conditions, and they would continue to be ruled by administrators, segregated by age, stigmatized according to language and perceived handicaps, and left to the mercy of other unruly students as provided by current law and principles of due process as applied by the courts. Students who choose, either by formal request, or by their own conduct, to leave the magnet classroom and enter a regular classroom, should be permitted, after an appropriate period, to apply for readmission to the magnet classroom.

Any legal challenge to the magnet class system would have to be based on the tautologically illogical argument that it is unfair for students declining to sign the waiver to be denied the right to be denied due process.

The public schools can still be saved, and policies of abandonment reversed, if we learn from others as well as from the mistakes of our own past, and are willing to reestablish the sound educational policies of our traditional American system long since abandoned in favor of the Prussian system. The solutions that we seek will not be found in more extravagant funding or more extreme judicial applications of due process. Rather, we shall find them in our own tradition and heritage.

Notes

PREFACE

1. David Tyack, *The One Best System: A History of American Urban Education* (Cambridge, MA: Harvard University Press, 1974).

2. *Id.*

3. Leonard, G. "The End of School: Changes in Current School Systems Needed," *The Atlantic Monthly*, May 1992, 24.

CHAPTER ONE

1. The National Commission on Excellence in Education, *A Nation at Risk: The Imperative for Educational Reform* (1983). (Hereinafter referred to as *A Nation at Risk*.)

2. See bibliography, *infra*.

3. See bibliography, *infra*.

4. J. Coleman, E. Campbell, C. Hobson, J. McPartland, A. Mood, F. Weinfield, and R. York, *Equality of Educational Opportunity* (Washington, DC: U.S. Office of Education, 1966). (Hereinafter referred to as the Coleman Report.)

5. Eric A. Hanushek, "When School Finance Reform May Not Be Good Policy." Symposium, Investing in Our Children's Future: School Finance Reform in the 1990s, *Harvard Journal on Legislation* 28 (Summer 1991), 423. This report acknowledges that the Coleman Report is "subject to a variety of interpretations," and refers to two other studies interpreting the conclusions citing F. Mosteller, and D. P. Moynihan, eds., *On Equality of Educational Opportunities* (New York: Random House 1972); D. P. Moynihan, "Educational Goals and Political Plans," *Pub. Interest* (Winter 1991), 32.

6. *Id.* at 4. Hanushek, *supra* note 5, at 4.

7. *Id.* at 6.

8. *Id.*

9. *Id.*

10. The Coleman Report *supra* note 4 at 325.

11. See, e.g., C. Jencks, *Inequality: A Reassessment of the Effect of Family and Schooling in America* (New York: Basic Books 1972), cited in Ronald F. Ferguson, "Paying for Public Education: New Evidence on How and Why Money Matters," Symposium, Investing in Our Children's Future, *supra* note 5.

12. *Id.*

13. Eric Hanushek, "The Economics of Schooling," *J. Econ Literature* 24 (1986), 1142.

14. Ferguson, *supra* note 11 at 3.

15. U.S. Department of Education, Office of Educational Research and Improvement, National Center for Education Statistics (1993).

16. *Id.* at 50, Figure 12.

17. *Id.* at 45.

18. Sam Peltzman, "Why Schools Fail: Political Factors, Remote Bureaucracies and Teachers Unions Have Dragged Down Student Performance," *San Diego Union* (August 1, 1993), G1.

19. Cited in Susan Chira, "The Big Test: How To Translate the Talk About School Reform into Action," *New York Times* (March 24, 1991), Sec. 4, at 1.

20. *A Nation at Risk, supra* note 1.

21. *Id.* at 8.

22. *Id.*

23. *Id.* at 8-9.

24. *MacNeil/Lehrer Report* (PBS television broadcast, July 6, 1994).

25. *A Nation at Risk, supra* note 1, at 11.

26. Arthur Fisher, "Science + Math + F: Crisis in Education," *Popular Science* (August 1992), 58.

27. *Id.*

28. *Id.*

29. Cited in *Id.*

30. *Id.*

31. *Id.*

32. *Id.*

33. *Id.*

34. *Id.*

35. *Id.*

36. *Id.*

37. "America's Quiet Crisis: Educating the Talented," *The Straits Times* (December 12, 1993), 1.

38. *Id.*

39. *Id.*

40. *Id.*

41. Ross Atkin, "U.S. Education Runs in Place," *Christian Science Monitor* (October 3, 1990), 12.

42. Clara Germani, "New School Year Rekindles Concern Over US Education," *The Christian Science Monitor* (September 4, 1990), 1.

43. *Id.*

44. Fisher, *supra* note 26.

45. *Id.*

46. *Id.*

47. Hanushek, *supra* note 13.

48. *See* Ferguson, *supra* note 11.

49. *Id.*

50. Elizabeth Mehren, "Reading, Writing, and Therapy," *Los Angeles Times* (April 25, 1994), E1.

51. *Id.*

52. *Id.*

53. *Id.*

54. *The Rocky Mountain News* (Denver), (June 27, 1994), A18.

55. *Id.*

56. *Id.*

57. Gerald Bracey, "The Third Bracey Report on the Condition of Public Education," *Phi Delta Kappan* (October 1993), 104.

58. *Id.*

59. *Id.*

60. Carol Innerst, "Schools Resist Major Reforms, Panelists Say," *Washington Times* (October 1, 1992), A1.

61. *Id.*

62. *Id.*

63. Carol Innerst, "New York Teacher of the Year Walks Out on System," *The Washington Times* (October 22, 1991), A1.

64. *Id.*

65. Harry Bernstein, "Labor: How Teachers Unions Hope to Improve the Schools," *Los Angeles Times* (March 6, 1990), D1.

66. Cited in *Time* (January 24, 1984), and in Benjamin Duke, *Lessons for Industrial America: The Japanese School* (Westport, CT: Praeger, 1986), 188.

67. *Id.*

68. Department of Education (U.S.), National Center for Educational Statistics, Office of Educational Research Law Improvement, *The Condition of Education* (Washington, DC: U.S. Government Printing Office, 1993), 141. (Hereinafter referred to as 1993 Department of Education Report.)

69. Office of Juvenile Justice and Preliminary Prevention, Federal Juvenile Delinquency Programs, Department of Justice (Washington, DC: U.S. Government Printing Office, 1988), 55.

70. Duke, *supra* note 66, at 188.

71. *Id.*

72. 1993 Department of Education Report, at 130.

73. Susan Ohanian, "Clinton Education Recipe: Reheat and Hash," *USA Today* (February 2, 1994), A11.

74. *Id.*

75. *Id.*

76. *Id.*

77. *Id.*

78. *Id.*

79. See Myron Lieberman, *Public Education: An Autopsy* (Cambridge, MA: Harvard University Press, 1993), 242. The author also cites other studies that revealed that the SAT score of the "typical preservice elementary teacher" was below even the average SAT for all college freshman. *Id.*

80. *Id.*

81. Tamara Henry, "Goals 200 Act Sets Forth Standards for Students and Schools," *USA Today* (March 28, 1994), D4. *See also*, Rich Lowry, "Reform and Democrats: Opportunity to Learn Means Opportunity to Spend, and the Old Democrats Are Rarin' to Go," *National Review* (July 19, 1993), 41.

82. Ohanian, *supra* note 73 at A11.

83. *Id.*

84. *Id.*

85. *Id.*

86. Jonathan Kozol, *Savage Inequalities* (New York: Crown, 1991), 198.

87. *Id.* at 63.

88. See Elena Neuman, "Reformers Seeking Key to Suburbia," *Insight* (April 15, 1993), 6, in which it is noted that the cost of educating students at Kansas City private schools was $2,000 in 1989-1990.

89. 1993 Department of Education Report, *supra* note 68 at 141.

90. Kozol, *supra* note 86 at 198.

91. See, *San Antonio Independent School District v. Rodriguez* 411 U.S. 1 (1973).

92. Carl Horowitz, "The Myth of Education Findings: More Money Does Not Translate to Better Scores," *Investor's Business Daily* (August 3, 1994), A1.

93. John McCormick, "'Separate But Equal' Again - Kansas City: Black Parents Look for Alternatives to Desegregation" *Time* (May 16, 1994), 31.

94. Neuman, *supra* note 88.

95. McCormick, *supra* note 93 at 31.

96. This figure is determined by multiplying the 34,000 in Kansas City schools by 3% (i.e., 1,110) and then dividing this number into 1 billion, (i.e., a little over 1 million dollars per student).

97. *Rivarde v. School District of Kansas City*, cited in Neuman, *supra* note 88 at 13.

98. *Id.*

99. McCormick, *supra* note 93 at 131.

100. *Id.*

101. Gary Orfield, "The Growth of Segregation in American Schools: Changing Patterns of Separation and Poverty Since 1986," *Equality and Excellence in Education*, (January 1994), 5; cited in *USA Today* (February 16, 1994), D4.

102. *Id.*

103. *Id.*

104. Richard Caldwell, *What's Really Wrong with Public Education* (Denver: Center for Public Policy and Contemporary Issues, University of Denver, 1991), 7.

105. *Id.*

106. *Id.*

107. McCormick, *supra* note 93 at 31.

108. Horowitz, *supra* note 92 at A1.

109. See, e.g., Kozol, *supra* note 86; Ohanian, *supra* note 73.

110. Rochelle L. Stanfield, "The Education President II," *The National Journal* (December 5, 1990), 2809.

111. *Id.*

112. See, Henry, *supra* note 81.

113. 1993 Department of Education Report, *supra* note 68 at 141.

114. Richard Lynn, *Educational Achievement in Japan: Lessons for the West* (Armonk, NY: M.E. Sharpe, 1985), 109, figure 7.6.

115. *Id.* at 16, Table 2.6.

116. *Id.*

117. H. Stevenson, *Mathematics Achievement of Chinese, Japanese and American Children* (California: Annual Report, Center for Advanced Study, 1983).

118. Lynn, *supra* note 114 at 128, citing Stevenson, *supra* note 117.

119. *See* Fisher, *supra* note 26.

120. Lynn, *supra* note 114 at 125.

121. H.J. Eysenck, *Personality and Individual Differences* (New York: Plenum Press, 1985); cited in Lynn, *supra* note 14 at 125.

122. *Id.*, citing data from T. Husen, *International Study of Achievement in Mathematics: A Comparison of Twelve Countries* (New York: John Wiley, 1967).

123. Lynn, *supra* note 114 at 105; citing data collected by, Comber and, Keeves, *Student Achievement in Nineteen Countries* (New York: John Wiley, 1973).

124. *Id.* at 105.

125. *Id.*

126. *Id.*, citing data from Husen, *supra* note 122 at 112.

127. *Id.* Table 7-8.

128. *Id.* at 110.

129. Duke, *supra* note 66 at 184. Although the $10,000 salary was for the year 1986, a low Japanese inflation rate would not translate into a 1994 salary of much more than $15,000 - 17,000, far below American salaries.

130. Lynn, *supra* note 114 at 107.

131. *Id.* at 108.

132. *Id.*

133. *Id.*

134. Duke, *supra* note 66 at 181.

135. *Id.*

136. *Id.*

137. *Id.* at 185.

138. *Id.*

139. *Id.*

140. *Id.*

141. *Id.*

142. *Id.* at 187.

143. Michael Lotito, "A Call to Action for U.S. Business and Education," *Employment Relations Today* (December 22, 1992), 379.

144. *Id.* at 379.

145. *Id.*

146. *Id.*

147. Lynn, *supra* note 114 at 128.

148. E.W. Turner, "The Effect of Long Summer Holidays on Children's Literacy," *Educational Research* (June 1972), 182-186; cited in Lynn, *supra* note 114 at 128.

149. Duke, *supra* note 66 at 191.

150. *Id.*

151. *Id.*

152. *Id.*

153. *Id.* at 192.

154. Yao Yaping, "American and Chinese Schools: A Comparative Analysis," *Education* (Winter 1992), 235.

155. See.e.g., Mehren, *supra* note 50 at E1.

156. Duke, *supra* note 66 at 192.

157. Lotito, *supra* note 143 at 37.

158. *See,* Duke, *supra* note 66.

159. 1993 Department of Education Report, *supra* note 68 at 356, Table 46-6.

160. *Id.*

161. *Id.* at 357, Table 46-7.

162. *Id.*

163. *Id.* 68.

164. *Id.*

165. *Id.*

166. Ohanian, *supra* note 73.

167. Fisher, *supra* note 26.

168. *Id.*

169. *Id.*

CHAPTER TWO

1. Elena Neuman, "Reformers Seeking Key to Suburbia," *Insight,* 9 (April 15, 1993). These figures are also cited in John E. Coons, "Choice Plans Should Include Private Option," in James Noll, ed. *Taking Sides: Clashing Views on Controversial Educational Issues,* (Guilford, CT: Dushkin, 1991), 137.

2. Marc Fisher, "Moving Schools to the Workplace," *Washington Post* (April 19, 1987), xii.

3. See, e.g., Henry M. Leven, "Education as a Public and Private Good," in Neal E. Devins, ed., *Public Values, Private Schools* (New York: Falmer Press, 1989), 221-222.

4. *Id.*

5. Myron Lieberman, *Public Education: An Autopsy* (Cambridge, MA: Harvard University Press, 1993), Table 6.1 (Hereinafter referred to as Harvard University Press Study.)

6. 163 U.S. 537 (1896).

7. 347 U.S. 483 (1954).

8. *Id.*

9. Harvard University Press Study, *supra* note 5 at 183-184.

10. *Id.*

11. *DeKanter and Baker Report* (1981), cited in Alberto M. Ochoa and Yvonne Caballero-Allen, "Beyond the Rhetoric of Federal Reports," in Noll, *supra* note 1, 310.

12. Diane Ravitch, "Politicization and Bilingual Education," in Noll, *supra* note 1, 324.

13. *Id.*

14. Cited in *supra* note 11. Rosalie Porter, *Forked Tongue: The Politics of Bilingual Education* (New York: Basic Books, 1990).

15. Leonard P. Ayres, *Laggards in Our Schools* (New York: Russell Sage Foundation, 1908), at 6, cited in Harvard University Press Study, *supra* note 5 at 184.

16. *Id.*

17. *Washington Times* (July 3, 1984), cited in S. I. Hayakawa, "*The Case for Official English*," in James Crawford, ed., *Language Loyalties: A Source Book on the Official English Controversy*, (Chicago: University of Chicago Press, 1992), 98.

18. Jonathan D. Hapt, "Assuring Equal Educational Opportunity for Language-Minority Students: Bilingual Education and the Equal Opportunity Act of 1974," *Columbia Journal of Law and Social Problems*, 209-293 (1983); cited in Ravitch, *supra* note 12 at 326.

19. *Id.*

20. Harvard University Press Study *supra* note 5, at 164.

21. *Id.*

22. Abagail Thermstrom, "Bilingual Miseducation," *Commentary* (February 1990), 46; cited in Harvard University Press Study, *supra* note 5 at 183.

23. *Id.*

24. For a discussion of this act, see Ravitch, *supra* note 12 at 322.

25. Pub. Law No. 94-149, 84 Stat. 773 (1975) (codified as amended at 20 U.S.C. §§ 1400-1416 (1988); for an excellent discussion of this act, see Marc C. Weber, "The Transformation of the Education of the Handicapped Act: A Study in the Interpretation of Radical Statutes," 24 *University of California Law Review* 349 (1990).

26. *State ex rel. Beattie v. Board of Education*, 172 N.W. 153.

27. Weber, *supra* note 25 at 355.

28. Pub. L. No. 89-750, 80 Stat. 1204 (1966).

29. Pub. L. No. 91-280, 84 Stat. 175 (1970).

30. 20 USC § 1412(1).

31. 20 USCA § 1400(A) (1988 & Supp. III 1991).

32. *Westchester County v. Rowley*, 458 U.S. 176 (1982).

33. 20 USCA § 1415(c).

34. 727 F.2nd 809 (9th Cir. 1983) *cert. denied*, 471 U.S. 1117 (1985).

35. Arval Morris, *The Constitution and American Public Education* (Durham, NC: Carolina Academic Press, 1989), 320.

36. Theresa Glennon, "Disabling Ambiguities: Confronting Barriers to the Education of Students with Emotional Disabilities," 60 *Tennessee Law Review* 295, 317 (1993); citing *Cole v. Greenfield*, 657 F. Supp. 56 (Ind. 1986).

37. Glennon *supra* note 36 at 318.

38. *Id.* at 319.

39. *Id.* at 326.

40. Sophfronia Scott Gregory, "Oprah! Oprah! in the Court," *Time* (June 6, 1994), 30.

41. Glennon, *supra* note 36 at 349; citing Jane Knitzer, et al., *At the Schoolhouse Door: An Examination of Programs and Policies for Children with Behavioral and Emotional Problems* (1990).

42. 753 F. Supp. 922 (Ala. 1990).

43. *Id.*

44. *Id.*

45. *Id.* at 932.

46. 484 U.S. 305 (1988).

47. Paraphrased by Glennon, *supra* note 36 at 329.

48. *Our Nation's Schools — A Report Card: "A" in School Violence and Vandalism*, U.S. Senate Committee on the Judiciary, Subcommittee to Investigate Juvenile Delinquency, 94th Cong., 1st Sess. (April 1975). Hereinafter referred to as *A Report Card*.

49. Cited in *Id.*

50. S. Rep. No. 168, 94th Cong., 1st Sess. 8 (1975), cited in Weber, *supra* note, 197 at 376.

51. *Id.*

52. Model School Disciplinary Code, quoted in *Inequality of Education* (Cambridge, MA.: Center for Law and Education, 1972), 47-49. For a discussion of the Fifth Amendment and the exclusionary rule, see Robert Hardaway, "Equivalent Deference: A Proposed Alternative to the Exclusionary Rule in Criminal Proceedings," 11 *Criminal Justice Journal* 37 (1989).

53. Interview with Dr. Thomas Hardaway, Assistant Chief of Child Psychiatry, in Ft. Hood, Texas (June 7, 1994).

54. 419 U.S. 565 (1975).

55. *Id.* at 580.

56. *Id.* at 581.

57. *Id.* at 581, n.9.

58. *Id.* at 582.

59. U.S. Constitution, Amendments V and XIV(i).

60. 583 F.2d 91 (3d Cir. 1978); paraphrased in Morris, *supra* note 35 at 277-347.

61. *A Report Card, supra* note 48. Sporadically, schools show a willingness to take on due process, as in Littleton, Colorado, which began expelling more students in 1994. See Janet Bingham, "Expelled" *Denver Post* (March 6, 1994), A1.

62. See, generally, Morris, *supra* note 35 at 277-347.

63. A. Jones, *Cruel Sacrifice* (New York: Windsor, 1994), 137.

64. *Id.* at 17-39.

65. *Id.* at 33.

66. *Id.* at 303.

67. *Id.* at 304.

68. *Id.* at 304.

69. *Id.* at 317.

70. *Id.* at 333.

71. *Id.*

72. *Gutierrez v. School Dist. R-1*, 585 P.2d 935 (Colo. App. 1978).

73. *Richards v. Thurston*, 424 F.2d 1281 (1st Cir. 1970); but see *Gfell v. Rickelman*, 441 F.2d 444 (6th Cir. 1971).

74. *A Report Card, supra* note 48.

75. *Id.*

76. *Id.*

77. *Id.*

78. *Id.*

79. *Id.*

80. Jon D. Hull, "Do Teachers Punish According to Race: That's the Charge in Cincinnati and the City Board Has Proposed an Explosive Remedy," *Time* (April 4, 1994), 30.

81. *Id.*

82. *Id.*

83. *Id.*

84. See Jones, *supra* note 68.

85. Cited in *A Report Card, supra* note 48.

86. See S. Report No. 168, *supra* note 50.

87. 457 U.S. 202 (1982).

88. *Id.*

89. *Id.*

90. Richard Lamm and Gary Imhoff, *The Immigration Time Bomb* (New York: Concord Books, 1985), 762-63.

91. Center for Immigration Studies, "Despair Behind the Riots: The Impediment of Mass Immigration to Los Angeles Blacks," *Scope* (Summer 1992), 1-3; generally, see also Robert Hardaway, *Population, Law and the Environment* (Westport, CT: Praeger, 1994).

92. Booker T. Washington, "The Atlanta Exposition Address," in *Booker T. Washington and His Critics* (1962, 1974) 21.

93. Robert Hardaway, "Give Me Your Tired, Your Poor, Low-Pay Workers," *San Francisco Examiner* (September 6, 1993), A17.

94. Cited in Vlae Kershner, "California Leads in Immigration and Backlash," *San Francisco Chronicle* (June 21, 1993), A1.

95. *Id.*

96. *Id.*

97. Hardaway, *Population, Law and the Environment*, supra note 91 at 142.

98. See *Digest of Education Statistics*, (U.S. Dept. of Education, 1993) at 72.

99. *Id.* at 45.

100. Richard Lynn, *Educational Achievement in Japan: Lessons for the West* (Armonk, NY: M.E. Sharpe, 1988), 109.

101. Nancy J. Perry, "What We Need to Fix U.S. Schools," *Fortune* (November 16, 1992), 132.

102. *Digest of Education Statistics, supra* note 98 at 72, Table 60.

103. See generally, William R. Hazard, *Education and the Law; Cases and Materials on Public Schools* (New York: Macmillan, 1978).

104. C. Emily Feistritzer, *The Making of a Teacher: A Report on Teacher Education and Certification* (Washington, DC: National Center for Education Information, 1984); cited in Micah Dial and Carla Stevens, eds., *Education and Urban Society* (Newbury Park, CA.: Corwin 1993), 36.

105. *Id.* at 36.

106. M. M. Kennedy, "Some Surprising Findings on How Teachers Learn to Teach," *Educational Leadership*, 49(3) (1991) 14-17; cited in Dial and Stevens, *supra* note 104.

107. J. B. Conant, *The Education of America* (New York: McGraw-Hill, 1963); cited in Dial and Stevens, *supra* note 104 at 8.

108. *Id.*

109. *Id.*

110. John Stuart Mill, *On Liberty* (London: Oxford University Press, 1859, 1966), 132; Cited in Harvard University Press Study, *supra* note 5 at 242.

111. Cited in Dial and Stevens, *supra* note 104 at 7.

112. *Id.*

113. Sam Peltzman, "Why Schools Fail: Political Factors, Remote Bureaucracies and Teacher's Unions Have Dragged Down Student Performance," *San Diego Union-Tribune* (August 1, 1993), G1.

114. *Id.*

115. *Id.*

116. *Id.*

117. *Id.*

118. Feistritzer, *supra* note 104 at 7-8.

119. Harvard University Press Study, *supra* note 5 at 242.

120. However, the average for preservice secondary teachers was 49 points higher than the average college freshman. *Id.*

121. Dial and Stevens, *supra* note 104 at 20.

122. *Id.*

123. J. E. Westerman, "Minimum State Teacher Certification Standards and Their Relationship to Effective Teaching: Implications for Teacher Education, *Action in Teacher Certification*, (1989) 25-32; quoted in Dial and Stevens, *supra* note 104 at 13.

124. Dial and Stevens, *supra* note 104 at 21, Table 1.

125. *Id.* at 20.

126. J. A. Boser and P. D. Wiley, "An Alternative Teacher Preparation Program: Is the Promise Fulfilled?" *Peabody Journal of Education*, 65(2)(1988),130-142; quoted in Dial and Stevens, *supra* note 104 at 13.

127. C. Emily Feistritzer, *National Overview of Alternative Teacher Certification* (Washington, DC: National Center for Education Information); cited in Dial and Stevens, *supra* note 104 at 24.

128. *Id.*

129. *Id.*

130. Susan Ohanian, "Clinton Education Recipe: Reheat Old Hash," *USA Today* (February 2, 1994), A11.

131. Perry, *supra*, note 101 at 132.

132. Thomas Toch et al., "The Perfect School," *U.S. News and World Report*, (January 11, 1993), 46; Perry, *supra* note 101 at 132.

133. Toch in *id.*

134. *Id.*

135. *Id.*

136. *Id.*

137. *Id.*

138. *Id.*

139. *Id.*

140. George Leonard, "The End of School: Changes in Current School Systems Needed," *The Atlantic Monthly* 269 (May 1992), 24.

141. *Id.*

142. David R. Colburn, "Better Schools: What Works, What Doesn't, and Why We Must Try," *Orlando Sentinel Tribune* (February 2, 1992), H3.

143. James Coleman and Thomas Hoffer, *Public and Private High Schools: The Impact of Community* (New York: Basic Books, 1987).

144. Marc Fisher, "Moving Schools to the Workplace," *Washington Post* (April 19, 1987), xii.

145. *Id.*

146. See Leven, *supra* note 3.

147. See note 87, *supra*, and accompanying text. 457 U.S. 202 (1982).

148. See Jones, *supra* note 63 and accompanying text.

149. See Kershner, *supra* note 94 and accompanying text.

CHAPTER THREE

1. John E. Chubb and Terry M. Moe, *Politics, Markets, and America's Schools* (Washington, DC: Brookings Institution, 1990); cited and discussed in Philip T. K. Daniel, "A Comprehensive Analysis of Educational Choice: Can the Polemic of Legal Problems Be Overcome?" 43 *De Paul Law Review* 1 (1993).

2. Milton Friedman, *Capitalism and Freedom* (Chicago: Univ. Chicago Press, 1962) 185-108; Milton Friedman, "The Role of Government in Education, in Robert Solo, ed., *Economics and the Public Interest* (1955); cited and discussed in Micah Dial and Carla Stevens, eds., *Education and Urban Society* (Newbury Park, CA: Corwin, 1993), 2.

3. Tom Chenowith, "Unanticipated Consequences of Schools of Choice: Some Thoughts on the Case of San Francisco," 7 *Equity and Choice* 33, 35 (1989), cited in Dial and Stevens, *supra* note 2 at 14.

4. Wis. Stat. § 119.23 (1990).

5. *Id.*

6. David L. Kirp, "What School Choice Really Means," *The Atlantic Monthly* (November, 1922), 120.

7. *Id.* at 127.

8. James S. Liebman, "Voice, Not Choice," 101 *Yale Law Journal* at 284-85, 297 (1991).

9. See Austin Swanson and Richard King, *School Finance: Its Economics and Politics* (1991), 340-41.

10. See *Rivarde v. School District of Kansas City*, cited in Elena Neuman, "Reformers Seeking Key to Suburbia," *Insight*, 9 (April 15, 1993).

11. Will Eglund, "The Battle of Paisley Grammar, Scotland Learns a Lesson About School Choice," *The Baltimore Sun* (March 19, 1989), Sec. 1, 34.

12. *Id.*

13. *Id.*

14. *Id.*

15. *Id.*

16. *Id.*

17. *Id.*

18. Amy Stuart Wells, "Choice in Education: Examining The Evidence of Equity," 93 *Teachers C. Rec.* 137, 147 (1991).

19. *Id.*

20. *Green v. County School Board*, 391 U.S. 430 (1968), quoted and discussed in William Lockhart et al., *The American Constitution*, 7th ed. (St. Paul: West, 1991), 966.

21. *Committee for Public Education v. Nyquist*, 413 U.S. 756 (1973).

22. U.S. Constitution Amendment I, providing that "Congress shall make no law respecting an establishment of religion."

23. *Mueller v. Allen*, 463 U.S. 388 (1983).

24. George Leonard, "The End of School," *The Atlantic Monthly* (May 1992), 24.

25. Steven B. Sample, "Say No To Our Schools' Status Quo," *Chicago Tribune* (November 30, 1993), 19.

26. Gershon M. Ratner, "A New Legal Duty for Urban Public Schools: Effective Education in Basic Skills," 63 *Texas Law Review* 777 (1985).

27. Thomas Toch et al., "The Perfect School," *U.S. News and World Report* (January 11, 1993), 46.

28. Jennifer Pitts, "Son of Edison," *The New Republic* (January 18, 1993), 218.

29. *Id.*

30. Susan Chira, "Study Confirms Worst Fears on U.S. Children," *New York Times* (April 12, 1994), A1; citing the Carnegie Report (1994); citing data from the U.S. Census Bureau, the Urban Institute, and the National Center for Children in Poverty.

31. *Id.*

32. *Id.*

33. *Id.*

34. *Id.*

35. Tamara Henry, "Goals 2000 Act Sets Forth Standards for Students and Schools," *USA Today* (March 28, 1994), D4.

36. *Id.*

37. See, Glennon, *supra* note 36, Chapter Two.

38. Robert Hardaway, "Reforming Education," *Atlanta Constitution* (August 1, 1991), A15.

39. See *U.S. v. Edwards*, 498 F.2d 496 (2nd Cir. 1974), quoted and discussed in Robert Hardaway, *Airport Regulation, Law and Public Policy* (Westport, CT: Quorum Books, 1991); and in Paul Dempsey, Robert Hardaway, and William Thoms, *Aviation Law and Regulation* (Salem, NH: Butterworth, 1993). For a general discussion of the development of constitutional principles, see Robert Hardaway, *The Electoral College and the Constitution* (Westport, CT: Praeger, 1994).

40. U.S. Constitution Amendment IV, set forth in Lockhart, *supra* note 20 at Appendix B.

41. *U.S. v. Edwards*, *supra* note 39, holding that an airplane passenger "consents" to a search of his or her bags by purchasing an airline ticket and entering the boarding area.

42. *U.S. v. Kroll*, 481 F.2d 884 (8th Cir. 1973); *U.S. v. Alberando*, 495 F.2d 799 (2nd Cir. 1974); see also discussion in Dempsey et al., *Aviation Law and Regulation*, *supra* note 39 at 145-146.

43. *U.S. v. Edwards*, *supra* note 39.

44. Committee on Policy for Racial Justice, *Visions of a Better Way: A Black Appraisal of Public Schooling* (Washington, DC: Joint Center for Political Studies, 1989), 36; cited in Liebman *supra* note 8.

45. Liebman, *supra* note 8.

46. *Hobson v. Hansen*, 269 F.Supp. 401, *cert. dism.* 393 U.S. 801 (1967).

47. Liebman, *supra* note 8.

48. *Hobson v. Hansen*, *supra* note 46.

49. *Id.*

50. See Carnegie Report, *supra* note 30.

51. *Id.*

52. In England, schools that would be called "private" in the United States (i.e., charging tuition) are called "public" schools.

53. John Dewey, *Democracy and Education* (New York: Macmillan, 1916), iii; quote paraphrased in Hilary Putnam et al. In, "Education for Democracy," *Educational Theory*, Vol. 43, No. 4 (1993), 373.

54. Velma La Point et al, "Dress Codes and Uniforms in Urban School," 115 *The Education Digest*, 32 (1993).

55. *Id.*

56. *Id.*

57. Putnam, *supra* note 53 at 373.

58. *Id.*

59. *Id.*

CHAPTER FOUR

1. See generally, Sheldon S. Cohen, *A History of Colonial Education, 1607-1776* (New York: John Wiley, 1974), 7-28.

2. *Id.* at 12.

3. *Id.*

4. *Id.*

5. *Id.* at 17.

6. *Id.* at 23.

. 7. *Id.* at 25-26.

8. *Id.*

9. J. Coleman et al., *Equality of Educational Opportunity* (Washington, DC: U.S. Office of Education, 1966) (see discussion in Chapter One, *supra*).

10. Cohen, *supra* note 1 at 17.

11. See, e.g., Ellwood Cubberly, *Public Education in the United States* (1919); Bernard Bailyn, *Education in the Forming of American Society* (New York: Norton, 1972); Lawrence Cremin, *American Education: The Colonial Experience, 1607-1783* (New York: Harper and Row, 1970) (all cited in Cohen, *supra* note 1 in his bibliographical essay, at 201-215).

12. Cohen, *supra* note 1 at 44.

13. *Id.*

14. *Id.* at 46.

15. *Id.* at 60.

16. See Joel Spring, *The American School, 1642-1990*, 2d ed. (New York: Longman, 1990), 30-31.

17. Burton J. Hendrick, *Bulwark of the Republic: A Biography of the Constitution* (Boston: Little, Brown, 1937) at 33; cited in Robert Hardaway, *The Electoral College and The Constitution* (Westport, CT: Praeger, 1994).

18. *Id.* at 33.

19. *Id.* at 36.

20. Spring, *supra* note 16 at 30.

21. *Id.*

22. *Id.*

23. Charles M. Wollenberg, *All Deliberate Speed: Segregation and Exclusion in California Schools, 1855-1975* (Berkeley: University of California Press, 1976), 30; cited in Spring, *supra* note 16 at 190.

24. *Id.* at 28-29; cited in Spring, *supra* note 16 at 190.

25. John McCormick, "'Separate But Equal' Again — Kansas City: Black Parents Look for Alternatives to Desegregation," *Time* (May 16, 1994), 31.

26. *Plessy v. Ferguson*, 347 U.S. 483 (1896).

27. *Id.*

28. Gary Orfield, "The Growth of Segregation in American Schools: Changing Patterns of Separation and Poverty Since 1986," *Equality and Excellence in Education*, (January 1994), 5; cited in *USA Today* (February 16, 1994), D4.

29. Elizabeth Mehren, "Reading, Writing and Therapy," *Los Angeles Times* (April 25, 1994), E1.

30. Carol Innerst, "New York Teacher of the Year Walks Out on System," *Washington Times* (October 22, 1991), A1.

31. Spring, *supra* note 16 at 382.

32. Merle Curti, *The Social Ideas of American Education* (Paterson, NJ: Pageant Books, 1959): 23-24; cited in Spring, *supra* note 16 at 382.

33. Andrew Gulliford, *America's Country School* (Washington, DC: Preservation Press, 1991); cited in Robert L. Leight and Alice D. Rinehart, "Revisiting Americana: One Room School in Retrospect," 56 *The Educational Forum*, 133 (Winter 1992).

34. U.S. Office of Education, *Biennial Survey of Education, 1928-1930* (Washington, DC: U.S. Government. Printing Office), Vol. 1, 65; cited in Leight and Rinehart *supra* note 33 at 138.

35. U.S. Office of Education, *Biennial Survey of Education*, 1956-1958 (Washington, DC: U.S. Government Printing Office, 1961), 26-27; cited in Leight and Rinehart *supra* note 33 at 138.

36. See, e.g., Leight and Rinehart *supra* note 33. This article documents many oral accounts and recollections of people who attended the early one room school houses.

37. *Id.* at 136.

38. Larry Cuban, *How Teachers Taught: Constancy and Change in American Education* (New York: Coleman, 1984), cited in *id.* 142.

39. *Id.* at 143.

40. Interview with James Gerhart (August 30, 1986), conducted by Leight and Rinehart and published in *id.* at 144.

41. *Id.*

42. Jesse Stuart, *To Teach, To Love* (New York: World, 1970), 314, cited in *id.* at 145.

43. Hamlin Garland, *A Son of the Middle Border* (New York: Macmillan, 1958): 113, cited *id.* at 145.

44. Leight and Rinehart, *supra* note 33 at 145-146.

45. *Id.* at 146.

46. Interview with Carrie Horne (August 21, 1986), conducted by Leight and Rinehart, *id.* at 146.

47. Stuart, *supra* note 42 at 313-314, cited in *id.* at 148.

48. *Id.* at 142.

49. Barbara Bush, cited in Gulliford, *America's County Schools*, *supra* note 33 at 5, and in *id.* at 142.

50. Elwood Cubberly, *Rural Life and Education* (Boston: Houghton Mifflin, 1941), cited in *id.* at 1.

51. Leight, *supra* note 33 at 140.

52. *Id.*

53. Jesse Stuart, *The Thread That Runs So True* (New York: Charles Scribner's Sons, 1949), 155, cited in *id.* at 140.

54. *Id.*

55. Horace Mann, *Seventh Annual Report to the Massachusetts State Board of Education* (1843); cited in Elwood Cubberly, ed., *Readings in Public Education in the U.S.: A Collection of Sources and Readings to Illustrate the History of Education Practice and Progress in the U.S.* (Boston: Houghton Mifflin, 1934), cited in Spring, *supra* note 16 at 137.

56. Spring, *supra* note 16 at 138.

57. Benjamin Duke, *Lessons for Industrial America: The Japanese School* (Westport, CT: Praeger, 1986), 184.

58. Raymond E. Callahan, *Education and the Cult of Efficiency* (Chicago: University of Chicago Press, 1912), 202, cited in Spring, *supra* note 16 at 236.

59. *Id.*

60. Quoted in David Tyack: *The One Best System: A History of American Urban Education* (Cambridge, MA: Harvard University Press, 1974), 61, cited in *id.* at 138.

61. Rosabeth Moss Kanter, "Women and the Structure of Organization: Exploration in Theory and Behavior," in Marela Millman and Rosabeth Moss Kanter, eds., *Another Voice* (Garden City, NY: Doubleday 1975), 14; cited in *id.* at 140.

62. Quoted in Tyack, *supra* note 60 at 60, and in Spring, *supra* note 16 at 141.

63. *Id.*

64. Leight and Rinehart, *supra* note 33 at 135.

65. Lotus Coffman's *Study of Teachers* (1911), quoted in Tyack, *supra* note 60 at 61, and cited in Spring, *supra* note 16 at 142-143.

66. See Robert Hardaway, "Transportation Deregulation (1976-1984): Turning the Tide," 10 *Transportation Law Journal* 101, 104-05 (1985).

67. Robert Hardaway, "The FAA Buy-Sell Rule: Airline Deregulation at the Crossroads," 52 *Journal Air Law & Commerce* 1 (1986).

68. See Paul Dempsey, Robert Hardaway, and William Thoms, *Aviation Law and Regulation* (Salem, NH: Butterworth, 1993).

69. Robert Hardaway, *Airport Regulation, Law and Public Policy: The Management and Growth of Infrastructure* (Westport, CT: Quorum Books, 1991).

70. Spring, *supra* note 16 at 272.

71. Quoted in David Tyack and Elizabeth Hansot, *Managers of Virtue: Public School Leadership in America* (New York: Basic Books, 1982); cited in Spring, *supra* note 16 at 270-271.

72. Quoted in Julia Wrigley, *Class Politics and Public Schools: Chicago 1900-1950* (New Brunswick, NJ: Rutgers University Press, 1982) at 127; and quoted in Spring, *supra* note 16 at 268.

73. *Id.*

74. Sam Peltzman, "Why Schools Fail: Political Factors, Remote Bureaucracies and Teachers' Unions Have Dragged Down Student Performance," *San Diego Union* (August 1, 1993), A1.

75. *Id.*

76. Julia Wrigley, cited in Spring, *supra* note 16 at 268.

77. A very small percentage of law professors are not members of the bar. There is no general certification requirement that a law professor even be a lawyer. At most law schools, however, a law degree is considered a requirement for law teaching.

78. American Association of Law School Statistics (Chicago: American Bar Foundation, 1993).

79. George Leonard, "The End of School: Changes in Current School Systems Needed," *The Atlantic Monthly* 24 (May 1992).

80. *Id.*

81. Peltzman, *supra* note 74 at G1.

82. Nancy Perry, "What We Need, to Fix U.S. Schools," *Fortune* (November 16, 1992), 132.

83. *Id.*

84. Peltzman, *supra* note 74 at G1.

85. *Id.*

86. Carnegie Institute Report (1994), citing data from U.S. Census Bureau, The Urban Institute, and the National Center for Children in Poverty. Tabulated and summarized in Susan Chira, "Study Confirms Worst Fears on U.S. Children," *New York Times* (April 12, 1994), A1.

87. *Id.*

88. Caroline Winterer, "Avoiding a 'Hothouse System of Education': Nineteenth-Century Early Childhood Education From the Infant Schools to the Kindergartens," *History of Education Quarterly* (Fall 1992), 289.

89. Curti, *supra* note 32 at 36; cited in Winterer, *supra* note 88 at 292.

90. *Id.*

91. John Williams Jenkins, "Infant Schools and the Development of Public Primary Schools in Selected American Cities Before the Civil War" (Unpublished Ph.D. dissertation, University of Wisconsin 1978), 111-113, cited and quoted in *id.* at 292-293.

92. *Id.*

93. *Boston Recorder and Scriptural Transcript* (July 9, 1829); cited and quoted in *id.* at 294.

94. Dean May and Maris Vinoyskis, "A Ray of Millennial Light. Early Education and Social Reform in the Infant School Movement in Massachusetts 1826-1840," in Tamara K. Haraven, ed., *Family and Kin in Urban Communities, 1700-1930* (New York: Macmillan, 1977); cited and quoted in *id.* at 294-295.

95. Quoted in *id.* at 295-296.

96. Carl F. Kaestle, *Pillars of the Republic: Common Schools and American Society, 1780-1860* (New York: Hill and Wang, 1983) at 48; cited in *id.* at 293.

97. *Id.*

98. Amariah Brigham, *Remarks on the Influence of Mental Cultivation and Mental Excitement Upon Health*, 2nd ed. (Boston, 1833), cited in *id.* at 297.

99. *Id.*

100. *Id.*

101. *Id.*

102. *Id.* at 297-298.

103. *Id.*

104. *Id.*

105. *Digest of Education Statistics* (U.S. Department of Education, Office of Educational Research and Development, 1993), 15 Table 6.

106. Friedrich Froebel, *Mutter-und Kose-Lieder*, quoted in Evelyn Weber, *The Kindergarten: Its Encounter with Educational Thought in America* (New York: Teachers' College Press, 1969), at 15; quoted in Winterer, *supra* note 88 at 301.

107. Michael Steven Shapiro, *Child's Garden: The Kindergarten Movement from Froebel to Dewey* (University Park, PA: Pennsylvania State University Press, 1983): 137-41, quoted in *id.* at 308.

108. *Id.* at 304-305.

109. J. W. Dickenson, "What Frobel's System of Kindergarten Education Is, and How It Can Be Introduced Into Our Public Schools," *National Education Proceedings* (Worcester, MA: 1873) at 235-236; quoted in *id.* at 306.

110. *Id.* at 304.

111. *Id.* at 313.

112. *Id.*

113. Spring, *supra* note 16 at 273-274.

114. Robert L. Shannon and Donna M. Shannon, "The British Infant School: A Reconsideration," 56 *The Educational Forum*, 62 (Fall 1991).

115. *Id.* at 65.

116. *Id.* at 66.

117. *Id.* at 67-68.

118. *Id.* at 68.

119. *Id.* at 62.

120. *Id.* at 63.

121. Robert L. Church and Michael W. Sediak, *Education in the United States: An Interpretive History* (London: Collier Macmillan, 1976), 455.

122. See Helen E. Rees, *Deprivation and Compensatory Education: A Consideration* (Boston: Houghton Mifflin, 1968), 228, cited in John U. Ogbu, *Minority Education and Caste: The American System in Cross-Cultural Perspective* (New York: Academic Press, 1978), 85.

123. Rees, *id.* at 215; Ogbu, *id.* at 86.

124. Rees, *id.* at 222; Ogbu *id.* at 86.

125. Church and Sediak, *supra* note 121 at 455.

126. *Id.* at 454.

127. Ogbu, *supra* note 122 at 93.

128. Church and Sediak *supra* note 121 at 454.

129. *Id.*

130. Arthur R. Jensen, "How Much Can We Boost IQ and Scholastic Achievement?" *Harvard Educational Review*, Reprint Series No. 2:1-123; cited in Ogbu, *supra* note 122 at 59.

131. Joel Spring, "Psychologists and the War: The Meaning of Intelligence in The Alpha and Beta Tests," *History of Education Quarterly* (Spring 1972); quoted in Spring, *American School, supra* note 16 at 239.

132. *Id.* at 239.

133. *Id.* at 246.

134. Joseph L. Tropea, "Bureaucratic Order and Special Children: Urban Schools, 1890's-1940's," 27 *History of Education Quarterly* 32 (Spring 1987); quoted and cited in *id.* at 246.

135. *Id.* at 245. According to Spring, a majority of studies during this period found that environment factors were "less important factors in predicting achievement than was measured native intelligence." *Id.* at 244.

136. Shannon and Shannon, *supra* note 114 at 63; citing Lauren B. Resnick and Leopold E. Klopper, *Toward the Thinking Curriculum: Current Cognitive Research* (Alexandria, VA: Association for Supervision and Curriculum Development, 1989).

137. Susan Ohanian, "Clinton Education Recipe: Reheat Old Hash: By Focusing Solely On Standards, The Real Needs of Children and the Problems of Education in the U.S. Are Overlooked," *USA Today* (February 2, 1994), A11.

138. Larry Cuban; cited in Leight and Rinehart, *supra* note 33 at 142.

139. "America's Quiet Crisis: Educating the Talented," *The Straits Times* (December 12, 1993), 9.

140. Spring, *supra* note 16 at 239.

141. Daniel P. Moynihan, "Can Courts and Money Do It?" *New York Times* (January 10, 1972), reprinted in Miriam Wasserman, *Demistifying School* (New York: Praeger, 1974) at 226-230; cited and quoted in Spring, *supra* note 16 at 359.

142. Spring, *supra* note 16 at 357.

CHAPTER FIVE

1. *Brown v. Board of Education*, 347 U.S. 483 (1954).

2. Gary Orfield, "The Growth of Segregation in American Schools: Changing Patterns of Separation and Poverty Since 1986," *Equality and Excellence in Education*, (January 1994), 5; cited in *USA Today* (February 16, 1994), D4.

3. William Peters, *A More Perfect Union: The Making of the U.S. Constitution* (New York: Crown, 1987) at 5, cited in Robert Hardaway, *The Electoral College and the Constitution* (Westport, CT: Praeger, 1994)

4. Burton J. Hendrick, *Bulwark of the Republic: A Biography of the Constitution* (Boston: Little, Brown, 1937) at 63; cited in Hardaway, *supra* note 3, at 70.

5. Hardaway, *supra* note 3, at 72.

6. Peters, *supra* note 3, at 97.

7. Hardaway, *supra* note 3, at 75.

8. *Id.*

9. U.S. Constitution Article I, Section 2, clause 3.

10. Peters, *supra* note 3, at 97.

11. *Id.* at 31.

12. *Id.*

13. *Id.*

14. *Id.* at 95.

15. *Id.* at 164, 168.

16. *Id.*

17. U.S. Constitution Article I, Section 9, clause 1.

18. Peters, *supra* note 3, at 175.

19. Bruce Catton, *The American Heritage History of the Civil War* (New York: American Heritage/Wings Books, 1988) at 29.

20. *Id.*

21. *Id.*

22. *Abelman v. Booth*, 62 U.S. 506 (1858), discussed in R. McCloskey, *The American Supreme Court*, at 95-97, and cited in John Nowak and Ronald Rotunda, *Constitutional Law*, 4th ed. (St. Paul: West, 1992) at 609-10.

23. *Id.*

24. *Dred Scott v. Sandford*, 60 U.S. 393 (1857).

25. McCloskey, *supra* note 22 at 609-10.

26. *Id.*

27. See Hardaway, *supra* note 3 at Chapter Four.

28. Catton, *supra* note 19 at 251.

29. D. Barber, W. Eskridge, and P. Frickey, *Constitutional Law* (St. Paul: West, 1993) at 14.

30. 17 Stat. 13 (April 20, 1971).

31. *Strauder v. West Virginia*, 100 U.S. 303 (1879).

32. *The Civil Rights Cases*, 109 U.S. 3 (1883).

33. *Loving v. Virginia*, 388 U.S. 1 (1967).

34. John Ogbu, *Minority Education and Caste: The American System in Cross-Cultural Perspective* (New York: Academic Press, 1978) at 106.

35. 59 Mass. 198 (1850).

36. Robert Church and Michael Sediak, *Education in the United States: An Interpretive History* (London: Collier Macmillan, 1976) at 211.

37. *Id.*

38. Horace Bond, *Negro Education in Alabama: A Study in Cotton and Steel* (New York: Atheneum, 1969) at 245; quoted in Ogbu, *supra* note 34 at 113.

39. Horace Bond, *The Education of the Negro in the American Social Order* (New York: Octagon Press, 1966) at 225-26; quoted in Ogbu, *supra* note 34 at 113.

40. *Id.*

41. *Id.*

42. Louis R. Harlan, *Separate and Unequal: Public School Campaigns and Racism in the Southern Seaboard States, 1905-1918* (New York: Atheneum, 1968) at 257, quoted in Ogbu, *supra* note 34 at 113.

43. The views of General S. C. Armstrong, paraphrased by Ogbu, *supra* note 34 at 114.

44. Robert Hardaway, *Population, Law and the Environment* (Westport, CT: Praeger, 1994) at 136.

45. *Id.*

46. *Id.*

47. *Id.*

48. Booker T. Washington, "The Atlanta Exposition Address," in *Booker T. Washington and His Critics* (New York: Penguin, 1974) at 21.

49. *Id.*

50. *Id.*

51. *Id.*

52. *Id.*

53. Richard Lamm and Gary Imhoff, *The Immigration Time Bomb* (New York: Concord Books, 1985) at 62-63; cited in Hardaway, *supra* note 44, at 138.

54. *Id.*

55. Vlae Kershner, "California Leads in Immigration and Backlash," *San Francisco Chronicle* (June 21, 1993): A1, A6.

56. Lamm and Imhoff, *supra* note 53, at 154.

57. *Id.* at 156.

58. *Id.*

59. *Id.*

60. *The Immigrants Business Week* (July 13, 1992), 119, see also Hardaway, *supra* note 44 at 141.

61. Kershner, *supra* note 55 at A-7.

62. *Id.*

63. Hardaway, *supra* note 44 at 139.

64. Center for Immigration Studies, "Despair Behind the Riots: The Impediment of Mass Immigration to Los Angeles Blacks," *Scope* (Summer 1992), 1-3.

65. *Id.*

66. *Id.*

67. *Brown v. Board of Education*, 347 U.S. 483 (1954); 349 U.S. 294 (1955).

68. 163 U.S. 537 (1896); see, e.g., Walter G. Stephan, "A Brief Historical Overview of School Desegregation," in Walter G. Stephan and Joe R. Feagin, eds., *School Desegregation: Past, Present, and Future* (New York: Plenum Press, 1980). "[Plessy v. Ferguson] defined the legal framework of race relations for the next 58 years, until it was eventually reversed in *Brown v. Board of Education.*" *Id.* at 7.

69. *Brown*, 347 U.S.

70. *Plessy*, 163 U.S.

71. *Id.*

72. *Id.*

73. *Plessy*, 163 U.S. at 78 (Harlan, J., dissenting).

74. *McLaurin v. Oklahoma State Regents for Higher Education*, 339 U.S. 637 (1950).

75. *Sipuel v. Oklahoma*, 332 U.S. 631 (1948); see discussion in Stephan and Feagin *supra* note 68, at 10.

76. 339 U.S. at 342.

77. *Gong Lum v. Rice*, 275 U.S. 78 (1927).

78. *Cummings v. Board of Education*, 175 U.S. 528 (1899).

79. *Berea College v. Kentucky*, 211 U.S. 45 (1908).

80. See, e.g., *Roberts v. City of Boston*, 59 Mass. 198 (1850). It should also be noted that this case was decided prior to the enactment of the Fourteenth Amendment.

81. *Buchanan v. Warley*, 245 U.S. 60 (1917).

82. Benno Schmidt, "Principle and Prejudice: The Supreme Court and Race in the Progressive Era," 82 *Columbia L. Rev.* 444 (1982); quoted and cited in Nowak and Rotunda, *supra* note 22, at 620.

83. *Brown v. Board of Education* actually consisted of five separate cases consolidated for decision by the Supreme Court. The other cases were against: Clarendon County, South Carolina; Claymont County, Delaware; Prince Edward County, Virginia; and the District of Columbia.

84. Stephan, *supra* note 68 at 14.

85. Richard Kluger, *Simple Justice* (New York: Knopf, 1976) at 495; cited in Stephan, *id.* at 15.

86. Kluger, *supra* note 85, at 363; cited in Stephan, *id.* at 13.

87. Stephan, *id.* at 13.

88. See K. B. Clark and M. P. Clark, "Racial Identification and Preference in Negro Children," in *Readings in Social Psychology* (New York: Holt, 1952) at 551-60; quoted in Stephan, *id.* at 11. See also N. H. St. John, *School Desegregation: Outcomes for Children* (New York: John Wiley, 1975); cited in Stephan, *id.* at 71.

89. Charles Black, "The Lawfulness of the Segregation Decisions," 69 *Yale Law Journal* (1960) at 421-30.

90. For example, psychologist Horace English testified that segregation is "prejudicial to the learning" of African Americans. Kluger, *supra* note 85 at 415.

91. It is this author's opinion, however, that the plaintiff's negligence on such conclusions was a tactical error. There were other studies which concluded that some separate schools were not in fact unequal—conclusions confirmed by Coleman et al., in *Equality of Educational Opportunity* (U.S. Office of Education, 1966), who showed that school resources had very little impact on student achievement. Indeed, some African American separatists have claimed that African American children learn better in a school where they can be the president, the council members, etc. Similar arguments have been made in favor of all-women's schools. By choosing to rely on controversial conclusions related to the effects of segregation on student achievement, the plaintiffs risked defeat, whereas their arguments about unequal treatment and stigmatization were clearly uncontrovertible and sufficient to find a violation of equal protection. Thus, the fact that the student in *McLaurin* who sat behind the railing might have been a high achiever should have no relevance to the fact that his treatment was "inherently" unequal and unfair under the Constitution.

92. *Brown*, 347 U.S. at 494.

93. *Id.*

94. P. Bergman, *The Negro in America* (New York: Harper and Row, 1969) at 555; cited and quoted in Stephan, *supra* note 68 at 17. Although this action was taken after *Brown II*, it is nevertheless indicative of the prevailing mood before *Brown II* as well.

95. Arkansas Constitution Amendment 44.

96. Ark. Code Ann. § 80-1519 to § 80-1524.

97. See *Griffin v. County School Board of Prince Edward County*, 377 U.S. 218 (1964).

98. *NAACP v. Button*, 371 U.S. 415 (1963).

99. See, e.g., Ala. Acts 1956, Spec. Sess. Act No. 42, at 70, (1956); Ga. Acts, H.R. 185, (1956); Miss. Acts, ch. 466, at 741 (1956); Va. Acts, S.J.Res. 3, at 1213 (1956).

100. *Aaron v. Cooper*, 156 F. Supp. 220 (E.D. Ark. 1957), *aff'd sub nom.*, *Faubus v. U.S.* 254 F.2d 797 (8th Cir. 1958), *cert. denied*, 358 U.S. 829 (1958).

101. Nowak and Rotunda, *supra* note 22, at 632.

102. *Brown v. Board of Education* (Brown II), 349 U.S. 294 (1955).

103. *Brown II*, 349 U.S. at 300.

104. Lino A. Graglia, "From Prohibiting Segregation to Requiring Integration: Developments in the Law of Race and the Schools Since Brown," in Stephan and Feagin, *supra* note 68 at 72.

105. The only Supreme Court decision on segregation issued between 1955 and 1963 was the *per curiam* decision (a decision without a signed opinion) of *Shuttlesworth v. Birmingham Board of Education*, upholding an Alabama plan. 358 U.S. 101 (1958).

106. 110 Cong. Rec. 6545 (1964); cited and quoted in Graglia, *supra* note 104 at 74.

107. 110 Cong. Rec. 12717 (1964); cited in *id.* at 74.

108. *Id.*

109. *Id.*

110. L. Friedman, ed., *Argument* (New York: Chelsea, 1969) at 402; cited in Graglia, *id.* at 71.

111. *Green v. County School Board*, 391 U.S. 430 (1968), see notes and annotations in Arval A. Morris, *The Constitution and American Public Education* (Durham, NC: Carolina Academic Press, 1989) at 446.

112. *Id.*

113. *Swann v. Charlotte-Mecklenburg Board of Education*, 402 U.S. 1 (1971).

114. Graglia, *supra* note 104 at 80.

115. The Supreme Court stated: "If we were to read the holding of the District Court to require, as a matter of substantive right, any particular degree of racial balancing, or mixing, that approach would be disapproved and we would be obliged to reverse." *Swann*, 402 U.S. at 37.

116. *Id.*

117. In fact, the Court of Appeals in *Swann* had upheld the district judge's order on grounds that busing was needed in order to redress racial discrimination in housing. *Id.* Even the Supreme Court could not swallow this rationale, stating that "we do not reach in this case, the question whether a showing that school segregation is a consequence of other types of state action . . . is unconstitutional." *Id.*

118. Friedman, *supra* note 110, at 402.

119. Morris, *supra* note 111, at 456.

120. Graglia, *supra* note 104, at 79.

121. *Id.* at 82 (ellipses indicating deletions have been omitted to avoid clutter but the meaning of quotation has not been altered).

122. See, e.g., *Columbus Board of Education v. Penick*, 99 S. Ct. 2941 (1979); *Dayton Board of Education v. Brinkman*, 99 S. Ct. 2971 (1979).

123. *Keyes v. School District No. 1*, 413 U.S. 189 (1973).

124. *Id.* (Powell, J., dissenting).

125. James Coleman, S. D. Kelley, and J. A. Moore, "Trends in School Segregation 1968-1973," Urban Institute, Paper # 722-03-01 (August 1975), cited and quoted in David J. Armor, "White Flight and the Future of School Desegregation," paper presented at the American Sociological Association (September 1978) sponsored in part by the Russell Sage Foundation, reprinted in Stephan and Feagin, *supra* note 68 at 187.

126. Jeffrey A. Raffel, *The Politics of School Desegregation* (Philadelphia: Temple University Press, 1980) at 115.

127. *Id.* at 116.

128. *Id.*

129. Thomas F. Pettigrew and Robert L. Green, "School Desegregation in Large Cities: A Critique of the Coleman 'White Flight' Thesis," 46 *Harvard Educational Review* (February 1976); reprinted in Nicholas Mills, ed., *Busing, U.S.A.* (New York: Teachers College Press, 1979) at 132.

130. *Id.*

131. *Id.*

132. Christine H. Rossell, "The Political and Social Impact of School Desegregation Policy: A Preliminary Report," paper presented at the Annual Meeting of the American Political Science Association, San Francisco (September 3, 1975), Table 10, cited in Pettigrew and Green, *supra* note 129 at 158-59. See also Christine Rossell,

"School Desegregation and White Flight," 90 *Political Science Quarterly* (Winter 1975-76); reprinted in Mills, *supra* note 129 at 214.

133. *Id*. Such factors include, according to Rossell, "reassignment of white students to formerly black schools, averaging for school districts with citywide two-way busing plans, a doubling of the normal loss in Northern school districts, and a tripling of the normal loss in Southern School districts." *Id*. at 227.

134. Pettigrew and Green, *supra* note 129, at 132.

135. Armor, *supra* note 125.

136. *Id*. at 191.

137. *Id*. at 221.

138. *Id*. at 214, 220.

139. *Gallup Opinion Index* (Princeton, NJ: American Institute of Public Opinion, February 1976); cited and quoted in Gary Orfield, *Must We Bus?* (Washington, DC: The Brookings Institution, 1979) at 109, Table 4-1.

140. *Gallup Opinion Index* (Princeton, NJ: American Institute of Public Opinion, November 1974; May 1975; and February 1978); quoted and cited in Armor, *supra* note 125 at 214.

141. Andrew M. Greeley, "School Desegregation and Ethnicity" (Chicago: National Opinion Research Center, 1987); cited in Stephan and Feagin, *supra* note 68 at 153.

142. David J. Armor, "Offer of Proof in Reference to the Testimony of David J. Armor in *Crawford v. Board of Education in the City of Los Angeles*," Supreme Court of the State of California for the County of Los Angeles (No. C22-854, June 6, 1977, Exhibit C), quoted in Armor, *supra* note 125 at 216.

143. *Rocky Mountain News* (July 24, 1994), 1A.

144. Thomas Sowell, *Race and Economics* (New York: McKay, 1975) at 43; cited and quoted in Greeley, *supra* note 141 at 151.

145. *Id*.

146. *Id*.

147. *Id*.

148. *Id*.

149. Malcolm X, *The Autobiography of Malcolm X* (New York: Clarity Press, 1964) at 272-273; quoted in Richard A. Pride and J. David Woodward, *The Burden of Busing* (Knoxville: University of Tennessee Press, 1985) at 7.

150. Greeley, *supra* note 141, at 153.

151. *Id*.

152. Black, *supra* note 89, at 421.

153. R. L. Crain, *The Politics of School Desegregation* (Chicago: Aldine, 1968) at 112; quoted in Arthur L. Stinchcombe and D. Garth Taybi, "On Democracy and School Integration," in Stephan and Feagin *supra* note 68 at 158.

154. Judith Bentley, *Busing: The Continuing Controversy* (New York: Franklin Watts, 1982) at 52.

155. *Id*.

156. *Id*.

157. *Id*. at 55.

158. Pride and Woodard, *supra* note 149 at 91.

159. See, e.g., the example of Florida described in Jeffrey Raffel, *The Politics of School Desegregation: The Metropolitan Remedy in Delaware* (Philadelphia: Temple University Press, 1980) at 176.

160. *Id.*

161. Orfield, *supra* note 2.

162. *Id.*

163. *Id.*

164. *Id.*

165. Clarence Lusane, *The Struggle for Equal Education* (New York: Franklin Watts, 1992) at 123.

166. John McCormick, "'Separate But Equal' Again — Kansas City: Black Parents Look for Alternatives to Desegregation," *Time* (May 16, 1994), 31.

167. Bentley, *supra* note 154, at 55-56.

168. *Milliken v. Bradley*, 418 U.S. 717 (1974).

169. *Id.*

170. *Id.* (Marshall, J., dissenting).

171. *Id.*

172. *Id.*

173. *Pasadena City Board of Education v. Spangler*, 427 U.S. 424 (1976).

174. *Id.*

175. *Freeman v. Pitts*, 112 S. Ct. 1430 (1992).

176. *Id.*

177. *Id.* (Scalia, J., concurring).

178. *Id.*

179. See, e.g., Reynolds Farley, "Residential Segregation and Its Implication for School Integration," 39 *Law and Contemporary Problems* (Winter 1975), 167; quoted in Orfield, *supra* note 2 at 91.

CHAPTER SIX

1. See, e.g., William R. Hazard, *Education and the Law: Cases and Materials on Public Schools*, (New York: Macmillan, 1978); E. Edmond Reulter, Jr. and Robert Hamilton, *The Law of Public Education*, 2nd ed. (Mineola, NY: Foundation Press, 1976); Arval A. Morris, *The Constitution and American Public Education* (Durham, NC: Carolina Academic Press 1989).

2. Morris, *supra* note 1 at xix.

3. *Marbury v. Madison*, 5 U.S. 137 (1803).

4. See, Chapter Four *supra* .

5. *Id.*

6. 414 U.S. 563 (1974).

7. Civil Rights Act of 1964, 42 U.S.C. §2000(d)(1988).

8. 35 Fed. Reg. 11 595 (1970).

9. *Lau v. Nichols*, 414 U.S. at 563.

10. Carol Penclas Whitten, "The Federal Role and Responsibility in Bilingual Education," in Gary Imhoff, ed., *Learning in Two Languages* (New Brunswick, NJ: Transaction, 1990) at 231.

11. Sally Peterson, "A Practicing Teacher's Views on Bilingual Education: The Need for Reform," in Imhoff, *supra* note 10 at 241.

12. Whitten, *supra* note 10, at 231.

13. *Id.*

14. *Id.*

15. Morris, *supra* note 1 at 592.

16. Whitten, *supra* note 10 at 229.

17. Peterson, *supra* note 11 at 241.

18. Myron Lieberman, *Public Education: An Autopsy* (Cambridge, MA: Harvard University Press, 1993) at 183-84.

19. Peterson, *supra* note 11, at 245.

20. *Id.*

21. *Id.* at 246.

22. *Id.* at 23-24.

23. *Id.* at 247.

24. *Id.*

25. *Id.*

26. *Id.* at 249.

27. *Id.*

28. Herbert A. Walberg, "Promoting English Literacy," in Imhoff, *supra* note 10 at 157.

29. *Id.*

30. *Id.*

31. *Id.*

32. *Id.*

33. *Id.* at 158.

34. *Id.*

35. *Id.*

36. K. Baker and A. De Kanter, *Effectiveness of Bilingual Education* (Washington, DC: U.S. Department of Education, 1981), cited in Walberg, *supra* note 28 at 158.

37. R. Venezky, "Non-Standard Language and Reading—Ten Years Later," in J. Edwards, ed., *The Social Psychology of Reading* (Silver Spring, MD: Institute of Modern Language, 1981), cited in Walberg, *supra* note 28 at 158.

38. E. Rotberg, "Some Legal and Research Considerations in Establishing Federal Policy in Bilingual Education," 52 *Harvard Educational Review*, 149-62 (1982).

39. Walberg notes that the "exception is willing (1985) who omitted two-thirds of the methodologically adequate studies and employed mistaken statistical adjustments of the estimates," citing A. Willig, "A Meta-Analysis of Selected Studies on the Effectiveness of Bilingual Education," 55(3) *Review of Educational Research* at 269-317 (1985); K. Baker, "Comment on Willig's 'A Meta-Analysis of Selected Studies of the Effectiveness of Bilingual Education," 57(3) *Review of Educational Research* at 351-62 (1987); C. Rossell, "The Effectiveness of Educational Alternatives for Limited English Proficient Children in the Berkeley Unified School District: A Report to the U.S. District Court in the Case of *Teresa P. et al v. The Berkeley Unified School District*" (Boston: Boston University, July 29, 1989).

40. Diane Ravitch, *The Schools We Deserve: Reflections on the Educational Crises of Our Time* (New York: Basic Books, 1985); cited in Whitten, *supra* note 10 at 229-230.

41. *Id.*

42. Walberg, *supra* note 28 at 153.

43. J. K. Hase, S. P. Rasher and H. J. Walberg, "English Mastery as a Diminishing Function of Time," *TESOL Quarterly*, 12(4) 1992 at 427-37, cited in Walberg, *supra* note 28 at 153.

44. "Interim Report of the Five Year Bilingual Education Pilot" (El Paso: Office for Research and Evaluation, 1987) cited and quoted in Rosalie Porter, "The Disabling Power of Ideology: Challenging the Basic Assumptions of Bilingual Education," in Imhoff, *supra* note 10 at 27-28. The evaluation showed no statistically significant differences in math achievement between the two groups. *Id.*

45. *Id.* at 28.

46. *Id.*

47. The article was adapted from her book, Rosalie Porter, *Forked Tongue: The Politics of Bilingual Education* (New York: Basic Books, 1990), and set forth in Imhoff, *supra* note 10 at 19.

48. Porter, *supra* note 44 at 29.

49. *Id.*

50. *Id.* at 30.

51. Editorial, *New York Times* (September 27, 1985); cited in Whitten, *supra* note 10 at 235.

52. Editorial, *Washington Post* (September 27, 1985), cited and quoted in Whitten, *id.* at 235.

53. *Id.* at 237.

54. Paraphrased and cited in *id.* at 238.

55. National Commission on Secondary Education for Hispanics, *Making Something Happen* (Washington, DC: Hispanic Policy Development Project, 1981), paraphrased and cited in Whitten, *id.* at 238.

56. W. McManus, W. Gould, and F. Welch, "Earnings of Hispanic Men: The Role of English Language Proficiency," *Journal of Labor Economics*, 1(2) at 121-122 (1983); cited and quoted in Whitten, *id.* at 238.

57. Brian Weinstein, "Political Goals of Language Policies," in Imhoff, *supra* note 10 at 163.

58. *Id.* at 165.

59. *Id.*

60. *Id.*

61. See *supra* discussion Chapter Four.

62. Morris, *The Constitution and American Public Education*, *supra* note 1 at 567.

63. 468 U.S. 992 (1984).

64. 20 U.S.C. § 1412 (1988).

65. 20 U.S.C. § 1400 (1988 & Supp. III 1991).

66. Jonathan Kozol, *Savage Inequalities* (New York: Crown Publishers) at 93.

67. 269 F. Supp. 401, *cert. dismissed* 393 U.S. 801 (1967).

68. *Id.*

69. *Id.*

70. Arthur Jensen, "How Much Can We Boost IQ. and Scholastic Achievement," *Harvard Educational Review* Series No. 2:1-123, cited in John Ogbu, *Minority Education and Cash: The American System in Cross-Cultural Perspective* (New York: Academic Press, 1978) at 59.

71. *Id.*

72. Carnegie Institute Report (1994, citing data from U.S. Census Bureau, the Urban Institute and the National Center for Children in Poverty. Tabulated in Susan Chira, "Study Confirms Worst Fears for U.S. Children," *New York Times* (April 12, 1994) A-1.

73. Harold C. Lyon, Jr., "The Other Minority," reprinted in Morris, *supra* note 1, at 587-589. Dr. Lyon is Director of Education for the Gifted and Talented.

74. *Id.*

75. Lyon, *supra* note 23, at 588.

76. *Id.*

77. *Id.*

78. *Id.* at 589.

79. *Id.*

80. *Id.*

81. *Id.* at 588.

82. *Bennett v. City School District of New Rochelle*, 497 N.Y.S. 2d 72 (A.D. 2 Dept. 1985).

83. "America's a Quiet Crisis: Educating the Talented," *The Straits Times* (December 12, 1993).

84. Morris, *supra* note 1 at 542.

85. Marian Scheifele, *The Gifted Child in the Regular Classroom*, cited in Morris, *supra* note 1 at 542.

86. Lyon, *supra* note 73 at 588.

87. Morris, *supra* note 1 at 542.

88. "Special Education Seen as a Trap for Many Minority Students," *New York Times* (April 6, 1994), A1, B8.

89. *Id.* at B8.

90. *Id.*

91. *Id.*

92. *Id.*

93. *Id.*

94. *Id.*

95. *Id.*

96. *Id.*

97. *Id.*

98. Rochelle Sharp, "To Boost IQ's, Aid Is Needed in First 3 Years," *Wall Street Journal* (April 12, 1994), B1.

99. *Id.*

100. *Id.* (paraphrasing a statement by William Greenough).

101. *Id.*

102. *Id.* at B1.

103. *Id.*

104. *Id.*

105. *Id.* (paraphrasing a statement by Edward Ziegler).

106. *Id.* (paraphrasing a statement by Craig Ramey).

107. *Id.*

108. *Id.*

109. *Id.*

110. Morris, *supra* note 1, at 591.

CHAPTER SEVEN

1. *San Antonio School District v. Rodriguez*, 411 U.S. 1, 35. "Education, of course, is not among the rights afforded explicit protection under our Federal Constitution." *Id*. See also *Hannible v. Husen*, 95 U.S. 465 (1877).

2. See, *State ex rel. Clark v. Haworth*, 23 N.E. 946 (Ind. 1890).

3. *Brown v. Board of Education*, 347 U.S. 483 (1954); of course, police and fire protection would also be high on the list.

4. See discussion and review of state public education laws in Arval A. Morris, *The Constitution and American Public Education* (Durham, NC: Carolina Academic Press, 1989) at 24-31.

5. Morris, *supra* note 4, at 27.

6. *City of Louisville v. Commonwealth*, 121 S.W. 411 (Ky. 1909).

7. See, e.g., *Mosier v. Thompson*, 393 S.W. 2d 734 (Tenn. 1965).

8. *Goss v. Lopez*, 419 U.S. 565 (1975).

9. *Id*.

10. *Id*.

11. *Id*.

12. *Libbs v. Board of Education*, 276 A.2d 165 (N.J., 1971).

13. *Id*.

14. Model School Disciplinary Code, in *Inequality of Education*, No. 12, at 47-49 (Cambridge, MA: Center for Law and Education, 1972).

15. *Id*.

16. *Id*.

17. *Id*. Justice Powell, joined by Justices Burger, Blackmun, and Rhenquist.

18. *Id*.

19. William Hazard, *Education and the Law* (New York: Macmillan, 1978) at 280.

20. *Id*. at 580.

21. *Id*. at 581.

22. *Id*.

23. *Givens v. Poe*, 346 F. Supp. 202 (W.D. N.C. 1972).

24. *Ingraham v. Wright*, 430 U.S. 651 (1977).

25. *Marlar v. Bill*, 178 S.W. 2d 634 (1944).

26. *O'Rourke v. Walker*, 128 A.2d (Conn. 1925).

27. *Wexell v. Scott*, 1786 N.E.2d 735 (Ill. 1971).

28. "Sexual or Textual Harassment," *Time* (May 9, 1994), at 56.

29. *Franklin v. Guinnett Co.*, 112 S. Ct. 1028 (1992).

30. Morris *supra* note 4, at 277, citing Blackstone.

31. *New Jersey v. T.L.O.*, 469 U.S. 325 (1985).

32. *Id*., citing *Ingraham v. Wright*, *supra* note 24.

33. *Id*.

34. *Id*.

35. *In re Williams, G.*, 709 P.2d 1287 (Cal. 1985).

36. Betsy Levin, "Educating Youth for Citizenship: The Conflict Between Authority and Individual Rights in the Public Schools," 95 *Yale Law Journal* 1647 at 1679 (1986).

37. *Cates v. Howell Pub. School*, 633 F.Supp 454 (1985).

38. Department of Justice, Office of Juvenile Justice and Delinquency Prevention, *Federal Juvenile Delinquency Programs* (Washington, DC, 1988) at 55.

39. Benjamin Duke, *Lessons for Industrial America: The Japanese School* (Westport, CT: Praeger, 1986), 188.

40. *Our Nations Schools—A Report Card: "A" in School Violence and Vandalism*, U.S. Senate Committee on the Judiciary, Subcommittee to Investigate Juvenile Delinquency, 94th Cong., 1st Sess. (April 1975).

41. S. Rep. No. 168, 94th Cong., 1st Sess. 8 (1975). Reprinted in United States Congressional Code Annotated.

42. *Tinker v. Des Moines School District*, 393 U.S. 503 (1969).

43. *Roberts v. Madigan*, 921 F.2d 1047 (10th Cir. 1990), *cert. denied*, 112 S. Ct. 3025 (1992).

44. David Tatel et al., "The 1991-92 Term of the United States Supreme Court and Its Impact on Public Schools," 78 *Ed. Law Rep.* 3, 7 (1992).

45. *Id.*

46. See, e.g., *Richards v. Thurston*, 424 F. 2d 1281 (1st Cir. 1970); *Owen v. Barry*, 483 F.2d 1126 (2nd Cir. 1973); *Massie v. Henry*, 455 F.2d 779 (4th Cir. 1972); *Zeller v. Donegal*, 517 F.2d 600 (3d Cir. 1975); *Karr v. Schmidt*, 460 F.2d 609 (5th Cir.), *cert. denied*, 409 U.S. 989 (1972), *King v. Saddleback*, 445 F.2d 932 (9th Cir.), *cert. denied*, 404 U.S. 979 (1971).

47. *Bannister v. Paracks*, 316 F.Supp 185 (1970).

CHAPTER EIGHT

1. See discussion, Chapter Five *supra*.

2. The Tenth Amendment provides that "the powers not delegated to the United States by the Constitution, nor prohibited by it to the states, are reserved to the States respectively, or to the people." U.S. Constitution Amendment X.

3. Chicago Panel on School Policy and Finance, cited and set forth in Jonathan Kozol, *Savage Inequalities* (New York: Crown, 1991), at Appendix, Table 7.

4. "Statistical Profiles of School Districts" (New York State Board of Education), cited and quoted in Kozol, *supra* note 3 at 237.

5. Educational Law Center), cited in Kozol, *supra* note 3, at 236.

6. *Serrano v. Priest*, 487 P.2d 1241 (Cal. 1971).

7. *San Antonio Independent School District v. Rodriguez*, 411 U.S. 1 (1973).

8. These expenditures were the result of combined contribution from local property tax revenues, state, and federal sources.

9. *Rodriguez, supra* note 7 at 25.

10. *Id.* at 27.

11. P. Ridenour and P. Ridenour, "Serrano v. Priest: Wealth and Kansas School Finance," 20 *Kansas Law Review* 213, 225 (1972); cited in *Id.* at 27, n. 64.

12. *Rodriguez* at 23, citing note, "A Statistical Analysis of the School Finance Decisions: On Winning Battles and Losing Wars," 81 *Yale Law Journal* 1303, 1328-29 (1972). The Court stated that it did not know whether a similar pattern would be found in Texas, but it had seen no evidence to suggest that the poorest people were concentrated in the poorest districts. *Id.*

13. *Id.* at 46-47, n. 101, citing and quoting R. Simon, "The School Finance Decisions: Collective Bargaining and Future Finance Systems," 83 *Yale Law Journal* 409, 439-40 (1973).

14. *Id.* at 47, n. 101.

15. *Id.* at 53, citing Simon, *supra* note 13 at 434-36.

16. *Id.* at 53, citing J. Conant, *The Child, the Parent, and the State* (1959), 27.

17. *Id.* at 28.

18. See, e.g., *Dupree v. Alma School District*, 651 S.W. 2d 90 (1983); *Rose v. Council for Better Education*, 790 S.W. 2d 186 (Ky. 1989); *Helena Elementary School Dist. No. 1 v. State*, 769 P.2d 684 (Mont. 1989); for discussion of recent school finance cases, see "Unfulfilled Promises: School Finance Remedies and State Courts," 104 Harvard Law Review 1072 (1991).

19. See *Edgewood Indep. School Dist. v. Kirby*, 777 S.W. 2d 391 (Tex. 1989); see discussion in Troy Reynolds, "Education Finance Reform Litigation and Separation of Powers: Kentucky Makes Its Contribution," 80 *Kentucky Law Journal* 309 (1992).

20. *Pawley v. Kelley*, 255 S.E. 2d 859 (W. Va. 1979).

21. Rodd Zolkos, *New Paradigms for Schools, City and State* (1994) at 1.

22. 1968 Haw. Sess. Laws, Act 38 § 1.

23. See e.g., *Serrano v. Priest*, 180 Cal. App. 3d 1187, *vacated and review granted sub. Placentia Unified School Dist. v. Riles*, 723 P.2d 1248, *transferred sub nom. Serrano v. Priest*, 763 P.2d 852 (1988); *Horton v. Meskill*, 486 A.2d 1099 (1985); cited and discussed at 104 *Harvard Law Review*, *supra* note 18 at n. 141.

24. Kozol, *supra* note 3 at 221.

25. *Id.* at 221.

26. See, e.g., Elena Neuman, "Reformers Seeking Key to Suburbia," *Insight*, Vol. 9 (April 15, 1993); 6.

27. See generally Benjamin Duke, *Lessons for Industrial America: The Japanese School* (Westport, CT: Praeger, 1986).

28. Arval A. Morris, *The Constitution and American Public Education* (Durham, NC: Carolina Academic Press, 1989), at 543.

29. In theory, the equal protection clause applies only to state action within a state's own jurisdiction. However, the Supreme Court held segregation in the District of Columbia to be unconstitutional by substituting the due process clause for the equal protection clause. *Bolling v. Sharpe*, 347 U.S. 497 (1954).

CHAPTER NINE

1. Thomas Sowell, "Tragicomedy," *Forbes* (June 6, 1994), 52.

2. Dennis Kelly, "Ex-educator's Illiteracy Is His Mission," *USA Today* (August 3, 1994), D5.

3. Arval Morris, *The Constitution and American Public Education* (Durham, NC: Carolina Academic Press, 1989), at 280.

4. *Id.*

5. *Rocky Mountain News* (Sunday, July 24, 1994), p. A1.

6. Sowell, *supra* note 1 at 52.

Selected Bibliography

Atkin, R. "U.S. Education Runs in Place," *Christian Science Monitor*, October 3, 1990, 12.

Ayres, L., *Laggards in Our Schools* (1908).

Barber, D.; Eskridge, W.; and Frickey, P. *Constitutional Law* (St. Paul: West 1993).

Bergman, P. *The Negro in America* (New York: Harper and Row, 1969).

Black, C. "The Lawfulness of the Segregation Decisions," 69 *Yale L.J.* 421 (1960).

Bond, H. *Negro Education in Alabama: A Study in Cotton and Steel* (New York: Atheneum, 1969).

Boser, J. A. and Wiley, P. D. "An Alternative Teacher Preparation Program: Is the Promise Fulfilled?" 65 *Peabody J. of Educ.* 130 (1988).

Bracey, G. "The Third Bracey Report on the Condition of Public Education," *Phi Delta Kappan*, October 1993, 104.

Caldwell, R. *What's Really Wrong With Public Education* (Denver: Center for Public Policy and Contemporary Issues, University of Denver, 1991).

Callahan, R. *Education and the Cult of Efficiency* (Chicago: University of Chicago Press, 1912).

Catton. B. *The American Heritage History of the Civil War* (New York: American Heritage, 1988).

Center for Immigration Studies, "Despair Behind the Riots: The Impediment of Mass Immigration to Los Angeles Blacks," *Scope*, Summer 1992, 1.

Chenowith, T. "Unanticipated Consequences of Schools and Choice: Some Thoughts on the Case of San Francisco," 7 *Equity and Choice* 33 (1989).

Church, R. and Sediak, M. *Education in the United States: An Interpretive History* (New York: Collier Macmillan, 1976).

Cohen, S. *A History of Colonial Education, 1607-1776* (New York: John Wiley, 1974).

Coleman, J.; Campbell, E.; Hobson, C.; McPartland, J.; Mood, A.; Weinfield, F.; and York, R. *Equality of Educational Opportunity* (U.S. Department of Education, 1966).

Coleman, J. and Hoffer, T. *Public and Private High Schools: The Impact of Community* (New York: Basic Books, 1987).

Committee on Policy for Racial Justice. *Visions of a Better Way: A Black Appraisal of Public Schooling* (Washington, DC: 1989).

Conant, J. B. *The Education of America* (New York: McGraw-Hill, 1963).

Cuban, L. *How Teachers Taught: Constancy and Change in American Education* (New York: Coleman, 1984).

Cubberly, E. *Readings in Public Education in the U.S.: A Collection of Sources and Readings to Illustrate the History of Education Practice and Progress in the U.S.* (Boston: Houghton Mifflin, 1934).

Cubberly, E. *Rural Life and Education* (Boston: Houghton Mifflin, 1941).

Curti, M. *The Social Ideas of American Education* (Paterson, NJ: Pageant Books, 1959).

Daniel, P. "A Comprehensive Analysis of Educational Choice: Can the Polemic of Legal Problems Be Overcome?" 43 *DePaul L. Rev.* (1993).

Department of Education (U.S.), National Center for Educational Statistics, Office of Educational Research Law Improvement, *The Condition of Education* (Washington, DC: U.S. Government and Printing Office, 1993).

Department of Justice, Office of Juvenile Justice and Preliminary Prevention, *Federal Juvenile Delinquency Programs* (1988).

Dewey, J. *Democracy and Education* (New York: Macmillan, 1916).

Dial, M. and Stevens, C., eds., *Education and Urban Society* (Newbury Park, CA: Corwin, 1993).

Dickenson, J. W. *What Froebel's System of Kindergarten Education Is, and How It Can Be Introduced Into Our Public Schools* (Worcester, MA: National Education Proceedings, 1873).

Duke, B. *Lessons for Industrial America: The Japanese School* (Westport, CT: Praeger, 1986).

Edwards, J., ed. *The Social Psychology of Reading* (Silver Spring, MD: Institute of Modern Language, 1981).

Eysenck, H. J. *Personality and Individual Differences* (New York: Plenum Press 1985).

Ferguson, R. F. "Paying for Public Education: New Evidence on How and Why Money Matters," 28 *Harv. J. on Legis.* 465 (1991).

Fisher, A. "Science + Math + F: Crisis in Education," *Popular Science*, August 1992, 58.

Friedman, M. *Capitalism and Freedom* (1962).

Garland, H. *A Son of the Middle Border* (New York: Macmillan, 1958).

Germani, C. "New School Year Rekindles Concern Over U.S. Education," *Christian Science Monitor*, September 4, 1990, 1.

Glennon, T. "Disabling Ambiguities: Confronting Barriers to the Education of Students with Emotional Disabilities," 60 *Tenn. L. Rev.* 295 (1993).

Gregory, Sophronia S. "Oprah! Oprah! in the Court," *Time*, June 6, 1994, 30.

Hanushek, "The Economics of Schooling," 24 *J. Econ. Literature* 141 (1986).

Hanushek, E. "When School Finance 'Reform' May Not Be Good Policy," Symposium, Investing in Our Children's Future: School Finance Reform in the 1990s, 28 Harv. *J. on Legis.* 423 (1991).

Hapt, J. "Assuring Equal Educational Opportunity for Language-Minority Students: Bilingual Education and the Equal Opportunity Act of 1974," 18 *Colum. J.L. & Soc. Probs.* 209 (1983).

Haraven, T. *Family and Kin in Urban Communities, 1700-1930* (New York: Macmillan, 1977).

Hardaway, R. *Airport Regulation, Law and Public Policy: The Management and Growth of Infrastructure* (Westport, CT: Quorum Books, 1991).

Hardaway, R. *The Electoral College and the Constitution* (Westport, CT: Praeger, 1994).

Hardaway, R. "The FAA Buy-Sell Rule: Airline Deregulation at the Crossroads," 52 J. Air. L. & Com. 1 (1986).

Hardaway, R. *Population, Law and the Environment* (Westport, CT: Praeger, 1994).

Hardaway, R. "Reforming Education," *Atlanta Constitution*, August 1, 1991, A-15.

Hardaway, R. "Transportation Deregulation (1976-1984): Turning the Tide," 10 *Transp. L.J.* 101 (1985).

Harlan, L. *Separate and Unequal: Public School Campaigns and Racism in the Southern Seaboard States, 1905-1918* (New York: Atheneum, 1968).

Hase, J. K.; Rasher, S. P.; and Walberg, H. J.; "English Mastery as a Diminishing Function of Time," *TESOL Quarterly* 12(4) (1992) 427.

Hazard, W. *Education and the Law: Cases and Materials on Public Schools* (New York: Macmillan, 1978).

Hendrick, B. *Bulwark of the Republic: A Biography of the Constitution* (Boston: Little, Brown, 1937).

Hull, J. "Do Teachers Punish According to Race: That's the Charge in Cincinnati and the City Board Has Proposed an Explosive Remedy," *Time*, April 4, 1994, 30.

Imhoff, G., ed. *Learning in Two Languages* (New Brunswick, NJ: Transaction, 1990).

Jones, A. *Cruel Sacrifice* (New York: Windsor, 1994).

Kaestle, C. *Pillars of the Republic: Common Schools and American Society, 1700-1860* (New York, 1983).

Kennedy, M. M. "Some Surprising Findings on How Teachers Learn to Teach," *Educational Leadership*, 49(3)(1991).

Kirp, D. "What School Choice Really Means," *Atlantic Monthly*, November 1922, 122.

Kozol, J. *Savage Inequalities* (New York: Crown, 1991).

Lamm, R. and Imhoff, G. *The Immigration Time Bomb* (New York: Concord Books, 1985).

LaPoint, V. "Dress Codes and Uniforms in Urban Schools," 57 *The Education Digest* 7 (1993).

Leight, R. and Rinehart, A. "Revisiting Americana: One School Room in Retrospect," *The Educational Forum*, Winter 1992, 133.

Leonard, G. "The End of School: Changes in Current School Systems Needed," *Atlantic Monthly*, May 1992, 24.

Levin, B. "Educating Youth for Citizenship: The Conflict Between Authority and Individual Rights in the Public Schools," 95 *Yale L.J.* 1647 (1986).

Liebman, J. "Voice, Not Choice," 101 *Yale L.J.* 284 (1991).

Lieberman, M. *Public Education: An Autopsy* (Cambridge, MA: Harvard University Press, 1993).

Lotito, M. "A Call to Action for U.S. Business and Education," *Employment Relations Today*, December 22, 1992, 379.

Lusane, C. *The Struggle for Equal Education* (New York: Franklin Watts, 1992).

Lynn, R. *Educational Achievement in Japan: Lessons for the West* (Armonk, NY: M.E. Sharpe, 1988)

McCormick, J. "Separate But 'Equal' Again — Kansas City: Black Parents Look for Alternatives to Desegregation," *Time*, May 16, 1994, 31.

McManus, W.; Gould, W.; and Welch, F. "Earnings of Hispanic Men: The Role of English Language Proficiency," 1(2) *J. of Labor Econ.* 122 (1983).

Mill, J. S. *On Liberty* (London: Oxford University Press, 1966).

Millman, M. and Kanter, R. M. eds. *Another Voice* (Garden City, NY: Doubleday, 1975)

Model School Disciplinary Code. *Inequality of Education*, no. 12 (Cambride, MA: Center for Law and Education, 1972) 47-49.

Morris, A. *The Constitution and American Public Education* (Durham, NC: Academic Press, 1989).

The National Commission on Excellence in Education. *A Nation at Risk: The Imperative for Educational Reform* (1983).

Neuman, E. "Reformers Seeking Key to Suburbia," *Insight*, April 15, 1993, 6.

Ogbu, J. *Minority Education and Caste: The American System in Cross-Cultural Perspective* (New York: Academic Press, 1978).

Orfield, G. "The Growth of Segregation in American Schools: Changing Patterns of Separation and Poverty Since 1986." *Equality and Excellence in Education* (January 1994).

Our Nation's Schools — A Report Card: "A" in School Violence and Vandalism, U.S. Senate Committee on the Judiciary, Subcommittee to Investigate Juvenile Delinquency, 94th Cong., 1st Sess. (April 1975).

Perry, N. "What We Need to Fix U.S. Schools," *Fortune*, November 16, 1992, 132.

Pettigrew, T. and Green, R. "School Desegregation in Large Cities: A Critique of the Coleman 'White-Flight' Thesis," 46 *Harv. Educ. Rev.* (February 1976).

Pitts, J. "Son of Edison," *New Republic*, January 18, 1993, 208.

Porter, R. *Forked Tongue: The Politics of Bilingual Education* (New York: Basic Books, 1990).

Pride, R. and Woodard, J. *The Burden of Busing* (Knoxville: University of Tennessee Press, 1985).

Raffel, J. *The Politics of School Desegregation* (Philadelphia: Temple University Press, 1980).

Ratner, G. "A New Legal Duty for Urban Public Schools: Effective Education in Basic Skills," 63 *Tex. L. Rev.* 777 (1985).

Ravitch, D., *The Schools We Deserve: Reflections on the Educational Crises of Our Time* (New York: Basic Books, 1985).

Rossell, C. "School Desegregation and White Flight," 90 *Political Science Quarterly*, Winter 1975.

Rotberg, E. "Some Legal and Research Considerations in Establishing Federal Policy in Bilingual Education," 52 *Harv. Educ. Rev.* 149 (1982).

Schmidt, B. "Principle and Prejudice: The Supreme Court and Race in the Progressive Era," 82 *Colum. L. Rev.* 444 (1982).

Shannon, R. and Shannon, D. "The British Infant School: A Reconsideration," *The Educational Forum*, Fall 1991, 62.

Shapiro, M. *The Kindergarten Movement from Froebel to Dewey* (University Park, PA: University of Pennsylvania Press, 1983).

Sowell, T. *Race and Economics* (New York: McKay, 1975).

Sowell, T. "Tragicomedy," *Forbes*, June 6, 1994, 52.

Spring, J. *The American School, 1642-1990* (New York: Longman, 1990).

Spring, J. "Psychologists and the War: The Meaning of Intelligence in the Alpha and Beta Tests," *History of Education Quarterly*, Spring 1972, 3.

Stanfield, R. "The Education President II," *The National Journal*, December 5, 1990, 2809.

Stevenson, H. *Mathematics Achievement of Chinese, Japanese, and American Children* (Annual Report, Center for Advanced Studies, 1983).

Stuart, J. *To Teach, To Love* (New York: World, 1970).

Stuart, J. *The Thread That Runs So True* (New York: Charles Scribner's Sons, 1949).

Tatel, D. "The 1991-92 Term of the United States Supreme Court and Its Impact on Public Schools" 78 *Ed. Law Rep.* 3, 7 (1992).

Toch, T. "The Perfect School," *U.S. News & World Report*, January 11, 1993, 46.

U.S. Constitution, Amendments, V, X, and XIV.

Washington, B. "The Atlanta Exposition Address." In *Booker T. Washington and His Critics* (New York: Penguin, 1974).

Weber, E. *The Kindergarten: Its Encounter with Educational Thought in America* (New York: 1969).

Wells, A. "Choice in Education: Examining the Evidence of Equity," 93 *Teachers C. Rec.* 137 (1991).

Winterer, C. "Avoiding a 'Hothouse System of Education': Nineteenth Century Early Childhood Education From the Infant Schools to the Kindergartens," *History of Education Quarterly* (Fall 1992).

Wollenberg, C. *All Deliberate Speed: Segregation and Exclusion in California Schools, 1855-1975* (Berkeley: University of California Press, 1976).

Wrigley, J. *Class Politics and Public Schools: Chicago 1900-1950* (New Brunswick, NJ: Rutgers University Press, 1982).

Yaping, Y. "American and Chinese Schools: A Comparative Analysis," *Education*, Winter 1992, 232.

Index

abandonment: inner-city schools,
    125-127, 129; public schools, x, 44,
    45, 49, 53, 164; traditional
    American model, ix, 87
abolitionist, 102, 103
achievement tests, student results
    U.S., x, 3, 4, 10, 22
activities: extracurricular, 20, 59;
    illegal, 62; within school, 74, 76
Adams, John, 70
Alexander, Lamar 3, 4
alternative education, 53
ambition, 22
American Civil Liberties Union, 62
American Council of Education, 25
American Federation of Teachers, 34,
    82, 83
American Revolution, 69, 70, 98, 102
antifederalists, 102
Armor, David, 123-124
Armstrong, S.C., 108
Articles of Confederation, 69, 99
assignments: homework, 60; to
    schools based on race, 117, 118,
    121, 129, 149; teaching positions,
    2, 3; to tracks, 57, 58
Association of Teacher Educators, 40
atomic bomb, 11
authoritarianism, 80, 81

authority: referring to school
    Prussianization, 43, 69-71, 94, 156,
    163-166; of state over classroom
    activities, 56, 114, 152; of teachers
    inside the classroom, x, 63, 73, 78-
    87, 148

back to basics, 7
Baird, Zoe, 112
Baker, K., 24, 25, 135
Bannister v. Paradis, 157
Basic Inventory of Native Languages,
    134
Beckman Institute, 146
behavioral problems, 29
Bennett, William, 137,
*Bennett v. City School District of New
    Rochelle*, 143
Berea College, 115
Bible, 67, 157
Biden, Joseph, 123
bilingual education 24-27, 131-138; as
    a basis for segregation, 53, 63;
    creating political debate, 95; and
    immigrants, 37
Binet, Alfred, 93
black codes, 107
Black, Charles, 116, 125
Blackmun, Harry, 32

Blackstone, William, 155
blue jeans, 34, 157
books, 2, 18, 22, 81, 82, 135-136
Boser, J.A., 41
Bridenbaugh, Carl, 68
Brigham, Amariah, 87-89, 91, 93
British Infant School, 90, 91
Brockhurst, School, 58-60, 77
brokers, 71, 72, 83
Brown v. Board of Education, 24, 97,
    113-128, 138, 152
Brown I, 117, 121
Brown II, 117, 118
Buchanan v. Warley, 115
budget: of Japanese schools, 17, 18;
    of U.S. schools, 15, 37, 38, 42
Bush, Barbara, 76
Bush, George, 10
busing, 13, 95, 119-128

Cales v. Howell Public Schools, 157
Carter, Jimmy, 95, 123
caste, 62, 91, 97, 107
Center for Immigration Studies, 36,
    113
Center for Law and Education of
    Harvard University, 30, 153
Center for Public Policy and
    Contemporary Issues, 11, 14
Center for the Study of American
    Pluralism, 124
certification, 21, 37-41, 63, 64, 165
Chris D. v. Montgomery County Board
    of Education, 29
Chubb, John, 45, 47
Chugani, Harry, 146
Church, Robert, 69, 92
Church of England, 68
Churchill, Winston, 142
Cincinnati Federation of Teachers,
    35
Civil Aeronautics Board, 81
Civil Rights Act of 1871, 107
Civil Rights Act of 1964, 1, 113, 118-
    122, 132
Civil War, 72, 80, 86, 102-104,
    106-108
Clark, Kenneth, 116
Cleveland, Grover, 109

Clinton administration, 21
Cohen, Sheldon, 68
Coleman, James: 1966 Report, 1-3,
    68; 1975 report on segregation,
    122-124; 1987 Report, 43-44
Committee v. Nyquist, 49
companies, 19, 36
compensatory education, 91, 92
competitors, 15, 16
compulsory public education, 69
Con Edison Co., 25
Conant, J. B., 38, 40
conduct, 31-34, 55, 157, 165, 166
Confederation Congress, 99, 100, 102
consolidation, ix, 73-80, 100, 149, 163
Convention of the Society of the
    Cincinnati, 99
counselors, 18, 53, 74, 147
creative minority, 142
crime, 9, 10, 35, 85, 107
criticism, 2, 11, 121, 154
Crittendon, John, 104
Cuban, Larry, 74
Cubberly, Elwood, 76, 78
cultural deprivation, 91
Cummings v. Board of Education, 115

dangerous students, 29
Darwin, Charles, 142
Davis, Jefferson, 105
de facto segregation, 15, 97, 113
de jure segregation, 97, 98, 113, 118-
    122, 129
De Kanter and Baker report, 24-25,
    135
Department of Education: Department
    of Education v. Katherine D., 27; its
    formation, 95; statistical
    information, 3, 10, 15, 20, 89
Department of Health, Education and
    Welfare, 50, 132
deregulation, 81
desegregation, 13, 72, 116-118,
    120-128, 161
Dewey, John, 62, 89
dinosaurs, 6
disabilities education act, 27-31, 140
disabled students, 27-30, 60, 78, 139,
    143-146

discipline, 28-35, 54, 60, 73, 152-158; 163-166
Dred Scott, decision, 103, 104, 114, 121, 151
drugs, 10, 20, 156
due process, 30-34, 52-56, 60-63, 151-158, 162-166
Duke, Benjamin, 17-18

Early Childhood Project, 91
Early School Admissions Project, 91
Economic Opportunity Act, 91
Edison, Thomas, 142, 144
Edison Project, 50
Education Alternatives, 50
Education for All Handicapped Children Act, 27, 30, 139
Education U.S.A., 30
educational establishment: and bilingual education, 38, 133; in need of reform, 8, 9, 43, 51, 52, 93-95; opposition to reform, 20-24, 79, 98; response to and sexism, 131, 147
Educational Excellence Network, 6
Educational Law of 1642, 68
Educational Testing Service, 4
Eighth Amendment, 155
Einstein, Albert, 142
Elementary and Secondary Education Act, 91
Emancipation Proclamation, 105, 106
equal protection: as a basis for desegregation, 9, 103, 106, 114-116, 120; and bilingual education, 131, 132; preschool education, 52; in school financing systems, 13, 159, 162; and sexism, 81; tracking, 142, 143, 148
expectations, 19, 26, 53, 57, 75
expenditures, public schools: on bilingual education, 27; compared to Japanese schools, 10-12; compared to private schools, 23, 38; inequalities, 115, 159-162; on magnet schools, 44; related to quality of education in U.S., 2-4, 15, 59, 60

Experimental Nursery School Program, 91
expulsion, 27, 31, 54, 153, 155

Families and Work Institute, 147
Farley, Reynolds, 123, 124, 129
federal aid, 15, 95, 140
Ferguson, Ronald, 2
Fifteenth Amendment, 106
Fifth Amendment, 30, 103, 151
financing, 4, 1, 12, 63, 159-161
First Amendment, 152, 157
Fourteenth Amendment, 34, 35, 106-108, 114, 115, 121, 131, 132, 140, 157
Fourth Amendment, 55, 156
Freeman v. Pitts, 129
Friedman, Milton, 45
Froebel, Friedrich, 89
Fugitive Slave Law, 103, 104
fundamental right, 55, 161

Gatto, John Taylor, 9, 73
Gerhart, James, 75
gifted children, 142, 143
gifted students, 46, 59, 143, 144, 148
Gladstone, William, 105
Goals 2000: Educate America Act, 10, 11, 15, 21, 94
Gong Lum v. Rice, 114-115
Goss v. Lopez, 32, 152, 158
Graglia, Lino, 118-121
Grant, Ulysses, 106
Great Cities Project, 91
Greeley, Andrew, 124, 125
Green, Robert, 123
Green v. County School Board, 48, 129
Greenough, William, 146
Gulliford, Andrew, 74
Gustus, Ted, 145

Haley, Margaret, 82
Hamilton, Alexander, 99, 100, 102
handguns, 10
Handicapped Act of 1970, 27
Harlan, John, 114
Harris, William, 82
Harris Poll, 1992, 112

Harvard Study, 1, 14
Hase, J.K., 136
Hazard, William, 154
Head Start, 91, 147
hearing, 31, 32, 152, 153, 166
Henry, Patrick, 99
Hernandez, Paquita, 7, 26, 73
Higher Horizons, 91
Hobson v. Hansen, 57, 60, 140, 144
Hoffer, Thomas, 43
Honig v. Doe, 29
Horne, Carrie, 76
Humphrey, Hubert, 119
Husen, T., 17

illegal aliens, 23, 35, 36
Immigration, 35-37, 108-113, 130, 139
Immigration and Naturalization
   Service, 111
In Re Williams, G., 156
Individuals with Disabilities
   Education Act, 27, 28, 140
inequalities, 1, 2, 12, 140, 159
infant schools, 86-90
International Assessment of
   Educational Progress, 4
interruption, 19, 42
invidious discrimination, 9
IQ, 92, 141, 146, 147

Javits, Jacob, 119
Jefferson, Thomas, 76,
Jensen, Arthur, 92, 141

Kanter, Rosabeth Moss, 79, 135
Kelley, S.D., 122
Kennedy, M.M., 38,
Keyes v. School District No. 1, 122
Kimber, Damon, 145
kindergarten, 41, 86, 88-90, 92
King George, 69
Koln-Holweide, 42-43
Kozol, Jonathan, 12, 140, 161

Lamm, Richard, 14
Lansing, John, 100
Lau Remedies, 132, 138
Lau v. Nichols, 132, 139

Learning English Advocates Drive,
   133
Leight, Robert, 75
Lee, Robert E., 105, 106
liberty, 32-36, 39, 62, 109, 152
Lieberman, Myron, 25, 40
limited-English-proficient (LEP), 132,
   134-137
Lincoln, Abraham, 104-105
Locke, John, 86
Luther, Martin, 100
Lynn, Richard, 17
Lyon, Harold, 142-144

Madison, James, 99-101
magnet classrooms, 53-58, 61-64, 148,
   165, 166
magnet schools, 18, 44, 46, 53, 54
Mann, Horace, 78
Marbury v. Madison, 117, 131
Marlar v. Bill, 155
Marshall, Thurgood, 119, 121, 128,
   141
masculine ethic, 79
Massarotti, Michael, 85
McClellan, General, 105
McKenna, George, 163
*McLaurin v. Oklahoma Board of
   Regents*, 114, 116
Mehren, Elizabeth, 6-7
Mendel, Gregor, 142
mentor, 58, 59
Mill, John Stuart, 39
Milliken v. Bradley, 127, 128
Milwaukee Parental Choice Program,
   46
Model School Disciplinary Code, 30,
   32, 153
Moe, Terry, 45, 47
Moore, J.A., 122
morals, 20, 21
Morris, Arval, 144
Morris, Gouvernor, 100
Motorola, 19
Moynihan, Daniel, 94
Mueller v. Allen, 49
multiculturalism, 26, 73, 88
multiple-choice tests, 75, 81, 87, 94,
   148

NAACP, 117, 119
Nation at Risk, A, 3, 4, 8, 12
National Advisory Council on
  Bilingual Education, 136
National Alliance of Business, 19, 20
National Assessment of Educational
  Progress, x, 4, 6, 15, 22
National Center for Education
  Information, 40
National Center for Education
  Statistics, 10
National Commission on Excellence
  in Education, 3
National Commission on Secondary
  Education for Hispanics, 138
National Education Association
  (NEA), 82, 89, 95
National Goals Panel, 9
National Institute of Education, 94
National Teachers Association, 82
neighborhood school, 54, 63, 124
New Jersey v. T.L.O., 156
New York American Schools
  Development Corporation, 50
Newton, Isaac, 142
Newton Public Schools Bilingual
  Program, 137
Nixon, Richard, 12, 94

O'Connor, Sandra Day, 35
O'Rourke v. Walker, 155
Office of Economic Education, 91
Office of Research and Evaluation,
  136
Old Deluder Laws, 69
one-room schools, 73-80, 84, 90, 148,
  163
Oppenheimer, Robert, 11

Paisley Grammar School, 46, 47, 53,
  62
Peabody, Elizabeth, 89
pedagogy, 76, 135
Peltzman, Sam, 40
Perry, Nancy, 85
Pestalozzi, Heinrich, 86
Peterson, Sally, 132-134
Pettigrew, Thomas, 123
Philadelphia Convention, 99, 102

philosophy, 14, 25, 52, 69-71
Phyler v. Doe, 35, 37
physiologists, 87, 89
Pierce v. Society of Sisters,
Plessy v. Ferguson, 24, 72, 113, 114
policy: administrative, 80; bilingual
  education, 133, 135; of Britain
  towards thirteen colonies, 69-72;
  Carter's involvement in
  formulation, 95; Center of Child
  Development and Social Policy,
  146; Center for Public Policy, 11,
  14; on grading and absences, 34-36,
  84; of higher expenditures, 3;
  immigration, 108, 109, 113;
  legislative policy, 159, 161, 165; on
  magnet schools, 55-57, 149; racially
  motivated, 98, 114, 117, 118; on
  segregation, 63-64, 81, 120, 122,
  123, 129, 130, 138; Sexism in
  School System, ix, 147; on teacher
  certification, 40; toward disabled
  students, 28, 60; on uniforms, 62
politicization, 25, 71-73, 94, 133, 163
Porter, Rosalie, 25, 136, 137
potential, 57, 71, 74, 142, 147
Powell, Lewis, 32, 122, 154
power brokers, 71, 72, 83
preschool, 51, 52, 57, 58, 64, 73, 85,
  86, 141, 146, 147, 165
privatization, x, 49, 50
professionals, 11, 32, 40, 41, 111
professors, 39, 43, 84, 115
property rights, 115, 152, 158
property taxes, 159-161
Prussianization, 83, 87, 123, 139, 156
psychologists, 7, 88, 93, 116, 143, 147
Puritans, 68

quota system, 13

racial discrimination: and *Milliken v.
  Bradley,* 128; and 1964 Civil Rights
  Act, 118; in public schools, 72,
  131; origins in U.S., 97, 98, 106,
  107; and *Swann v. Charlotte
  Mecklenburg*, 120-122
racism: in immigration policies, 36,
  108; inherent in the constitution,

100; as part of segregation, 113,
    124, 163; and quota plans, 14, 15,
    19
Ramey, Craig, 147
Rasher, Diane, 13
Ravitch, Diane, 25, 27, 135
Reagan, Ronald, 95
recitation, 74, 75, 142, 151
reconstruction, 106, 107
reform(s), 1-3, 10, 13, 21, 45, 49, 63,
    67, 70, 79, 81, 85, 95, 130
reformers, 12, 23, 46, 63, 74, 76-78,
    81, 90, 162
Rehnquist, William, 32, 35
remuneration, 18
revenues, 22, 42, 77, 99, 159
Rinehart, Alice, 75
Roberts v. City of Boston, 107
Roberts v. Madigan, 157
Rodak, John, 34
Ross, Rosell, 135
Rossell, Christine, 123, 124
Rotunda, Ronald, 115
Rousseau, Jean-Jacques, 86
Rutledge, John, 101

salaries, 1, 10, 15, 17, 37, 38, 44, 50,
    52, 77, 83, 108, 147, 160
San Antonio v. Rodriguez, 160-162
Schmidt, Benno, 115
Scholastic Aptitude Tests (SATs), 4,
    6, 11, 15, 16, 40, 85, 163
school choice, 45-47, 164, 199
school discipline, See expenditures
school expenditures, See expenditures
School Public Relations Association,
    30, 35
schoolhouse, 29, 68, 69, 74, 76
Science Report Card, 4, 22
segregation: based on age, 61, 74, 78,
    162, 163; based on sexism, 81;
    based on special education, 144,
    147, 148; and bilingual education,
    24, 25, 138, 139; and Brown v.
    Board, 115-118; and Civil Rights
    Act of 1964, 119; and compulsory
    attendance laws, 93; de jure, 97,

113; de facto, 97; definitions, 125;
    present frauds, 4, 15, 53, 72, 164;
    and Swann v. Charlotte
    Mecklenburg, 120-122, 126; in terms
    of resegregation, 128-131
self-esteem, 7, 20, 26, 73, 87
Senate Education and Labor
    Committee, 147
Senate Subcommittee on Juvenile
    Delinquency, 33
seniority,
separate but equal doctrine, 103, 107
Serrano v. Priest, 159-161
sexism, 79-81, 163, 164
Sexual Harassment Task Force, 155
Seylar, Margaret, 75
Shanker, Albert, 7
Shannon, Robert & Donna, 90, 94
Shays, Daniel, 69
Sherman, Roger, 102
simplicity, 19
slavery, 97, 100-108, 151, 152
Smith v. Robinson, 139
Society for Infant Children, 86, 88
Sowell, Thomas, 124, 125, 163
special education, 57, 59, 61, 139,
    144-147
Speer, Hugh, 116
Spring, Joel, 70, 78, 94
standardized tests, 10, 11, 57, 94, 142
Statue of Liberty, 36, 109
Stevenson, Harold, 16
Stigler, James, 4
stigmatization, 59, 63, 116, 145, 148
strikes, 40, 83
Stuart, Jesse, 75-76
student achievement, 1-3, 8-17, 21, 22,
    44, 83-85
Studies: on bilingual education, 24,
    25, 133, 135, 136; on compensatory
    education, 91-94; on disabled
    students, 27, 146; on immigration,
    36; and its effect on employment,
    111, 113; on segregation, 116, 123,
    124; on tracking, 57; on uniforms,
    61; on U.S. schools performance, 1-
    3-, 6-12, 16, 20, 143
Swann v. Charlotte Mecklenburg Board
    of Education, 120-122, 125-128, 141

talented students, 143
teacher education, 1, 2, 38, 41
teacher experience, 2
teachers' unions, 7, 50
television, 4, 13, 20-22, 51, 60
Tenth Amendment, 159
testing, 5, 75, 81, 93, 140
textbooks, 12, 18, 44, 53, 151
Thirteenth Amendment, 106
Tinker v. Des Moines, 157
Title VII, 133, 137
tracking, 54, 60-62, 87, 140, 143
Trager, Helen, 116
Tropea, Joseph, 93
truant, 51
tuition, 23, 35, 46, 49, 58
Turner, E. W., 19
Tyack, David, ix, 79-80

unemployment, 36, 110, 111, 138
uniforms, 47, 61-63
unionization, 40, 41, 82-85
Urban Institute, 51, 85, 122, 141
U.S. Office of Education, 43, 68, 74,
    116, 142

vandalism, 18, 30, 34, 44, 157
Van de Kamp Education
    Commission, 49

Venezky, R., 135
Vietnam, 94, 123
violence, 10, 30, 32-35, 62, 77
violent students, 37, 52
vouchers, x, 45, 48, 53, 95, 164

Walberg, Herbert, 135, 136
Washington, Booker T., 36, 37,
    109-113, 130
Washington, George, 70, 87, 99, 101
weapons, 10, 11, 20, 44, 156
Weinstein, Brian, 138
Wexell v. Scott, 155
Whitney, Eli, 102
Whittle, Chris, 50
Wiley, P.D., 41
Williamson, Hugh, 100
Winterer, Caroline, 89
Wood v. Strickland , 153
Wright, J. Skelly, 140-142, 148

Yale University Center in Child
    Development and Social Policy,
    146
Yerkes, Robert, 93
Young, Ella, 82-83

Ziegler, Edward, 146-147

About the Author

ROBERT M. HARDAWAY is Professor of Law at the University of Denver. He is the author of *Airport Regulation, Law and Public Policy* (Quorum, 1991), *Population, Law and the Environment* (Praeger, 1994), and *The Electoral College and the Constitution* (Praeger, 1994).

ISBN 0-275-94951-6

90000>

EAN

9 780275 949518

HARDCOVER BAR CODE